R00223 04925

CHICAGO PUBLIC LIBRARY
HAROLD WASHINGTON LIBRARY CENTER

R0022304925

DISCARD

QP
85
.G54

Psychological
immortality

DATE			

BUSINESS/SCIENCE/TECHNOLOGY
DIVISION

© THE BAKER & TAYLOR CO.

Psychological Immortality

By the same author

MONEYLOVE
TRANSCENDENTAL SEX
FRIENDS: THE POWER AND POTENTIAL OF THE
COMPANY YOU KEEP
MY NEEDS, YOUR NEEDS, OUR NEEDS

Psychological Immortality

Using Your Mind
To Extend Your Life

by Jerry Gillies

Richard Marek Publishers
New York

TO GAYLE HALLENBECK STONE

Gifted and beautiful writer
Enriching, encouraging, immortal friend

Copyright © 1981 by Jerry Gillies
All rights reserved. No part of this book may be reproduced in any form or by any means without the prior written permission of the Publisher, excepting brief quotes used in connection with reviews written specifically for inclusion in a magazine or newspaper. For information write to Richard Marek Publishers, Inc., 200 Madison Avenue, New York, N.Y. 10016

Grateful acknowledgment is made for permission to use the following copyright material:

Excerpt from *Anatomy of an Illness* by Norman Cousins. Copyright © 1979 by W.W. Norton & Co., reprinted by permission of the publisher.

Excerpt from *The Coming of Age* by Simone de Beauvoir. Copyright © 1972 by G. P. Putnam's Sons, reprinted by permission of the publisher.

LIBRARY OF CONGRESS CATALOGING IN PUBLICATION DATA

Gillies, Jerry, date.
    Psychological immortality.

    1. Longevity.   2. Longevity—Psychological aspects.
3. Will.   I. Title.
QP85.G5   613'.01'9   80-28676
ISBN 0-399-90103-5

PRINTED IN THE UNITED STATES OF AMERICA

BST

Contents

4 *Contents*

Acknowledgments

For the book that this turned out to be, much of the credit must go to the many people who were willing to be interviewed and quoted, to those who offered their support and suggestions, and to those men and women of vision who were so willing to share their view of the way things can be for all of us.

Most especially, I am indebted to Norman Cousins, Ray Bradbury, Leonard Orr, Dr. Richard G. Cutler, and Dr. Peter Steincrohn for stimulating my own imagination by sharing their knowledge, insight, and speculations about the possibilities of psychological immortality.

A. Stuart Otto was most generous in opening up to me the voluminous files of the Committee for an Extended Lifespan. F. M. Esfandiary's provocative ideas were most helpful. Reverend Terry Cole-Whittaker's optimism was contagious. Many thanks to five brilliant therapists and valued friends: Dr. Barton Knapp, Nancy Bristol, Vicki Johnson, Maria Fenton, and Dolly Lavenson. Former astronaut Wally Schirra inspired a lot of thought with his comments.

For our far-ranging conversations on the biological and psychological opportunities afforded by an extended lifespan, I am deeply grateful to the following scientists, physicians, psychia-

7

trists, and psychologists: Dr. Bernard Strehler, Dr. Lawrence Casler, Dr. Ken Dycktwald, Dr. Elmer Green, Dr. Naira Dalokishvili, Dr. Sula Benet, Dr. Arthur Falek, Dr. Roy Schenk, Dr. George Pollock, Dr. Robert Butler, Dr. Harold Bloomfield, Dr. Ron Parks, Dr. William J. McGrane, Dr. Sonya Herman, Dr. Claude Nolte, Dr. Dorothy Nolte.

And for their many suggestions, continuous support and inspiration, warm appreciation to my agent, Julia Coopersmith, my editor, Joyce Engelson, and my friend, Maggie Davis.

INTRODUCTION: DYING IS NOT THE WAY TO GO

This book was triggered by a series of seemingly unrelated incidents and encounters which illuminated for me the basic awareness that we human beings are fighting for our lives and, for the first time in recorded history, starting to win that battle.

The seed was planted about six years ago in Miami, when I met Leonard Orr, the creator of several innovative human development techniques, who suggested that physical immortality was an attainable goal. As with so many shocking new ideas, I filed this one away in some dusty corner of my subconscious mind. Then, in 1977, when I started interviewing people for my book, *Moneylove*, and especially working on the chapter Worklove, about the importance of doing work one loves and loving the work one does, I came across a fascinating phenomenon: Those people who were absorbed and pleasured by their work seemed to be younger than their years. This was particularly true of people who, at 65 or 70, were still vigorously engaged in the living/working process. When I examined some of these people more closely I found that they were often ignoring the dictums of society that they start retreating from an active life at a certain age; some were even ignoring the advice of their personal physician that they slow down and retire.

Something obviously was going on here. And it wasn't just that

they believed they were younger and more vital—they *looked*
younger. When I interviewed even older people and found that
those who survived much longer than the average human lifespan
were people who had also been absorbed, excited, and pleasured
by their work, an inescapable conclusion emerged: *The way in
which these people lived their lives had a physical impact on their
health and longevity*.

The concept of Psychological Immortality evolved out of these
interviews, stimulated and expanded by dozens of conversations
with physicians, biologists, gerontologists, geneticists, psychologists, psychiatrists, and long-lived individuals. What started out
as a rather abstract idea began to take on some very clearly
defined properties. It soon became apparent that the idea of
substantially increasing the human lifespan wasn't just the
province of visionaries and philosophers but had become the life
work of thousands of dedicated and respected scientists. Much of
the medical and biological research now going on around the
world is clearly inspired by the basic premise that dying at 65 or
70 is dying prematurely.

I have divided this book into three parts because, as the
research for it continued, I realized that the life-extension effort
must be threefold. First, there is the mind-boggling scientific
investigation running the length and breadth of biological knowledge and speculation from studying the long-lived peoples of the
world to looking at the ability of the DNA molecule to repair itself
and exploring the intricate and mysterious secretions released by
the brain itself. This section of the book covers a lot of territory,
but it could have gone on for thousands of pages since each
scientist I interviewed had one or more suggestions of other
scientists I should talk to and other projects I should look into.
Part One of the book is not, therefore, an attempt to present a total
picture of all the longevity and anti-aging research now underway
around the world, but rather a look at some of the most promising
research and comments from some of the most innovative and
respected of researchers. This scientific medical research also has
a psychological dimension, since knowing that this work is now

going on can reinforce the healthy attitude that anything really might be possible and that, at the very least, we will know much more about our own biological opportunities than ever before in human experience.

Part Two looks at the very powerful and profound effect the human mind has on health and longevity. Though in popular mythology we often see the grumpy, lonely old person surviving to very old age, those who generally do survive longer have certain psychological attitudes, above all, perhaps, one of optimism and exuberance. The most exciting aspect of this psychological approach is the new knowledge, backed up by impeccable laboratory research, that one's emotional approach to life affects body chemistry.

Part Three is the first attempt ever to develop strategies which will create in the individual a supportive emotional climate conducive to achieving a longer life. Once one knows of the biological and psychological opportunities and possibilities, these strategies can help turn that knowledge into a positive action program. This type of positive action is necessary to counter all the negative conditioning we constantly receive about death and aging. Many of us may now be harboring a self-destructive belief system which could very well be called "death consciousness." For instance, most people believe that they have to start falling apart at a certain age, that there is a fixed limit to the number of active years they can expect to enjoy. This is "death consciousness." Life consciousness involves becoming aware of the infinite possibilities and living our lives without preconceptions about sickness, deterioration, and death. This is at the core of Psychological Immortalilty, and the awareness that these limitations are not considered insurmountable by the scientists now engaged in longevity research coupled with the use of positive psychological strategies can promote exactly the physical and mental processes necessary to achieve a triumphantly long and active life.

Gathering the raw material for this book has had a profound effect on my own life consciousness. At this moment, I have the absolute conviction that I can live as long as I want to, that sickness and debilitation will not overtake me prematurely at 75 or 80, and that with each succeeding year I grow more youthful, vigorous, and alive. If I can pass this conviction on to others, this book will have more than served its purpose.

PART
ONE

BIOLOGICAL OPPORTUNITIES

WE LIVE in a society where death is glorified, commemorated, anticipated. Psychological Immortality is a repudiation of this death consciousness. It is not so much a denial of death as a reaffirmation of life. This is not to say that you, as an individual, will live forever. But certainly, by preparing yourself emotionally and making use of the scientific advances now in sight, you will be able to substantially increase your own lifespan.

We are now witnessing a panoramic human quest, complete with villains and heroes. The villains are the preconceived and archaic notions about death and aging. The heroes are largely unsung, but there are thousands of them quietly working with dedication and hope in their laboratories, aiming at nothing less than the complete obliteration of the villains. It is time for all of us to take sides. Are you determined to hold onto old beliefs about the inevitability of death and the aging process, or will you join the biologists, biochemists, gerontologists. geneticists, and other scientists who, whatever their divergent views and fields of research, offer one basic and common prediction: *You will have the opportunity to live longer than you've ever before supposed.*

The purpose of examining this quest, this large body of research, in what is basically a book about psychological

13

attitudes, is twofold. First, the more aware you become of the efforts to increase your biological opportunities, the more you'll be willing to adopt the life consciousness attitudes that will enable you to take full advantage of these opportunities. Second, the optimism of the scientists as illustrated by the time and energy they are putting into these life-extending explorations can act as a model for your own expectations. If so many prominent researchers think it's possible to extend your life, how can you justify holding onto the belief that it's limited?

HOW OPTIMISTIC ARE THE SCIENTISTS?

Generally speaking, scientists are rather cautious about making flamboyant predictions. It is therefore surprising and encouraging that so many are so willing to offer up strongly optimistic expectations about the life-extension research they are now engaged in.

Dr. Bernard Strehler, for instance, Professor of Biology at the University of Southern California, believes that gerontologists will soon understand the causes of aging, and be able to *reverse* the process. Without aging, Dr. Strehler believes a healthy person could well live more than 2000 years!

Dr. Paul Segall, a researcher in the Department of Physiology at the University of California, Berkeley, says:

> *If life-extension becomes a national priority like the space program, if there were a $200 billion assault on aging and death, this could produce dramatic results in five years. A program that would put such a dent in death we might wipe it off the face of the earth.*

The likelihood of such a crash program seems remote while research funds stay under the control of bureaucrats with limited vision, and while the vast majority of the population remains apathetic. A number of the scientists interviewed for this book expressed concern over this public ignorance and apathy. Most people *are* ignorant about the research now underway and about the very real possibilities for a breakthrough in the near future. Of course, once some actual breakthroughs are announced, many more distinguished scientists will jump on the longevity bandwagon, the public's imagination will be captured, and, eventually, the bureaucratic machinery will start moving. Meanwhile, in the vanguard, physicians and scientists continue to make their optimistic predictions.

Dr. W. E. Stonebraker of the VA Hospital in Seattle, Washington, says:

> *Normal life expectancy will increase to 120 to 140 years in the next few decades, but this will require increasing the retirement age to 100. Within twenty-five years we should see a sharp increase in longevity accompanied by a high degree of competency.*

In the face of this hopefulness, it becomes more apparent than ever that the apathetic and pessimistic viewpoint is one fostered by negative conditioning inflicted on us by parents and significant others at an early age, and perpetuated by radio, television, movies, and books. Though we humans have dramatically increased our horizons in many areas, this is one facet of life—its prolongation—in which our beliefs are fixed and rigid. As Dr. Benjamin Schloss, a pioneer in aging research, said:

> *People dismiss the possibility of living indefinitely because of the belief that evolution has given us roughly seventy years and this is what we're stuck with. This kind of thinking is inconsistent with the generally held and valid belief that man can work almost any kind of miracle upon his environment. Too many people seem to think that man himself is somehow an exception, that our bodies can't be tampered with. That's nonsense!*

Many scientists see a synergetic effect, whereby one anti-aging or life-extending breakthrough will give an individual enough extra time to live until the next breakthrough. Thus, it is possible to conceive of a pyramiding effect that will permit people to live almost indefinitely. If, as many researchers predict, we can add twenty years to the human lifespan by the year 2000, then many more scientists will join in the effort, and perhaps add another twenty or thirty years by 2020. One gerontologist told me: "The best advice I can give anybody is to stay fit and stick around awhile . . . the big prize is just around the corner."

In his book, *Slowing Down the Aging Process,* biochemist Dr. Hans J. Kugler says:

> *I personally believe that in the near future man will be able to extend his lifespan thirty to fifty years by simply taking a daily pill. I also believe that he will be able to stay physically fit and mentally alert for both his daily and nightly tasks. Actually my projections are conservative in light of information that is available on this subject.*

It's important here to underline Dr. Kugler's emphasis on "physically fit and mentally alert." We are not talking about giving people thirty to fifty years more of "old age," but rather an additional period of youthfulness. In fact, much of the apathy and antagonism surrounding this subject may be due to the fact that people do not realize that life-extension actually means *youth*-extension. The same biological and psychological tools which will add years will also add vitality. This specific concern was examined in a conversation with Dr. Lawrence Casler of the State University of New York, who says:

> *I don't think we envision people 100, 110, 120 creeping around. We see them as vital and vibrant. So the preparation must include not just the idea, "I am going to live longer," but, "I am going to live longer and have complete control of all of my mental and physical capacities." If we get individuals to believe **both** of these ideas, not just intellectually, but at a very deep emotional level as well, then I think older persons will be prepared for this gift that they'll soon have available.*

Our belief systems are firmly entrenched at a very deep level of consciousness. Many researchers agree with Dr. Casler's declaration that we have to go beyond intellectual acceptance of the idea that we are going to live longer and stay younger. This is a fantastic gift we are receiving, and it requires emotional preparation. Part of that preparation is resisting the negative beliefs that hold us back, the beliefs that dismiss the conquest of aging and death as farfetched fantasies. Many people are so locked into their rigid belief systems that they feel threatened whenever a new idea comes along to challenge those old beliefs, even such an obviously positive idea as life-extension. In Belgium, for instance, noted gerontologist Dr. Herman LeCompte stirred up a great deal of controversy with his claim that it's possible to increase the human lifespan to 500 years and that he personally hopes to make it to 1000! Dr. LeCompte actually landed in jail when he ran up against the conservative Belgian Medical Council, which deplored the sensational media coverage of his lifespan statement. The Council found LeCompte guilty of "unethical conduct by advertising" and barred him from practice for six weeks. When he defied that order, he was arrested and put in jail. There was such a public outcry, however, that he was released within forty-eight hours. LeCompte formed an organization called the International Association on the Artificial Prolongation of the Human Specific Lifespan, and became affiliated with Dr. L. V. Komarov of the USSR Academy of Sciences. Dr. Komarov shares LeCompte's optimism and states:

People can and must live not by decades but by centuries!

This optimistic lifespan view is certainly not new. Albrecht von Haller, the famous Swiss physiologist of the eighteenth century, considered the limit of man's life to be not less than two hundred years. Christoph Wilhelm Hufeland, the German nineteenth-century physician, named the same figure:

An animal lives eight times longer than the time it takes to grow up. To achieve complete growth man needs twenty-five years. Therefore, his proper lifespan without a doubt may be considered as two hundred years.

Today, these highly positive predictions are not coming from just a few iconoclastic scientific mavericks, but from the most prestigious and respected researchers and institutions.

Several years ago, the Rand Corporation polled eighty-two of the world's foremost gerontologists. They said that by 1992 science will be able to add at least twenty years to our lifespans.

Dr. Irving Oyle, author, physician, and faculty member at the University of California at Santa Cruz, believes the normal lifespan can be doubled.

Dr. Ken Dycktwald, a pioneer in working with the elderly, and founding president of the Association for Humanistic Gerontology, says:

My expectation is that within the next twenty years the average lifespan will jump up to about 100 for men, 105 to 110 for women. Most people who are 60 or 70 right now and healthy can probably expect to live to somewhere between 89 and 100.

THE CURRENT RESEARCH

In attempting to provide an overview of the current research by biologists, biochemists, gerontologists, geneticists, behavioral geneticists, etc., into longevity, the aging process, and ways of retarding or eliminating death, I was fortunate in talking to some scientists who shared information not readily available elsewhere, and pleasantly surprised at their willingness to speculate on life-extension possibilities. Some of those speculations are off-the-record, anonymous. It is unfortunate that in this bastion of freedom, some researchers have to be circumspect in their comments so as not to jeopardize government grants. There is even currently some research being done on the capability of human beings to actually achieve physical immortality. The scientists working in this area wouldn't dare be so foolish as to announce their true goals, but label their research as "anti-aging." A number of scientists investigating cancer, for instance, are also looking into longevity. It is indicative of the bureaucratic focus that twenty to thirty times the amounts spent on longevity research are being spent on cancer research. Several gerontologists told me they feel certain that had the same amounts been spent on longevity as have been spent on cancer over the past twenty years, we not only would have seen a twenty- to thirty-year lifespan extension, but may well have come up with more effective cancer treatments. It surely makes more sense to study healthy people and the reasons for longevity than it does to study disease and the reasons for death. Of course, these areas of research often overlap, but what we're talking about is where the emphasis is placed. Focused attention tends to reinforce whatever it's focused on. Spending billions on studying disease instead of health reinforces the idea that disease is an undefeatable foe. One former astronaut-engineer told me that one of the reasons the goal of putting an American on the moon first succeeded was that research was focused on how to do it rather than on overcoming the obstacles. This enabled the space scientists to always move forward, and the actual obstacles were overcome faster than they would have been had most of the attention been focused on negative issues.

Quite a few of the scientists interviewed mentioned that research efforts are starting to pay off in terms of accumulated knowledge. Several stated that more was accomplished in 1979–1980 alone than in all the preceding twenty years. And since it often takes one or two years for the results to find their way into print, the breakthrough you read about today may well have been surpassed by the time you do so.

Dr. Richard G. Cutler: A Few Genes

One of the most respected scientists studying life-extension is biological gerontologist Dr. Richard G. Cutler of the Gerontology

Research Center of the National Institute on Aging in Bethesda, Maryland. He told me:

> *The most solid thing we've shown in our research is that there certainly isn't any reason to believe that the length of lifespan that man presently has is some finite, fixed number. There's no biological process that we've uncovered yet that says, "This is the bottleneck and something really radically has to be changed in order to get more lifespan." At least we've shown that. We do have other data indicating that it might just be the degree of expression of a few genes that could maybe double lifespan.*

Dr. Cutler's statement is echoed by a number of other scientists, who agree that there is no complicated bottleneck to break through, but that the answers, once found, will turn out to be simple ones. This isn't to say that it will be easy to find those simple answers. It may take another ten or twenty years, millions of dollars, and millions of research hours. But, on several fronts, the focal point seems to be narrowing. Dr. Cutler says:

> *Most gerontologists are predominantly involved in determining what the biological nature of aging is. My field of interest is a little different in that I am looking at what the biological nature is of those processes that promote longevity. It's sort of the opposite, but very closely related. The way this links in is that the processes that determine lifespan mainly are those that are involved in aging. Our idea is that there might be specific genes or specific biochemical processes whose role is specifically to maintain the functional integrity of the organism.*
>
> *The reason why man lives twice as long as the chimpanzee is not because there are basic building-block differences in terms of physiology, biochemistry, and so forth, but simply because there might be a few gene differences. This was sort of a wild idea at the beginning, and we then went ahead and tried to determine whether there was any scientific basis to*

this. And so far, we've been reasonably successful in finding data to support the idea that there might indeed be a rather simple set of genes and/or biochemical processes which determine whether you live to be 2 or 3 years of age, or up to 100. Now, if this really proves to be the case, then the consequences would be very far-reaching.

Far-reaching indeed. What Dr. Cutler is saying is that if the initial indications hold up, a few genes responsible for longevity may be isolated. Then, of course, the work will involve ways of modifying those genes, ways of enhancing their longevity properties. I asked Dr. Cutler whether he had any thoughts on what kind of time-frame was possible, how long it might be before people could start to benefit from this research.

Well, we are dealing with a lot of unknown factors, but more importantly than that, the time-frame business also depends on how many competent scientists you have working in the field. If one were able to establish the scientific basis that there's really a good possibility of a few genes underlining general health maintenance, if that really becomes convincing, then, of course, one could easily imagine that scientists throughout the world would rapidly jump on the bandwagon.

*The second problem is whether or not, after this is shown to be a reasonable possibility, it might be determined by our government and others that it wouldn't be a good idea to finance the research toward this, in the sense that the economical, political, theological consequences might be so overwhelming that it might be thought that it would be best to work on other things. So, unfortunately, there's lots of problems involved other than just the scientific. I look at that as the main determinant of the time-frame of when something like this might come about, **if** everything works out and assuming the theory is right. There are only five or six laboratories working on this throughout the world right now.*

At that pace, if no more get involved, then it would be a very long time before anything came out of it.

Just as the medical profession is moving from prescribing cures for disease to perpetuating health, gerontology, in the hands of such people as Dr. Cutler, is starting to look toward longevity rather than aging. After all, if you wanted to discover how to extend life would you study someone who lived a long and healthy life, or would you study people who aged quickly and died young? This approach also dictates that life-extension include youth-extension. The public apathy toward longevity research is due in part to the belief by many that extending life would merely mean more years spent in old age. I asked Dr. Cutler if he saw a way of enlisting public support for his type of research.

*There have been surveys on how the general public feels about lifespan research. Do they support it? Do they think it's a good thing? Would they like to have another ten or fifteen years of **good** health? And when it's explained in that way, they overwhelmingly answer yes. What we're talking about is not living older longer but living **younger** longer. And that's a new concept. People think of being **senile** longer when they think of life-extension. And the trouble is that that's really what medical science is doing, keeping us older longer, not younger longer. The concept that there might actually be something to keep you younger longer people find unbelievable. But those individuals to whom this is made clear really are all for it.*

STAYING ALIVE LONGER *AND* YOUNGER

There does seem to be a lot of medical effort devoted toward keeping people older for longer periods of time. Science has learned how to keep life going with mechanical and chemical assistance. But this is not really what we mean when we talk about life-extension. A few more months or a few more years of life in a feeble state is not so grand a prize. It may well be that medical efforts in this area have held back real longevity progress. The more we see very old people kept artificially alive the less desirable life-extension seems as a concept. But all the scientists interviewed for this book agree that they are working toward keeping people young and alive rather than just alive. It is important that this dual purpose be made clear, for what we're saying is that there are possibilities and, if people will understand and support them, they will become more possible. In addition to the false belief that life-extension means people will more or less be living longer in a feeble state, Dr. Cutler points out some other negative beliefs that hold back public support and involvement in longevity research:

> *There's also the idea that you become bored with life and that by the time you're 50 or 60 years old you've pretty well been exposed to everything. There's also the belief that nature has a reason, that there's a reason for you having a finite lifespan that's beyond our comprehension, and that if you were somehow or other able to live longer there're going to be all kinds of problems that we cannot foresee.*

This rather superstitious view that some ominous fate awaits anyone tampering with the natural order of things has been perpetuated by popular entertainments such as *Frankenstein,* wherein the mad scientist gets his just rewards for tampering with nature. This overlooks, of course, the fact that if human beings were somehow not meant to expand their horizons there would be no reason for the natural intellectual capacities which allow for this exploration. This belief that it's natural to grow older, sicker, and die, severely hampers medical science as well as clinical treatment of disease. If an individual believes, deep within his subconscious mind, that deterioration is a natural state at a certain age, he will not be able to fully mobilize the body's natural healing processes or take adequate advantage of medical treatment. Several scientists go so far as to suggest that individuals create their own debilitating illnesses in order to fulfill their own expectations that life is finite and that death is natural at a certain age.

Being emotionally prepared for a longer life will also mean a major change in our whole social structure. People living to the age of 120 certainly wouldn't want to slow down at 65 and take a backseat for the next fifty-five years. Along with the false belief that it's somehow natural to start fading at 50 and dying at 70 or 80, we have to eliminate the idea that life gets less interesting as it goes on, that there are few choices available after a certain age, and that the natural course of events is to slow down and have a less active lifestyle as the years progress.

Becoming "civilized" has locked us into some very narrow boundaries. In certain primitive societies, life-extension is a highly desirable goal, and those who achieve great longevity are the most respected citizens. Our more sophisticated culture has provided us with other priorities, such as intellectual and scientific development, complex economic structures, political freedom, and physical comfort and security. Dr. Cutler feels that the slowing down of the natural evolution toward a longer lifespan may be a negative by-product of increasing civilization, and is therefore *abnormal*. That somehow we have slowed down a very natural life-expansion process, and the life-extension work now going on is getting us back to the biological norm, back on the track again. I asked Dr. Cutler whether he feels a good part of the thrust of his work is to prove that a longer lifespan is indeed a natural biological event:

Of course, this is the attitude we take. Actually, we ask the question: "Why is man so long-lived as compared to other primate species?" Man being the longest-lived of all mammals, twice as long-lived, essentially, as the next one down the line, in terms of actual years. So the real question is, "What is the biochemistry behind our unusual ability not only to keep our neurophysiological system going, but everything else?" Our ability to maintain our mental competence, hearing, seeing, everything across the board is maintained in

*a much more active state for a longer period of time than any
other species. Everything is slowed down for man in terms of
the rate of aging. The functional ability of every behavior trait
is longer than in any other species. Now the question is: What
do we have that's unique? What do we have, for instance, that
keeps our immune system going and our nervous system going
longer than our next of kin, say the chimpanzee?*

This attitude is linked to the emerging humanistic view in
health care and psychology, a view that produces more effective
results, a view that says "You are well and let's help you get even
better," rather than "You are sick and let's get you back to
normal." Dr. Abraham Maslow, the father of what is now known
as humanistic psychology, revolutionized the study of human
behavior by the simple, commonsense approach of studying
super-healthy people instead of mentally disturbed patients. He
called these people self-actualized, and found that their attitudes
and behavior provided clues to help everyone take more complete
charge of their emotional lives. So studying why man is the
longest-lived species, looking at why we live so long rather than at
why we die, seems to be the far more desirable and effective
approach. In the specific work done by Dr. Cutler, he and his
research team came up with some fascinating results:

*So far, the most interesting thing that came out of all of this
is the similarity between us and the chimpanzee. Everything
seems to be the same. There is no one hormone that has been
found to be different. In fact, even the amino acid sequences
and the structure of the molecules and so forth are essentially
identical. Which means that whatever the difference might be
that seems to govern the aging rate of the various primate
species, it **doesn't** seem to be **too** different, because everything so far seems to be the same. In terms of genes, we're 99
percent chimp or vice versa. So there's only about a 1 percent
genetic difference that could possibly account for **everything,
all** the differences between us and the chimpanzee, including
longevity.*

*The thing we would **like to do** and **are** doing is to measure the various hormones, and the stimulating factors that we find in the plasma in man, and compare it to the different primate species, and see if we can possibly relate that to their aging rate. But I doubt very much that we'll find that we have something unique that accounts for our longevity. I think that it's more likely that we'll find we just have more of the same thing, that man has more of whatever it is that controls the aging rate.*

The hunt is on, therefore, for that certain something that enables us to outlive other species. Though the task is far from an easy one, at least this particular research group has its sights sharply focused. I asked Dr. Cutler whether this didn't indicate that the real breakthrough will come when we learn how to turn on some internal switch, something that will activate whatever it is that we have more of than the other primates.

That's right. This is the fascinating idea here, I think: that we might already have the genes in our chromosomes that are necessary to double our lifespan, if only we knew how to turn them on more. Most of the longevity research in the past, and even now, is involved in trying to develop something new and inject it into animals. Antioxidants, free radical scavengers, hormones of some kind or another. There are many things people are injecting and seeing what effect this might have on longevity. The idea that we may already have a set of genes that govern our aging rate whose further stimulation might further increase our lifespan is somewhat new. If we could only identify those genes and learn how to further increase their activity, then you might be able to substantially increase lifespan.

THE BASIC PREMISE

The basic premise of Psychological Immortality is that we *do* have the capacity right now to live longer, that we already possess whatever chemicals or physiological processes are necessary to substantially increase our lifespan, and that certain emotional attitudes, certain psychological techniques can help activate that inner fountain of youth. We know now *absolutely* that psychological attitudes affect the body's biochemistry. And while such research as Dr. Cutler's may turn up some biochemical methods of stimulating these longevity processes, it seems just as likely that they can be stimulated through changes in behavior and attitude. Norman Cousins has inspired a lot of the current research into secretions of the brain which can be activated by certain emotional stimuli. We'll discuss his work and hear some of his views on this subject further along in this section. The important thing here, I think, is that we don't have to know all the intricate operating mechanisms of the body in order to effect change. In some of the work done at the Biofeedback Institute in 1971 and 1972, one of the most fascinating factors was that people learning to control such physiological functions as brain wave frequency, skin temperature, and muscle tension did not have to know anything about the biochemical or physiological processes involved. They just had to know their goal, and have some way of monitoring their rate of success. For example, if you have an electromyographic biofeedback unit (which measures the rate of muscle firings) attached by electrodes to the frontalis muscle at your forehead, you can learn to relax that muscle efficiently merely by trying different mental/emotional techniques, and simultaneously measuring your results. If you think about an argument you had with your boss, and the needle jumps to a high level, you have learned something about what affects muscle tension. If you imagine a peaceful beach scene, relax your body, and see the needle go to lower levels, you have effectively learned to lower that muscle tension. And you don't need any in-depth knowledge about the biochemical and bioelectrical intricacies involved. While this might be an important awareness in terms of the internal attitudes people have and how they will affect longevity, it is also useful in the kind of research going on at the Gerontology Research Center. As Dr. Cutler puts it:

You really don't have to understand everything about what's going on. An analogy might be in the prevention of polio. You have polio as a disease, and of course we still don't understand how it works. It's very complicated. But we had an idea that the polio virus that causes the disease might be used. There's also the immune system, which we also don't understand, but we felt we might be able to protect it. So, without understanding too much of anything, we're able to at least prevent a very complex disease by stimulating the defense. There might be the same possibility for aging. We might be able to somehow or other fool our cells into believing that we're aging faster than we ought to and thereby somehow stimulate the genes governing the aging, without understanding all of them, but increasing their rate of expression. That's the kind of things we're working on. I think that lifespan extension will probably occur in this way and not by identifying some hormone factor or plasma factor or something of this nature.

The approach taken by Dr. Cutler seems to be an effective one: to look at why man has been able to live more years than other species. But there is still the fact that most species live proportionately longer in terms of their lifespan compared to their maturation rate. I asked whether, in fact, there is a connection between aging and the amount of time it takes us to mature. Could the same genes be involved?

That's a very interesting question. There's certainly some kind of relationship here, I think, a very important one. And, of course, one can ask another question: Is the rate of development limited by the rate of brain development? Because it seems as if there's also a good correlation between the dependence of a species in terms of its learned behavior for success, and longevity. The more the animal requires learned behavior for its survival, the longer it seems to be able to live. One could say, well maybe that's because there's a certain length of time required for learned behavior, and this was one of the selective forces involved in evolution. Anyway, there certainly seems to be a link between rate of development and longevity. Almost any biochemical process that we've been able to devise, and that any other laboratory has devised, that lengthens lifespan, seems to also reduce rates of development. So, if you were able to reduce rates of development, slow them down and thereby lengthen the development process, I would almost guarantee that you're going to increase the lifespan. There's really a close correlation there.

One of the processes that is responsible for determining an animal's longevity is its rate of development. Now let me give you a biochemical explanation of why we think that is true. It appears that many of the biochemical processes that govern the size of an animal can eventually hurt the animal. As you're growing, your cells are dividing all the time, and then there is something that occurs that stops cell growth, some kind of hormone or something that limits the organ size. The liver's a certain size, every organ is a certain size. This process occurs somewhere around the age of sexual maturation. It may be related to growth hormones. There are many steroids that are also related to sexual maturation. All these growth-limiting processes and hormonal processes that are related to sexual maturation have been shown to have long-term detrimental effects on tissues. They're necessary factors for the successful development of the species, but long-term, *they do the animal in. Therefore, if there were selective pressure for the evolution of longer lifespan, one way would be simply to postpone the biochemical appearance of these hormone factors that are necessary for the final differentiation and development of the organism. For instance, we know we can prevent the sexual maturation of certain species, it's very spectacular in salmon and eels and octopuses, and if you prevent the sexual maturation, you can almost double lifespan.*

While no one is suggesting sexual maturation in humans be prevented, the postponing of puberty might be a side effect of dramatically increasing lifespan. This might very well be a way of balancing some of the other factors in a society filled with long-lived people. If puberty were delayed until 25, and lifespan were extended to 110–120, an individual would have more of an opportunity to know family members on a multigenerational level. Grandparents might work alongside grandchildren. The delayed sexual maturation might also help balance overpopulation problems caused by extended childbearing periods. There is every indication that increasing the lifespan, and having people live longer younger, will also lengthen the span of sexual activity. Lifespan extension might not necessarily mean a delay in sexual maturing, but if it does, it may very well solve some of the other difficulties connected with longevity.

In terms of psychological attitudes, Dr. Cutler and I agreed that it might be useful to study people who are "late bloomers," who naturally seem to have a delay in their sexual maturing, at least psychologically. Do these people live longer?

If, as Dr. Cutler states, certain processes or substances connected with slowing down cell growth as we reach our full size and full maturation do have long-term harmful effects on our bodies, then it seems to follow that slowing down our rate of development may diminish that harmful effect. If, for instance, the very substance that at puberty prevents our organs from getting any bigger is by necessity also an aging substance, then we have to find a way to delay and prolong its delivery. If substance X is released into the system as part of the sexual maturing process, and large amounts of it are released in a relatively short time, and substance X also is involved in eventual physical deterioration, then it may be that slowing down this process so that smaller quantities of X are released over a longer period of time will eliminate its negative effects.

The connection between learned behavior and longevity is also an interesting area for exploration. The longer we take to learn what we need to know, the longer we live, it's thought by some. We humans require the most learned behavior for our survival, and we survive the longest. Human beings seem to be the only species with the capacity and desire to learn throughout the entire lifespan. Once simple survival skills are learned, there are wide-ranging new areas of knowledge to be developed, and in a healthy functioning individual, the learning continues. Almost all human beings learn new things, little and big, every day. We can learn new skills, new ways of understanding ourselves, new ways to communicate with others. In a rapidly changing world, we learn to adapt. Does this mean that the more learning we absorb the longer we will live? Certainly, those older persons I've interviewed who have lived longest in mental and physical alertness seem to be people who have never stopped learning new things. Scientists who have studied the long-lived residents of certain remote villages around the world tell me that these people, while not sophisticated by Western standards, do learn a lot about how to survive and govern their lives in healthy and successful ways. And they never stop this learning!

It may well be that one of the answers lies in slowing down the rate of physical/biological development, and, at the same time, expanding mental/emotional development, so that it continues for a longer period of time. I asked Richard Cutler if he agreed that certain psychological attitudes will be compatible with the coming scientific breakthroughs.

There is something in relation to attitudes that I find very fascinating, and that is the general field of stress. I opened my eyes to this because new biochemical data's been coming out that in terms of stress there are various hormones, particularly the adrenocorticals, that are found to accelerate when they exist in high stress for any length of time, and seem to have a very broad effect in accelerating aging. So one can easily see that if one has a high stress level, and these hormonal levels are high all the time, more often than for other people, then this person may have a higher rate of aging. There really is something to attitudes, therefore, in terms of taking it easy, taking life in stride, and not getting excited over everything. There's really a biochemical basis for that.

In terms of attitudes, I think that bad attitudes can certainly accelerate the aging process. There are unhealthy attitudes, people who lose the will to live. There's good documentation that these people come down with all types of diseases, cancer and everything else. That's clear. If you want to ensure that you'll at least live up to your biological potential, there are certainly positive attitudes that will being you up to that point, up to your full biological potential. Though this is your field more than mine, I don't know if there's any attitude that you can have that would be able to decelerate your aging rate beyond what would be considered normal for the species.

But what is normal for the human species? Here, Dr. Cutler talked about a fascinating awareness: that though the human lifespan has increased over the centuries, in some ways it really hasn't.

*Throughout history, as far as we know it for the Homo sapiens species, it appears that our bodies are only geared to keep us healthy up to the age of 30 or 40, in terms of optimum physical health. As far as we can see, today this is still true. Even though we **live** longer, the duration of good health has remained the same. So it seems to be predominantly a species characteristic. Now certainly poor attitudes, stress, and many things like this can result in accelerated aging.*

We were probably one of the few research groups that, in order to get clues on what might be the basis of aging and the processes governing aging rate, undertook an evolutionary study. To ask the question: How did longevity evolve? Most researchers were thinking that aging evolved, that somehow way back among our ancestors there was no aging at all, and that aging evolved for some good reason, perhaps to have a turnover in the population, or to kill you before you got too old, or something like that. What came out of these studies is the fact that almost all animals, when you look at them in

their natural ecological niche, in their natural environment,
you will not find senescent animals, animals that have lost
some of their peak health due to their age. In other words, if
you go into the wild, you can't find an old mouse, you can't
find an old monkey, you can't find an old fish, you can't find
an old bird. There's a natural balance in nature, so that an
animal is normally killed by its natural predators before it has
a very high probability of living long enough to be affected by
the aging process. And that is even true for man. The Homo
sapiens species has probably been around for twenty or thirty
thousand years. Throughout that period of time, except for the
last few hundred years, very few humans ever lived past the
age of 30 or 40 years. Very rarely did anyone live to be 50,
60, or 70, although the genetic potential existed to do so. It
seems as though longevity was maintained or health was
maintained to the point where further maintenance wouldn't
be of any benefit. What has happened in man's situation is
that by radically lowering our environmental hazards through
the advent of civilization, we have been able to live really
longer. So our mean lifespan then radically began to increase
from 30 or 40 up to where we find it now.

Does this mean that we can only expect good health up to the
age of 40, that no matter how much longer we live it's downhill
from then on? Of course not, these researchers are not interested
in extending old age. But it is true that we have some leftover
attitudes and ancient biological processes from the former periods
of history in which we were unlikely to need to survive much
longer than forty years. It is also true that medical science has
helped extend life but not necessarily youth and optimum health.

Perhaps we are still in the midst of an evolutionary process in
which our bodies have yet to catch up to our lifestyles. Now that
most human beings live safer lives, with less chance of starving to
death or being eaten to prevent another creature's starving, certain
built-in processes needed in a less safe environment may
eventually diminish. The "fight or flight response" which activates
a number of bodily processes is a throwback to the prehistoric era,

when these processes were needed to enable man to either run from a deadly threat or do battle for survival. Now that this kind of direct threat has been eliminated (such a current threat as being mugged calls for a totally different response, as both running and fighting might be the least appropriate responses), the fight or flight response is more destructive than helpful, leading to much of the stress which has become mankind's single most dangerous enemy. Part of this evolutionary process may include the use of our minds to achieve greater longevity. Once people feel safe, they expand in all sorts of ways, and life-expansion is one of the most natural and obvious manifestations of this. The fact that some people are frightened by much less direct and deadly threats may merely be the normal resistance to change built into the human psyche. If someone realizes that a safe environment presents a number of new challenges, but is unwilling to face those challenges, then imaginary threats are invented to once again make survival rather than growth the major issue.

THE LONGEVITY ENZYME

How close are the scientists to answers? Well, there do seem to be several substances that might be directly responsible for helping us to live longer than other species. Dr. Cutler talked about one of these:

> *Man makes the most of a particular enzyme called superoxide dismutase, which is thought to be very important in governing the aging rate. In fact, there's a beautiful correlation between longevity and the amount of this enzyme that's in tissues. This particular enzyme is used to remove the production of free radicals that result from us breathing oxygen. All organisms among all mammals utilize oxygen. The evolution of the utilization of oxygen is to make a very efficient production of energy. It's much more efficient than not. There*

is a disadvantage, however, in this utilization of oxygen. Oxygen is very toxic, and in the metabolism of oxygen, a number of by-products are produced. One of these are the superoxide free radicals. A natural by-product, and all organisms produce it, but it's very toxic. So all organisms that use oxygen have also evolved superoxide dismutase to get rid of this toxic by-product. It appears that the more long-lived species have more of this enzyme (superoxide dismutase) in direct proportion to their longevity. That's a beautiful example of simplicity. In other words, there's probably no aging gene—aging is a by-product of living. But there are specific genes whose duty is to protect the organism, and expression of these genes, the amount of enzyme produced, could very well determine how long an organism is able to maintain optimum health. This is actually the first example where an enzyme has been shown to be directly involved in longevity.

TWO DIFFERING VIEWS

There are two basic schools of thought among gerontologists. One is that death is somehow biologically programmed into the organism. The other is that death is the result of a breaking down of the system, a failure somewhere along the line, perhaps in the immunological system, perhaps in the ability of certain cells to repair themselves. Some scientists skirt the issue of deciding between the two by assuming both are true. They see the breaking down of the system as something inherent in the species, as the means by which death is programmed into the organism. All the scientists agree that all of this theorizing is based on a good deal of unsupported speculation. We really don't *know* enough about longevity, death, and the aging process to make definitive statements.

It is my contention that many scientists find exactly what they are looking for. In other words, if a scientist has a basically pessimistic viewpoint and believes that death is inevitable, that aging is a natural process, then he will no doubt focus on areas that will tend to support this premise. The scientist who has a grander vision of the human potential, who understands that *anything* is possible until proven otherwise, rather than believing that *nothing* is possible until proven so (a subtle but vital difference), will tend to have an open mind, and be more alert to those wonderful serendipitous moments that are the foundation of most scientific achievement. For example, a number of gerontologists and biologists have considered the superoxide free radicals as the villain and focused all their attention on studying these unstable fragments and their negative effects. Dr. Cutler, on the other hand, while certainly paying attention to the free radical activity, focuses most of his attention on the heroes of this internal melodrama, the enzyme superoxide dismutase which seems to have been beautifully designed just to do successful battle with the free radicals. In more simplistic terms, some scientists think it natural for the free radicals to win the battle, and others are rooting for the protective enzyme. While the former may learn something about the aging process, it's the latter who seem more likely to come up with realistic procedures for enhancing longevity.

Again, this research is itself possibly all part of the natural evolutionary process. The correlation Dr. Cutler cites between longevity and species more dependent on learned behavior can be taken one step further, so that some of the learned behavior we are quite naturally evolving may be that which will enable us to perfect the organism itself. Since, for instance, we humans have more superoxide dismutase than other species *and* more dependence on and capacity for learned behavior, then a logical supposition might be that we have naturally been biologically programmed with the capability to increase the production of that enzyme and thus prolong life even further.

While superoxide dismutase may not be the final answer, it does lend support to the hope that someday in the not too distant future we might see the development of an "enzyme pill" that will promote longevity.

PROGRESSIVE RELAXATION

As Dr. Cutler was talking about the toxic effects of oxygen utilization, I was reminded of a discussion I had at a Biofeedback Research Society meeting in 1972 with Dr. Edmund Jacobson, who created the concept of Progressive Relaxation in the 1930s. His book on that subject is still studied by physicians around the world. Jacobson was both a medical doctor and a psychologist, having studied at Harvard with pioneering psychologist William James. In 1972, Jacobson was 84 and very youthful. He taught people to use their muscles more efficiently. For example, he might spend a month working with someone so that they learned how to completely relax their arms. Because when you tell someone to relax an arm, what they usually actually do is focus attention on it and end up tensing the muscles. His premise was that we use many muscles we don't need in such tasks as sitting down or standing up, and that if we learn more efficient use of the muscles, we become healthier. In the course of our discussion, I asked Dr. Jacobson what his views were on meditation, which was then just emerging as an antistress tool and being backed up by research indicating that it had positive organic effects. Jacobson told me that he saw meditation merely as deep relaxation, and that it achieved its positive effects simply because it cut down on oxygen intake by relaxing the muscles, which thereby needed less oxygen for oxygenation. He obviously felt Progressive Relaxation did this more effectively and efficiently than did meditation. I told Dr. Cutler about Dr. Jacobson's comments and asked him whether he felt more efficient operation of our bodies, which would cut down on oxygen utilization, wouldn't leave more superoxide dismutase in the system to affect longevity, since the enzyme wouldn't be needed in as great quantity for its primary function.

Oh, definitely so! The thing is that, right in line with this, there is a constant that characterizes each species. For man, if you take the total amount of oxygen consumption on a per-day basis, and you multiply that by his maximum lifespan potential, you'll get the lifespan calorie consumption for man on a per-gram basis. This is a very high figure for man. We are able to burn more energy per gram than any other species, and that follows because we are **the longest-lived.** *There's a constant in the sense of the amount of energy you've been programmed to utilize for your lifespan. If you were able to somehow or other decrease your oxygen consumption on a per-day basis, or spread it out to maybe make more efficient use of all your cells, and divide it up so that no particular cell fibers would be more exerted, then there's no doubt in my mind that you're going to increase longevity. We've done that already in flies and other species. If you can decrease oxygen consumption then you will increase longevity. This was an observation that was known thirty years ago. It gave rise to what I guess is the oldest theory in aging, the wear and tear theory. That theory was that there are so many calories that an animal has been programmed to be able to utilize and, depending on whether or not that animal has a high oxygen consumption or low oxygen consumption, the lifespan will vary accordingly. For instance, it's usually true that bigger animals live longer, such as elephants. But* **elephants** *have very low oxygen consumption and it's right in proportion to* **their longer lifespan.**

PROPER BREATHING—LONGER LIFE

In terms of oxygen consumption, a number of physicians interviewed have stated that one of the major impediments to good health is the fact that most people do not breathe properly. Proper breath control, more efficient breathing, might well cut down on total oxygen consumption. Leonard Orr has developed a breathing process known as Rebirthing—aimed at creating a natural rhythm between inhaling and exhaling. (We'll explore this technique further when we look at Psychological Opportunities in Part Two of this book.) A lot of the body therapies involve methods that help people make more efficient use of their basic physiology. The Oriental technique of T'ai Chi, for example, is a system of slow but precise movements that enable one to gain more control over bodily actions, and has proven very health-enhancing when practiced by the elderly in China and in some limited application in the U.S. The emergence of body-mind approaches to physical and emotional health may also be a natural evolutionary step, with our internal genetic programming somehow leading us in the right exploratory directions. And while we've known for some time that a high-stress lifestyle can shorten life, we are only just receiving biological confirmation that a low-stress existence can help people transcend the so-called average life expectancy figures. And, again, we do not have to be aware of all the internal processes involved: Relaxing more, and lowering your oxygen consumption, will help you live longer whether or not you ever heard of superoxide dismutase. In fairness to Dr. Cutler, I must state that he has seen no indication that any behavior changes will increase superoxide dismutase levels, and his work is aimed at trying to enhance that level directly in the lab. But he does agree that we may just not have discovered yet the connection between this enzyme and behavior and attitude patterns. I suggest that a future research project worthy of consideration might be to teach a number of people to relax and develop life-enhancing attitudes and then measure oxygen consumption levels and superoxide dismutase levels. Of course, this sort of human testing is the next evolutionary step in the gerontological research, followed by actual application of the knowledge.

In winding up our conversation, I said to Dr. Cutler: "It seems, with biofeedback research and control of the autonomic nervous system, that we are learning more and more about the connection between the mind and the body, and there are probably many more levels to discover about how we can possibly intervene in our own processes. I feel there has to be a partnership between developing the psychological attitude that will be receptive to scientific breakthroughs and the scientific research itself. If you do start to tell yourself that you'll begin aging at the age of 40 or 50 and are going to go downhill, and when you are 60 they discover a way of prolonging life, you may not be able to take advantage of that biological opportunity."

There's no doubt about the power of positive attitudes in that, and I think that's very important.

"If you think in a youthful manner you're not going to spend all your time sitting in a rocking chair, you're going to get up and walk. You're going to, in some way, keep active. So, if people get away from that negative emotional programming that says that they have to slow down so much that they can't work and they're going to be in a period of debilitation at the age of 65 or 70, they may increase their span of optimum health and longevity."

Yes, and I think that, in that particular sense, what you have to say is probably more pertinent anyway. It has the most immediate application because there is a tremendous loss of manpower in the nation simply because of the attitude that they're supposed to be old, and they're 65 so nothing is expected of them and they don't do anything. Indeed, many people probably do senesce much faster than they should. This forms one of the basic thrusts of the National Institute on Aging, that is to try to reverse the common idea that many people have that at a certain age you're supposed to be old, and you're not supposed to remember well. If you look at the stereotypes on television of the aging you can see this. I think it's very important to try to reverse that, and take optimum advantage of what potential we do have for longevity. So what you say is probably true: that by proper line of thought and behavior one can more fully take advantage of his basic biochemical potential for longevity.

It might be useful here to underline and speculate on several of Dr. Cutler's comments. While it is true that searching for a few genes that may be responsible for increasing longevity is a much simpler procedure than the shotgun type of anti-aging efforts that have been undertaken by many other researchers, this is not to say that it will be easy and that you can expect those genes to be identified and isolated anytime soon. Of course, one of the exciting facets of scientific research is that almost anything is possible, and Dr. Cutler and his team may well have made major strides by the time you read this. The next step would be to discover ways of affecting those genes, of stimulating them or enhancing their positive attributes. This could involve a lot of years of solid scientific investigation. As Dr. Cutler says, the more scientists who get excited about the prospects and jump on the bandwagon, the more likely a solution.

Biologists and gerontologists involved in this kind of research have to be optimists at heart, they have to believe, as Richard Cutler believes, that a longer lifespan is a natural biological event, and that their work is part of the natural evolutionary process of man using his natural talents to affect his organism and his environment.

In psychological terms, I like the focus expressed by Dr. Cutler on realizing that we already live longer than all other mammals and most other creatures. This awareness can give us an appreciation for the marvelous human mechanism, and an understanding that, if we have come so far, there is certainly a lot further to go.

This long interview with a leading biological gerontologist was included in its entirety because of the breadth of the subject, and the rare opportunity it provided to have the possibilities discussed by a scientist as eminent and articulate as Dr. Cutler. Look at some of the hopeful ideas expressed:

> *. . . there might . . . be a rather simple set of genes and/or biochemical processes which determine whether you live to be 2 or 3 years of age, or up to 100.*

The scientific searchlight is lit and here is a hopeful place on which to shine it. Just think what could be accomplished if Dr. Cutler could be joined by hundreds more dedicated researchers and tens of millions of dollars! Once we know a direction, once we have a goal, the task may not be easy, but it *is* simple. What a prodigious effort it's taken to narrow the field this far, to discover that perhaps 99 percent of our genes are identical with those of the chimp. Dr. Cutler is too precise an investigator to offer any false hopes, but there is much in what he says to stimulate optimism about the next decade or two of scientific effort.

> *What we're talking about is not living **older** longer but living **younger** longer.*

As Dr. Cutler says, that *is* a new concept, and one of immense importance. The more this is made clear to the general public, the more damage will be done to the destructive psychological belief that prolonged life means prolonged old age. Many other scientists have understood all along that one cannot discover the secrets of increasing lifespan without also finding ways of expanding the period of youthful vigor, but this has not been made sufficiently clear.

> *What do we have, for instance, that keeps our immune system going and our nervous system going longer than our next of kin, say the chimpanzee?*

What this comment really says is that we are already superior practitioners in the art of surviving. We already have the capacity for longevity far surpassing that of any other species. The raw materials are there, the functional system is in place. Now we just have to learn to understand and harness it. This attitude of "Look how much we've got going for us" certainly seems more productive than one of "Look at the odds against us."

> *. . . man has more of whatever it is that controls the aging rate.*

This statement is really at the heart of the research now going on at the Gerontology Research Center: to look at the positive factors and study ways of enhancing and stimulating them. This takes no more effort and wastes far less time with far more results than trying to eliminate the negative factors of aging and disease before considering longevity. Once you learn how to turn on the light switch, you don't ever again have to worry about fighting darkness.

What do we have more of? That remains to be uncovered in the lab, but it will be a far more inspired hunt than would be one looking for something we have too little of.

We might be able to somehow or other fool our cells into believing that we're aging faster than we ought to and thereby somehow stimulate the genes governing the aging, without understanding all of them . . .

For psychologists and psychiatrists what has emerged as the single common denominator among people who have difficulty coping and suffer from emotional disturbances is their feeling that they are not in charge, that they have no control over the circumstances of their lives. We have all had this feeling from time to time; it can be frightening. Part of the process of growing emotionally is to become aware that we are indeed in charge of our own lives. Learning how to actually govern our genes, biochemically or otherwise, can create a great sense of this self-responsibility. In biofeedback training, we know that one doesn't have to understand the process in order to control a certain physiological function. One of the characteristics that has held back some scientific development is the desire to know it all before putting it into action. The desire to have it all together before doing anything. This eliminates one of the great factors in any learning process: trial and error. We *don't* have to understand all of the operations of the human cell before starting to take charge of some of those operations. The sad danger here is that some brilliant biologist may discover a biochemical substance that will prolong life, and if he doesn't know exactly why it works there may be little chance of getting it accepted for general usage. By all means, we need careful laboratory research in this area, and precisely kept records, but it's important to understand that we might not know all there is to know about the human organism in another hundred years, and we don't have to wait until then to do something about improving our lives and our potential right now.

The more the animal requires learned behavior for its survival, the longer it seems to be able to live.

This fact certainly lends credence to the theory that we only use a small proportion of our intellectual capacity, and that the natural evolutionary flow is for us to use more of this mental energy. We are living longer today in our protected environments, and this gives us the opportunity to research ways of living still longer and having still more control over our environments, both externally in the outside world, and internally within our own physiological systems.

. . . if you were able to reduce rates of development, . . . I would almost guarantee that you're going to increase the lifespan.

This brings up an interesting philosophical question: If you were offered a lifespan of two hundred years, but this would require that it take you forty years to "grow up," would you take up the offer? It is within the realm of possibility that scientists will find some way of slowing down the developmental process, thus lengthening it. In another section of this book, we'll examine the lifestyles and attitudes of those people who seem to live much longer as a group in various remote settings. One of the factors that perhaps indirectly affects their longevity by eliminating the stress of uncertainty seems to be that they have very definite rules and instructions about all aspects of life. They are rarely at a loss for what to do. It is certainly true that in our Western culture, we are not very well prepared for life. There is virtually no instruction on the really important aspects of living: how to get along with people, how to choose a lifestyle, how to become successful, how to love. If we had forty years to mature, this could be a period of profound learning and preparation. And with another 160 years of vigorous life ahead of us, with perhaps several different careers and lifestyles during that long stretch of time, we'd need all the preparation and instruction we could get. And it might be that with a slowing down of intellectual development, we would find ways of untapping that vast storehouse of unused intellectual potential we all have.

If you want to ensure that you'll at least live up to your biological potential, there are certainly positive attitudes that will bring you up to that point . . .

This, of course, is the major focus of Psychological Immortality—that, at the very least, certain psychological attitudes will help you get closer to what almost every biologist sees as the current maximum lifespan potential: 120 years.

There are specific genes whose duty is to protect the organism and we don't yet know whether changing lifestyles or attitudes will affect these, but we can certainly suppose that a stress-free, emotionally positive existence will enhance whatever process we eventually use to activate and stimulate these specific genes.

. . . aging is a by-product of living.

It's interesting to speculate on this comment. Could it be that once we learn how to live in total harmony with our environment we will automatically eliminate much of what we now consider normal aging? I would go a step further than Dr. Cutler and state that aging is a by-product of unhealthy living. As we evolve toward taking better care of ourselves—physically, emotionally, spiritually, environmentally—perhaps we can eliminate that by-product. Just as the amazing enzyme superoxide dismutase evolved to get rid of the toxic by-product of oxygen utilization, so might certain psychological skills emerge to deal with the toxic by-product of living: aging.

If you can decrease oxygen consumption then you will increase longevity.

We know that living in a high-stress situation raises oxygen consumption, as does operating with a physically unfit body. This produces inefficient oxygen utilization. We already have tools and skills, such as relaxation techniques and meditation methods, that will help individuals reduce oxygen consumption. What effect this might have on longevity is yet to be fully documented, though there is documented research to the effect that meditators live longer than those who don't meditate. This may very well have something to do with more efficient oxygen consumption. As we develop more precise ways of measuring these physiological changes, we will be able to develop more skills to take charge of our own organism.

Norman Cousins: The Brain's Secretions

A number of the scientists interviewed for this book expressed support and enthusiasm for the work now being inspired by Norman Cousins, a man never trained as a scientist who may end up having the greatest impact of all on the scientific community. In 1964, Cousins, long interested in medicine and science, developed a disease known as ankylosing spondylitis, a crippling condition involving the deterioration of the spine's connective tissue, and one which specialists gave him only a 1-in-500 chance of recovering from. With the cooperation and encouragement of his physician, Cousins developed his own self-treatment program, part of which consisted of massive doses of vitamin C, and part of which consisted of lifting his spirits with laughter, stimulated by old Laurel and Hardy and Marx Brothers movies. Here was a disease which was thought to be hopeless, but Cousins recovered fully. What he later found out was that laughter triggers the secretion by the brain of a substance known as endorphins. These are a morphine-like substance which, once the brain was triggered into secreting them, replaced the need for a number of painkilling drugs. Thus Cousins was able to activate his powerful will to live with an alert, undrugged mind. This underlines some of the dangers of overmedication during debilitating illnesses. If the mind has the power to cure the body, a drugged mind would obviously not be as effective in unleashing the immunological processes built into the human organism.

Since Norman Cousins first reported on his recovery/discovery, a lot more research has been undertaken in this area. In one experiment, for example, dental patients were given a placebo—a nonactive, harmless pill—after a tooth was pulled. A large proportion of these patients had minimal pain and major relief after receiving the placebo pill. What was happening was simply the fact that their brains, absorbing the suggestion that these pills would counteract the pain, produced endorphins to make that suggestion come true. Some of these patients were then given naloxone, a drug which blocks the action of the brain-secreted endorphins. Those given naloxone reported that the pain returned. This effectively showed that these patients weren't just imagining that the placebo eliminated pain, but were actually producing chemical changes in their bodies to fight that pain.

Norman Cousins wrote an article on his experience, and became one of the few laymen ever to be published in the prestigious *New England Journal of Medicine*. That article, appearing in December of 1976, was widely reprinted and discussed in medical and scientific circles around the world. It's now being used as text material by some two dozen medical schools. Cousins expanded the article, and in 1979 it was published as *Anatomy of an Illness as Perceived by the Patient*, quickly achieving best-seller status. In that book, Cousins wrote:

I have learned never to underestimate the capacity of the human mind and body to regenerate—even when the prospects seem most wretched. The life-force may be the least understood force on earth. William James said that human beings tend to live too far within self-imposed limits. It is possible that these limits will recede when we respect more fully the natural drive of the human mind and body toward perfectibility and regeneration. Protecting and cherishing that natural drive may well represent the finest exercise of human freedom.

Norman Cousins is now senior lecturer at the School of Medicine, UCLA, and lectures to doctors and medical students around the world. He is directly involved in inspiring and supporting research into the brain's many secretions. When he first arrived at UCLA in 1978, he asked for a list of all the secretions produced by the brain and was astounded when the medical researchers gave him a list of thirty-eight such secretions. Within a year the list had doubled; at this writing it is approaching four hundred separate substances! Cousins has had a profound effect on medical and biological thinking in that more and more scientists are now viewing the brain in its role as the most prolific gland in the human body.

In a conversation with Cousins, I asked him whether he thought one or more of these secretions from the brain might turn out to be an inner fountain of youth:

They may well have a great deal to do with the optimal functioning of the human body, another way of defining youth. Aging is a matter of the body's regulatory system failing to keep the rebuilding or retardation process on an even keel with the natural processes of cell breakdown. That regulatory system has its center in the human brain. Many medical scientists believe that the lifespan of a human being is about a hundred and twenty years. And it's rather artificial that humans don't fulfill that potentiality. I have no doubt that Richard Berglund is right when he describes the brain not just as the seat of consciousness but as a gland. Other medical researchers like Jon Levine and Howard Field of the University of California at San Francisco have been identifying the products of the gland.

What happens in the brain is, therefore, not merely the processing of thoughts, but actually the production of numberless secretions. The emotions or attitudes can trigger or retard those secretions. The will to live is a powerful stimulant on the endocrine system and on the capacity of the brain to carry out its secreting functions. We're talking about a complicated process which involves not just the endocrine system but perhaps the body's basic energy system. The body is something of a fuel cell which converts chemical energy into electrical energy. All these processes, mysterious but real, are involved in the body's economy.

A number of physicians have expressed the opinion that Norman Cousins may provide the vital link between traditional medicine and the new holistic approaches to healing. He is respected and has made valuable contributions in both areas.

BIOCHEMICAL SIGNIFICANCE OF THE WILL TO LIVE

We cannot begin to measure the impact Cousins will have on human health and longevity. Imagine the implications of this research into the brain's secretions. We do not know the purpose of all of these substances, but it is fair to assume that some of them can have a direct relationship to longevity. By creating a certain mood or attitude, therefore, it might be possible to trigger the secretion of a life-extending chemical. Doctors and other intelligent observers have known all along that the will to live was a potent force in self-preservation and the healing process, but now it can be measured scientifically and we know that it has biochemical significance. The will to live is no longer an abstract psychological theory but a biochemical reality. Now that we have proof positive that this force stimulates actual changes in the body's chemistry, a greater number of people will be more receptive to developing the skills needed to enhance and perpetuate the will to live. With the medical and scientific establishment recognizing the validity of Cousins's perceptions and discoveries (he's now writing articles for the AMA Journal), we'll see more emphasis on building supportive psychological environments and less on pumping bodies full of drugs. And if the will to live can indeed be fortified, as seems likely, dramatic life-extension and even physical immortality come closer to being realistic expectations.

This new awareness of the brain's function as a secreting gland can change the course of human history. With my own background in biofeedback training and research, I can see the eventual development of devices which will actually measure and identify specific secretions and feed back the information to an individual so that he or she knows which specific thoughts or feelings trigger which specific substances. As human beings become more adept at taking charge of their own healing mechanisms, the medical profession will evolve toward greater diagnostic capabilities. We can probably look forward to a day when your doctor can tell you exactly which secretions are necessary for your individual health, whereupon you will program your brain to release those particular secretions. In an era when we have learned to control the autonomic nervous system through biofeedback training, this is not really too farfetched.

It is possible that there may be an eventual link-up between the research being done by such scientists as Dr. Richard G. Cutler and the brain secretion work. If, as he expects, Dr. Cutler narrows the search down to one or two genes that control longevity, then it may be possible to find specific secretions that affect these genes along with ways to trigger those specific secretions.

Perhaps the most profound and important contribution Norman Cousins's work will have is on developing the connection between positive attitudes and actual chemical changes in the body. In a discussion I had with one of the world's most respected gerontologists, Dr. Robert Butler, Director of the National Institute on Aging, he said:

> It is to me generally amazing how little attention we've paid to successful aging, how little we study positive emotions such as joy and affirmation, and how little we've devoted to studies to understand types of changes and rates of changes over time looking at successful populations of adaptive people. I'm extremely positive about Norman Cousins's contribution. I think it helps, and will continue to help, people to begin to think that we can't just study pathology. Sigmund Freud, unfortunately using a wonderful turn of phrase, said that it's often deviation that teaches us. When you take a look at the huge number of dollars that are devoted to health, we spend relatively little trying to understand human growth, develop-

ment, creativity, success, positive elements such as Norman is trying to bring people's attention to.

It's very promising that the head of the National Institute on Aging, one of the eleven major arms of the National Institutes of Health, is so clearly focusing on positive attitudes. As mentioned, the Gerontology Research Center, where Dr. Cutler is doing his research on longevity, also comes under the jurisdiction of the National Institute on Aging. The willingness of this major medical research facility to consider positive and varied approaches to increasing longevity offers a much greater chance of eventual success than merely studying the processes of aging and disease.

LOOKING FOR THE BREAKTHROUGH

In a number of other laboratories around the world, scientists are exploring their own individual theories about aging, death, and longevity. It is certainly possible that one of these projects will produce the explosive breakthrough which will provide the human species with tools to create longer lifespans. Right now, much of this research is unrelated and disconnected.

Many U.S. scientists would like to see more longitudinal studies, research carried out over a longer period of time. This is, in fact, now going on in Soviet Georgia, where four major longevity institutes are conducting a wide range of studies, including some that involve following up the life of one person over a long period. There are also some cooperative efforts between Soviet scientists and U.S. scientists in this area. We'll discuss some of these in Part Two of this book, when we look at some of the long-lived citizens of the Soviet Union and the U.S., as well as other isolated longevity pockets.

Dr. Naira Dalokishvili: Broad-Range Soviet Longevity Studies

I talked to a top Soviet biologist, Dr. Naira Dalokishvili, of the Department of Gerontology, Institute of Experimental Morphology of Academic Sciences in Soviet Georgia. She is involved in the medical/biological part of a massive study which is looking at the Soviet population as a whole in the area of longevity, and says:

> *There are quite a few separate issues that we're looking at. Anthropological studies, ethnography, and a great deal having to do with medical/biological studies, which includes ecological, biochemical, genetic, psychological, medical, and many physiological studies of the cardiovascular, pulmonary, and the nervous system. This all emerged as the result of our conclusion that this phenomenon of longevity is extremely complex and obviously there are many factors to be taken into account, not just one. We are trying to connect all these factors together and determine what are the peculiarities or special features of those who live long. Therefore, we're not just studying those who live long, but the population as a whole.*

The value of studying a population as a whole—the Soviet study is a first of its kind, looking at total populations which have a large percentage of people who live long—is to be able to see the differences between those who do live long and those who don't. What do those who live long and vigorous lives have in common? And what do they have that other people in the same environment may not have?

Though it has been said that the Soviet scientists are not terribly innovative by our standards, they are doing valuable groundwork in building a foundation of solid research into longevity, and they do seem willing to share this information with their counterparts in the U.S. There is, moreover, a parallel between the conservative approach Soviet scientists take and that of those U.S. scientists working primarily under government auspices. Some of the same biologists and gerontologists who complained to me of the stodgy character of the Soviet studies also said that U.S. scientists dependent on grants for their funding tend to play it safe, to continue work already begun, to pick projects with a large possibility of success rather than ones with a lot of unknown factors. People who dispense money for research want results. The iconoclastic inventor working out of his basement and experimenting with a lot of far-out research is not the one getting funded today.

FREE RADICALS

Though it sounds like the cry of a crowd of demonstrating students, free radicals is in fact the term applied to a specific type of molecules. As Dr. Richard Cutler mentioned, free radicals are a by-product of the metabolism of oxygen. They are called free radicals because they are unattached and unstable fragments which zip around the body tissue, entering into reactions with other chemical compounds. These free radicals are thought to be responsible for a lot of so-called cellular garbage. Dr. Denham Harman of the University of Nebraska believes the critical factor in aging may be lipid peroxidation, which involves the formation of certain nonfunctional molecules when free radicals react with unsaturated fatty acids. This results in lipofuscin being produced, a fatty pigment which can take up over 30 percent of the cellular space, leading to an unstable and not very healthy situation. Dr. Harman contends that compounds called antioxidants, which inhibit free radical damage, may be able to slow the aging process. (Vitamin E works at cleaning up the free radicals when taken in conjunction with vitamin C.) Studies have shown that high doses of antioxidants given to laboratory mice may protect them against cancer and certain aging processes. While the mean, or average, lifespan of mice has been reportedly extended through these high antioxidant doses, there are no reports of actually raising the maximum lifespan. It apparently will be several years before any sort of antioxidant drugs will be available for humans in the high doses that seem necessary for results.

AVERAGE VERSUS MAXIMUM LIFESPAN

The difference between average and maximum lifespan sometimes seems confusing. To clarify it, let us simply say that the
average lifespan is the one that is based on the death rate from all
causes, and is slowly going up as medical advances continue.
This is the figure that insurance companies use in their actuarial
studies. This figure has climbed in the past several decades from
the upper 60s to the lower 70s for both men and women. The
maximum lifespan is what biologists see as the general upper
limits we can attain, with some exceptions, the maximum age our
current biological structure seems to prepare us for, which is
somewhere between 110 and 120 according to most scientists.
The work of longevity research is twofold, therefore: to get the
average lifespan closer to our maximum potential, and to raise the
maximum potential itself. So, when we look at the extension of
lifespan of laboratory mice through high antioxidant doses, we are
looking at a raising of the average lifespan, bringing it closer to
the maximum current biological lifespan potential of those mice.

Another way to look at this is to see maximum lifespan, say 120
years, as the potential we now have if we maintain a healthy
psychological and physical lifestyle. A number of the research
projects are aimed at helping people take fuller advantage of this
biological potential. The average lifespan, say 73 years, is what
we can hope to obtain if we *don't* change current attitudes about
aging, if we *don't* realize there is a built-in potential to live longer.
Of course, really unhealthy attitudes and physical habits will
prevent certain individuals from even reaching the average
lifespan.

There is an overlapping effect here. As we move toward getting
more people to reach their full biological potential of over a 100
years, we will simultaneously be working toward raising that
maximum potential even higher.

One of the purposes of Psychological Immortality is to get
people to pay more attention to the maximum lifespan potential as
a goal, rather than to the more widely publicized average lifespan

figures. It's simply a matter of expanding expectations. How many successful actors would have entered the profession if they were constantly told that the average actor earns less than $5,000 per year? The few who earn millions are the inspiration for all those who follow. How many people would write books if they were constantly bombarded with the information that the average book does not even pay for its own printing costs? We reach for the best in ourselves when we have goals of heroic proportions. Not impossible goals. But goals that give us a reason for going on, for wanting to build momentum in our lives. And it can be done one step at a time. The first step is to live as active and involved a life as possible, no matter what your age. The next is to lift your personal horizons beyond the "average" lifespan.

THE MAGICAL DNA

Deoxyribonucleic acid, or DNA, is a microscopic chemical computer. The form and the function of every living thing are dictated by molecules of DNA. Whenever cells divide, the DNA duplicates itself, passing on its genetic information to the new cells. DNA also guides the cells in the production of proteins necessary for life itself, including hormones such as insulin, antibodies that fight disease, hemoglobin that carries oxygen, and enzymes that produce chemical reactions in the body. For some as yet unknown reason, the DNA molecules break down, eventually causing the body to age. In terms of the relationship of aging to the length of developmental time mentioned by Dr. Richard Cutler, it seems that the DNA is programmed to break down once an animal reaches maturity and reproduces. One theory has it that some specific factor of the DNA molecule no longer operates once the body's reproductive period is over and that learning how to keep that specific factor functioning would retard the aging process.

Research has shown that those species with longer lifespans have an increased internal capacity to repair DNA damage. This research therefore has considerable implications in terms of eventually raising the maximum lifespan potential.

As the cells in the body continue to divide, DNA transmits genetic messages to the new cells via RNA, or ribonucleic acid. In someone who is young and healthy, these messages are sent clearly and accurately. With bodily deterioration, however, the messages can get mixed up. It's as if you were dependent for all your communication with the outside world on one switchboard manned by one operator who was slowly getting more and more senile. The more mixed up the messages would get, the more mistakes you would make. The same is true with the cells. Inaccurate messages from the DNA can prevent them from reproducing correctly and can limit the effective defense system that helps the body ward off degenerative diseases. The immunological system is also dependent on these DNA messages.

If, as some scientists theorize, aging is caused by some part of the DNA process being shut down once a person reaches a certain age, then one way to substantially increase lifespan would be to learn to turn that process back on. This might be done by injecting new DNA material into the body. It may also be possible to increase DNA efficiency by eating foods high in nucleic acids. DNA and RNA are both nucleic acids, and some physicians suggest that a diet focused primarily on fish and certain other foods will provide the necessary nucleic acids to reinforce the natural DNA and RNA, thereby helping the body increase DNA repairability.

This is all very new. DNA research was almost nonexistent before the dramatic work of James Watson and Francis Crick in 1953. These two Cambridge University scientists, along with Maurice Wilkens at nearby King's College, made perhaps the most exciting breakthrough in the entire history of genetic research, actually discovering and proving the double helix structure of DNA. It was like finding the instruction booklet for all living organisms. Much of the research in the following three decades has been aimed at reading that booklet.

RECOMBINANT DNA

In the past several years, a new technology known as recombinant DNA has emerged. This involves taking genes from one organism and planting them into another, in effect splicing genes. In 1978, a group of California scientists used this process to make human insulin. Up to now, insulin for the diabetics who need it to stay alive has been produced from pancreatic tissue of cattle or pigs. In addition to its high cost, animal insulin causes an allergic reaction in many diabetics, so that the California project has some immediate benefits in sight. Recombinant techniques have also been used to produce interferon, a natural antivirus substance. David Baltimore of the Massachusetts Institute of Technology feels that any of the body's basic proteins will be able to be produced through recombinant DNA in unlimited quantities in the next fifteen years. Scientists say that this new science will enable them to identify every single one of the 100,000 genes in the human cell, so that eventually healthy cells could be produced to replace unhealthy ones.

SNOWBALLING BREAKTHROUGHS

The breakthroughs are occurring faster than anyone can predict them. In September of 1979, for instance, a group of experts at a recombinant DNA conference predicted it would take at least three years to produce human interferon in bacteria. That breakthrough was announced just four months later. While most genetic engineering has involved transplanting genes into cells outside bodies in laboratory dishes, or into bacteria, in April of 1980 scientists at UCLA reported that they had inserted into adult mice a gene that makes cells resistant to a specific drug. In September of the same year, a group of Yale scientists announced they had injected foreign genes into a fertilized mouse egg. They did this by isolating genes from two viruses and then producing those genes in large quantities. Using glass needles thinner than a hair, biologist Francis Ruddle, with research colleagues Jon Gordon and George Scangos, microinjected from 1,000 to 20,000 copies of the genetic material directly into the nuclei of newly fertilized mouse eggs kept alive in laboratory dishes. The eggs were then transferred to the wombs of female mice, and these foster mothers gave birth to 150 infant mice. When DNA was extracted from the tissue of these newborn mice, portions of the transplanted viral genes were found in two of the mice. This experiment lends credence to the genetic engineering dream of someday eliminating many inherited diseases by changing the genetic material in the human egg. Of course, this is an issue fraught with controversy, ethical implications, and potential dangers.

When the April 1980 UCLA experiments were announced, many scientists said experimentation with humans was still a great many years away. But then (in October of 1980) it was revealed that in July of that year UCLA hematologist Martin Cline and colleagues in Jerusalem and Naples performed gene transplants on two female patients suffering from an inherited blood disorder in which the bone marrow produces red blood cells with defective hemoglobin. Cline and his colleagues removed small amounts of bone marrow and combined it with genes that were capable of directing the production of normal hemoglobin. The genes had been manufactured by bacteria altered by recombinant DNA technology. The marrow, now including these new genes, was injected back into the patients' bodies. At this writing, there's no sign yet that healthy hemoglobin is being produced by the newly reinforced bone marrow, but the mere fact that this type of experiment was carried out on human subjects years ahead of a timetable predicted only months before has astounded scientists around the world and awakened many to the snowballing effect of breakthrough genetic research.

If scientists locate the right chromosomes, they could conceivably repair defective genes in individuals or insert new healthy genes into the cell. This process is called gene therapy. Genetic engineers hope eventually to be able to repair many hereditary defects in humans. One of these defects may be aging itself. There are two ways of doing this repair work. One would be to infect patients with viruses that carry the correct healthy genes. Another would be to remove actual cells from the particular individual, repair those in culture in the lab, reproduce the repaired cells, then reinsert them into the body, as was done in the Jerusalem and Naples experiments.

While it was once thought that genes were passive creatures, passing on their hereditary messages, scientists over the past several years have been shocked by one discovery after another indicating that instead of just carrying the coded messages to the cells, genes can rearrange themselves in the first few months of life, producing new codes, which in turn can produce new biological substances. It now appears that some genes are dynamic and some are passive. The dynamic genes seem to belong to the immunological system. Biologists feel that this new awareness will lead to their discovering the causes of diseases of the immunological system in the very near future.

So far, we have no idea how this all fits in with those natural brain secretions mentioned by Norman Cousins. Truly, this whole area of science is in its infancy. No one knows where it is going, and no scientist involved in any of this research is declaring that there are any limits to the possibilities.

RESEARCH AS BIG BUSINESS

There is a major controversy going on now because the ability of DNA recombinant techniques to produce human proteins is proving a spectacular boon to the drug companies, which are pouring money into the basic research with the hope of developing a number of commercially successful substances. This could possibly mean that should this research produce an anti-aging substance, some pharmaceutical firm could hold the patent on it. There are many scientists who feel this work should be above commercial considerations. The other side of the argument is that some of the research wouldn't get done if it weren't for the large sums being poured into labs by the drug companies.

One side effect of all this activity is what could be called the dehumanization of some of these processes. The media gets excited about the announcement that interferon is produced in the lab, but hardly anyone knows that this is one of those natural secretions Norman Cousins talks about, one of the substances released by the brain. Perhaps if more research were devoted to finding ways of internally producing more of these substances we would be further along in increasing biological opportunities. Of course, the drug companies, funding a great deal of the recombinant DNA research, would have nothing to sell if people learned to produce these substances within their own bodies.

One of the inherent dangers therefore in focusing so much attention on substances produced either in the lab artificially or from animals is that research into how humans can internally learn to control these processes may suffer. If a substance called XYZ were found to inhibit aging, was produced by one of the body's many glands, and could also be produced in a lab, a major drug company might pour millions of dollars into synthetically producing XYZ, patenting this process and eventually reaping windfall profits, while efforts to learn more about how the body produces it and how its production could be stimulated might fall by the wayside for lack of funding.

Dr. Arthur Falek: DNA Repairability

One of the areas of research which looks most promising and seems to make a lot of sense is that aimed at repairing the natural breakdowns of the DNA. I talked to Dr. Arthur Falek, Director of the Behavioral Genetics Laboratory at the Georgia Mental Health Institute, who said:

The possibilities are as wide as the imagination can go. We know that the DNA, sitting even under standard neon lights, does break down. This ultraviolet light does have an impact on our cells and on the DNA repair of our cells. We repair this damage. We have demonstrated in the lab that we have individuality of repair. I repair that ultraviolet light damage at a different rate than you repair it. There's a difference in the repairability. Our next step is to measure the genetics of the DNA repairability. The question to ask is: Do individuals who repair DNA damage from ultraviolet light, or from large chemicals, which is a different repair kind of phenomenon, or from small chemicals, which is still a different repairing phenomenon—do individuals who have this capability of repairing in all three instances, let's say at a very high level, are these the people who survive?

We can now demonstrate that there is a relationship between levels of DNA repair and levels of chromosome damage—that those people who have a greater difficulty in repairing DNA have a greater frequency of chromosome damage.

The implications for what the biology of the mechanism is seem very real, as do the implications for those people who fortunately have the positive aspect of this biology in terms of length of life. What now needs to be considered is how we can impact upon that to prevent abnormal division of cells that has been considered as the basis of aging.

Obviously, if certain people have more DNA repair capabilities than others, *and* live longer, then a major factor has been revealed. The studies to prove this would be complex and long-ranging. It seems a logical conclusion, but many such logical conclusions have been disproved in the objective world of research. Enough scientists, however, accept the idea that DNA repairability is related to longevity to suppose it will be substantiated by further experiments. One can see here why some of the massive studies undertaken by the Soviet Union are useful. If we could take one thousand people, somehow measure their DNA repairability, and then see how long they live and how youthful they remain, we could easily measure the correlation between the two factors: DNA repairability and longevity. The next step, and one already being studied by a number of biologists and geneticists, is, as Dr. Falek puts it, how to impact upon that, how to improve DNA repairability. If, as some scientists suggest, it could be done by injecting DNA material into the body to reinforce the already present DNA material, then everyone could have optimum DNA repairability. This means that as we would grow older, the DNA messages to the cells would remain youthfully clear and accurate, and the cells would divide in normal ways, maintaining the body in healthy and youthful condition perhaps indefinitely.

Again, the possibilities are limitless, especially if we find that one of the nearly four hundred brain secretions either contains or affects the nucleic acid content of the body. If laughing, as has been proven, can stimulate release of painkilling endorphins from the brain, then who knows what emotional attitude or activity might affect the release of nucleic acid; perhaps DNA or RNA material itself could be increased. This period in research history could be likened to the early days of flying: The dreams are boundless, but the actual current effort involves much speculation, risk, hard work, and a great deal of adventure.

Dr. Bernard Strehler: Ribosomal DNA

For the past twenty-five years, one of the most daring and respected of all the "pilots" in the field of aging and longevity research has been Dr. Bernard Strehler, Professor of Molecular Biology at the University of Southern California, and one of the scientists instrumental in helping to set up the National Institute on Aging. Dr. Strehler, who is also focusing on the DNA factor, is dedicated, innovative, and optimistic:

I think we can extend the lifespan by some ten years by the turn of the century. By 2025, we ought to be able to increase it by a total of thirty to forty years, and after that it's anybody's guess. It depends on how the research turns out. We have to understand how a car is made before we can tell how long it's going to last. You have to know what you can fix in it and what you can't.

Dr. Strehler also believes DNA repairability can be the key to longevity:

We're looking at damage to DNA, particularly loss of particular kinds of DNA called ribosomal DNA, or rDNA, which manufactures ribosomal RNA, which in turn is used in the production of proteins. You find about a 40 to 60 percent loss during the lifetime in cells such as brain cells and heart cells. We think that this loss may account for the decreased vigor that older individuals have.

If the loss of ribosomal DNA does affect the deterioration of the brain and heart cells, what can be done to counteract it?

Well, there's a 10 to 25 percent possibility that additional copies of such genes might be inserted through genetic engineering, carried by a viral carrier, such as has been proposed for individuals that have a specific defect in some of their enzymes.

Dr. Strehler is talking here about the very essence of life. rDNA is the main component of ribosomes, which are any of several minute particles composed of protein and RNA and found in cells. As to the current focus of his research team, Dr. Strehler says:

I'd like to know how the ribosomal DNA is lost, the degree to which the loss of a given amount impairs a specific cell's function. If you know how it's lost, one might be able to counteract or reduce the rate of loss. Dogs lose the same percentage of this material in about one-seventh of the time that we do, which corresponds to the rough ratio of our lifespans. Dogs live to about 15, we to about 105. It probably has to do with the efficiency of repair mechanisms for single-stranded DNA damage.

Here again we see the vital impact of DNA repairability. If dogs lose rDNA seven times faster than we humans do, and die seven times faster, then we can easily see the direct connection. If rDNA loss affects the repair capability, then preventing that loss, or somehow replacing the rDNA, will help the organism operate more efficiently, and repair damage over a longer period of time.

In the lab, Dr. Strehler has come up with still another fascinating connection between rDNA and aging:

> *You can almost predict the age of tissue from the amount of rDNA that is present in the DNA. Since it's a key material, it may be the reason for the decreased rate of response of older humans and other kinds of animals to severe challenge. It's the speed of response frequency rather than the absolute maximum response obtained that is decreased in older animals.*

In other words, though older humans may have the same response capacity, it just takes them longer to use it. This relates to the findings of a number of scientists studying the connections between behavior and longevity, health, and aging. It seems that one of the factors determining whether someone will successfully survive is his or her ability to *quickly* meet and overcome stressful challenges. It isn't that they don't respond to stress, but that they respond more quickly, and therefore recover faster. How fast your system responds with necessary and appropriate responses, whether physical or emotional, can make all the difference in whether your life is successful or not. Dr. Strehler agrees:

> *It can be very tough on you if you're running from a lion, and that extra burst of speed is a matter of life and death. Similarly, in an infection, if your immune system responds 50 percent as rapidly, even though it responds properly, then it can't keep up with the infection, you can't win. In order for one to respond to a severe challenge like an infection, you have to make antibodies and kill off the invading bacteria faster than they can grow. If the immune system is deficient in its rate of response, suppose it responds at 50 percent the rate of a younger person, then, depending on the magnitude of the infection that one is dealing with, an older person will not be able to manufacture the defenses rapidly enough to take care of it. I think the loss of the ribosomal DNA is what limits the rate of response.*

Again we see that the immunological system has an important role to play. Many researchers feel that the body's natural defense system is operating at only a fraction of its true potential, and that if this efficiency could be boosted by either some internal process as suggested by Norman Cousins, or by external application of some substance—introduction into the body of some immune-enhancing gene or hormone or enzyme—then perhaps aging itself could be eliminated. Dr. Strehler says:

If *you eliminated aging, since death due to accidents in young people is about one in ten thousand per year, you'd have an average lifespan, if you stayed exactly as you were when you were 11 years old, of five to ten thousand years, depending on the environment.*

Dr. Strehler emphasizes that the "if" is a big one, and we are nowhere near actually eliminating aging. He likens predicting this to trying to predict the weather a year or two from now. As to whether we will ever be able to enlist the brain's secretions in the effort to replace lost DNA, he says:

I would be reluctant to make that kind of connection. I do think the area of neurosecretions, for example the endorphins, these relatively simple peptides that have remarkable effects in relieving pain and so forth, I think that there may be a whole group of undiscovered things that affect other physiological functions.

As for the belief expressed by Dr. Richard Cutler that just a few genes may be responsible for longevity, Dr. Strehler feels that this theory is predicated on random selection as an evolutionary process, that human beings naturally evolved into a longer lifespan. One theory that is quite provocative and has been written up for various journals by Dr. Strehler is that we have early polygamy to thank for our current lifespan. As he told me:

The amazing thing is that the life expectancy of humanoids has doubled in the last couple million years at most, and that's a remarkably fast evolution of longevity. What it may mean is that the social structure of early human societies provided means such as polygamy as a way of increasing the rate of evolution of vigor and mental capacity and longevity. That is that the smartest and strongest males in the tribe had access to most of the females. Then the rate at which those genes that confer vigor become common to the species is increased roughly in proportion to the degree of polygamy that's exercised. I suspect that most of our ancestors were polygamists, which is probably why men still have a greater tendency than women to be polygamists today, officially or unofficially.

This is one of those digressions that make this area of study so fascinating. Despite its implications to those of us committed to equality between the sexes, this theory does raise some interesting questions. What Strehler is saying, basically, is that the early male member of a human tribe who had exceptional vigor and a long survival rate would tend to mate with more of the tribal women, thus conferring those qualities on the offspring of such unions. If true, this could answer the question asked by many biologists: Why did this remarkably fast evolution of longevity seem to slow down over the last few hundred years? Could it be that this somehow coincides with the emergence of monogamy as the preferred social state?

Furthermore, if we agree that it is natural for the species to evolve to higher and higher levels of health and longevity, then might this not indicate that polygamy is a more natural state for males than monogamy? And can't this be supported by the fact that there are more women than men in most populations? If this were to be studied, it would also be interesting to examine tribes in which women were dominant and able to mate with as many of the men as possible, depending on the women's vigor and proven superiority of strength and intelligence. Would the offspring of these polygamous women also inherit these genetic strengths? No one is suggesting a social upheaval and return to polygamy, but this does provide some food for thought if not for further scientific investigation.

HORMONAL AGING

There is yet another school of scientific and gerontological thought that considers the primary factor in aging to be hormonal. This group feels there is indeed an internal biological clock and that it's made up of hormones, various internally secreted compounds. Dr. W. Donner Denckla, formerly of the Harvard Medical School and Roche Laboratories, and now with the Institute of Alcohol and Alcoholism, has been seeking to identify the hormone he believes is directly responsible for aging and death. He's been focusing his attention on a pituitary extract containing eighteen proteins, but hasn't yet uncovered the one hormone he is hunting for.

Dr. Richard C. Adelman of the Fels Research Institute at Temple University's School of Medicine believes that hormonal regulation of enzyme activity is the key to halting or slowing down the aging process. He feels breakdowns in neural or endocrine regulatory capability may be the cause of the decreased performance and lower immunity to disease noted in the elderly. So while Dr. Bernard Strehler is looking into the loss of ribosomal DNA as the factor that might be responsible for the deterioration in the speed of response of older people, Dr. Adelman is focusing on hormones. Note that a lot of this research is interconnected, but that different scientists choose different aspects of these processes on which to base their studies. It could conceivably be that if Dr. Strehler finds a way to prevent the loss of ribosomal DNA, this would affect breakdowns in hormonal regulation, while finding a way to correct hormonal breakdowns might affect the loss of ribosomal DNA.

Dr. Adelman's hypothesis reminds me again of the work of Norman Cousins at UCLA. Cousins believes the brain can secrete endocrinal and hormonal substances that will fortify and optimize the body's basic immunological defenses. If old age itself is a disease, something that can be fought and cured, then any buildup of the body's defense mechanisms has to have a positive effect. Also at UCLA Medical Center, Dr. Roy L. Walford has suggested that the immunological system is the key. He notes that artificial disruption of the system produces many of the same effects as does the aging process. These include degeneration of internal organs, skin wrinkles, loss of brain cells, and weight loss. Cancer researchers have stated time and time again that a breakdown in the normal immunological functions may well be the spark that ignites the spread of cancer. There's a good chance we'll soon see specific drugs and techniques designed to enhance the body's natural immunity processes and thus have a clearer idea of whether this will have an effect on aging.

THE THYMUS

The primary immunological gland is the thymus, which programs cells from the lymph nodes and spleen to combat attacking organisms. The thymus gland is about the size of a half dollar at birth, and grows to about three times its original size during puberty. Then, for no known reason, it begins to shrink and virtually disappears in old age. Until 1961, scientists assumed the thymus gland, located just over the heart, was useless—a sort of nonfunctioning anatomical leftover from some earlier period in human evolution, like the appendix. Then researchers were amazed to find that when the thymus gland was surgically removed from young animals in the lab, the animals got massive infections and literally wasted away, also getting a much higher than normal rate of cancer. At the Albert Einstein College of Medicine in New York, the noted endocrinologist Dr. Abraham White came to the conclusion that the thymus was secreting a hormone. Dr. Allan Goldstein, now chairman of the Department of Biochemistry at George Washington University, had just arrived for postdoctoral training under Dr. White. White and Goldstein studied this theoretical hormone, and finally isolated it in 1965. Dr. Goldstein is one of the scientists who has now manufactured the hormone thymosin, which can increase the number of white blood cells so important in the body's defense system. Scientists working on some 150 thymosin research projects around the world feel this development is akin to the creation of antibiotics in the early 1940s in terms of its impact on human health. In studies by Dr. Paul Chretien of the Tumor Immunology Section at the National Cancer Institute, cancer patients given high doses of thymosin lived far longer than groups given placebos and groups given low doses of thymosin. When Dr. Takshi Makinodan of the National Institute on Aging transplanted thymus glands and bone marrow from young mice into older mice, the older mice were rejuvenated, in terms of their disease-fighting capability, to the level of mice one-fifth their age. The mice with the transplants also lived at least one-third longer than their normal lifespans.

There's little doubt that one reason people get older is because of a breakdown in the immunological system. As the thymus gland shrinks, the immunological system weakens. Scientists are optimistic about eventually regenerating the entire immunological system with doses of thymosin. A lot more research needs to be undertaken; it will probably be several years before enough tests are completed and evaluated for thymosin to be made available to the general public. Thymosin is believed to have the capability of repairing the immunological system when it is damaged by the chemotherapy and radiation therapy used in cancer treatments. Most researchers think this is why the cancer patients studied by Dr. Chretien lived longer after receiving high doses of thymosin.

Manipulation of the immunological system with such drugs as thymosin is the fastest growing new field in biology. Yet one of the reasons a lot more work is needed in this area is that thymosin is not merely a single hormone, but rather a whole family of hormones with many different components. Dr. Goldstein's team at George Washington University is now trying to identify and characterize all of thymosin's components.

There is a theory called "immunological surveillance" popularized by Nobel laureate and biologist Dr. MacFarlane Burnet of England. This theory is simply that we humans are constantly getting all sorts of diseases every single day of our lives, but that our immunological system successfully battles these illnesses before we even know they exist. Cancer researchers extend this theory to encompass the idea that cancer cells are constantly being created in the body and constantly being destroyed by the immunological system. If this theory is correct, then being able to build up the immunological system with thymosin can have very great consequences for human health and longevity. The Hoffmann-LaRoche pharmaceutical labs in Nutley, New Jersey, have a major role in the development of thymosin. Dr. Allan Goldstein assigned patent rights on his discoveries to the universities where the discoveries were originally made. In turn, the universities have signed licensing agreements with Roche, the only producer of thymosin in the United States. Dr. Armin Ramel, one of Roche's leading biochemists, feels thymosin can have a stunning impact on anti-aging efforts:

After all, what is aging? It is getting more and more sick. Sicker and sicker. More and more often.

Dr. Allan Goldstein himself says:

This would be a whole new way of treating disease. The exciting thing is that these discoveries offer us the opportunity to deal with disease the way God has dealt with it. That is, from within.

The fact that so much research is now centered on thymosin, a substance not even imagined in 1960, indicates the explosive evolution of biological research. One thing that seems apparent is that these thousands of scientists around the world are really writing the repair manual for the human body. And whether it's learning how to repair DNA or the immunological system or cellular deterioration, it seems certain that the next ten to twenty years will see astounding progress in terms of enhancing health and promoting longevity.

FOOLING THE BODY

As we learn more about the inner processes of the body, we see that it is an even more intricately and remarkably designed mechanism than ever before imagined. *The human body in fact seems to produce all it needs to combat most breakdowns.* As we learn more about those internal healing processes, the body will become an even more effective self-maintaining organism. One theory is that the body can produce additional amounts of some of the anti-aging substances it already produces *if* we create circumstances which will, in effect, fool the body into thinking it has undergone a major pathological attack. Dr. Richard Cutler, for one, speculates that we could stimulate a barrage of DNA repair processes by inserting into the cell structure a highly damaged piece of DNA with everything possible wrong with it, thus activating all the internal mechanisms for repairing DNA damage. Another way Dr. Cutler sees to trick the body is to inject some kind of simulated aging material, a sort of anti-aging vaccine, which would activate all the protective enzymes and the entire immunological system. As he said in reference to the polio vaccine, we don't even have to know exactly how and why it works.

If scientists discover exactly why the thymus gland shrinks in old age, then we could conceivably send it false messages that the body was, in fact, not aging at all. Sexual maturation may have some side effects that trigger the shrinking process, and this may be one of the reasons scientists such as Dr. Cutler see some parts of the body's biology starting to break down with sexual maturation. If the thymus could be fooled into thinking that sexual maturation has not yet occurred, then perhaps the body's immunological system will stay youthful and effective for a much longer period.

It seems likely that we will become more knowledgeable about the brain's secretions through the research inspired by Carmine Clemente and Norman Cousins at UCLA Medical School and at other research facilities. It is therefore entirely possible that someday we will discover a certain mental/emotional trigger that can produce more of these protective enzymes and hormones. The human brain is a biochemical factory and we are like cavemen suddenly transported into a modern computer complex in terms of our grasp of the situation and its potential. But one thing has been true throughout human history: We continue to learn.

CANCER AS A CURE

One scientist who requested anonymity suggests that cancer may be the answer to the search for a life-extension substance. Currently the number two killer of human beings, next to heart disease, cancer, this biologist thinks, might eventually be turned around and enlisted in the battle against aging. He feels that once we have learned enough about cancer to cure it, we will also have learned enough to use it positively. He bases this speculation partly on the fact that cancer cells are more indestructible than regular cells.

Now, it used to be thought that all cells were virtually indestructible. It was only about twenty years ago that this was proven to be a false premise. Dr. Leonard Hayflick of Stanford University was the scientist who rocked the biological establishment by proving that cells divide and redivide a limited number of times in tissue culture. (There's an excellent account of this research in Albert Rosenfeld's *Pro-Longevity*.)

As so often is true when science tries to declare anything absolutely so, the entire medical-biological community was wrongly convinced that cells could reproduce indefinitely in culture outside the body. Until Leonard Hayflick came along, no one dared question the integrity or accuracy of the late Nobel Prize-winning Alexis Carrel of the Rockefeller Institute, who apparently had continuously maintained a culture of chicken cells for thirty-four years. What eventually turned up, after Hayflick's initial research, was that Carrel's culture was contaminated by fresh stray cells contained in the embryonic chicken heart substance added to the culture to keep it fresh. What's especially fascinating is that a number of other researchers had discovered that Carrel's hypothesis was wrong but were either afraid to say so or disbelieved their own research results, so powerful was the Carrel mystique. This is one of the reasons we have a reasonably healthy scientific milieu today in which many different scientists are doing their own basic research in many different areas, and not depending on the reputation of only one or two scientists. And for the most part scientists researching longevity seem to be on excellent personal and professional terms, even when disagreeing about each other's theories.

THE HAYFLICK LIMIT

What Hayflick found was that cells will divide, double their population, about fifty times before they stop dividing. This is now known as the Hayflick Limit. It is invaluable information for those studying aging and longevity. It indicates a possible reason for our apparent maximum lifespan of 110 to 120 years. In fact, once Hayflick found that human cells could divide about fifty times without dying, he estimated that, on the basis of those fifty divisions, the human lifespan should be about 110 to 120 years, since that's how long it would take for those fifty divisions to occur inside the human body.

Scientists do not yet know why cells just stop reproducing at some point, both in the body and outside it in tissue culture. Once *this* secret is uncovered, there may be no limits as to how long a human being may live. In a sense, all of the work mentioned so far in this section may be seen as attempts at overcoming the Hayflick Limit. Whether genes, hormones, enzymes, or some other brain secretions will eventually prove to have the major effect on longevity, there is a good chance that all of this current research will eventually have an impact on the solution to the longevity problem. One reason Hayflick's work is monumental is the simple fact that once we know the limits, we can start working toward expanding them.

Now, while we know there is a limit to the life of normal cells in tissue culture, we also now know that there is, so far, no limit to the life of cancer cells in culture. In fact, the longest continuously maintained human cell strain is the HeLa strain, started with samples from a woman named Henrietta Lacks who had cancer of the cervix. Dr. George O. Gey of Johns Hopkins was the man who began this strain in 1951, and it is still thriving in labs around the world, proving invaluable in cancer research. Cancer cells are obviously not immortal *inside* the human body, since they will eventually kill off their own life-support system. Cancer cells seem to be able to turn on switched-off genetic processes. Certain cells stop dividing once maturity is reached, with a built-in "stop dividing" switch. Dr. Bernard Strehler says most aging effects occur in these cells that have stopped dividing. Some of the damage caused by cancer evidently occurs when the cancer cells intervene in this natural process. If cancer cells could somehow be programmed, be *trained* to intervene, but in healthy ways rather than destructive ones, they indeed might prove the ironic key to extended life.

Another farfetched but not impossible theory is to fool the body into thinking it is under massive attack by cancer cells, so that the immunological system is totally alerted and activated, thus perhaps counteracting some of the aging process.

There are some interesting correlations between cancer and aging. We humans double our susceptibility to cancer every nine years between the ages of 45 and 80. When skin cells from middle-aged mice are exposed to chemical cancer-inducing agents, they are more likely to become malignant than skin cells similarly exposed from young mice. Processes that have successfully expanded the lives of laboratory animals have also reduced the amount of malignant tumors in those animals, and the severity of those tumors which did occur. Aging, then, seems to impair the ability of the immunological system to respond quickly, as noted by Dr. Strehler in our interview. Dysfunctional immunological processes also seem to be related to cancer, with people having damaged immunological systems being much more likely to get that disease.

A lot of the basic longevity research emerged out of discoveries made during cancer research. One cancer researcher told me that "once we have the secret of cancer, we'll have the secret of life." Not all scientists are so hopeful, but many agree that cancer research and longevity research are very much interconnected, and that some of the research projects now going on, such as that involving thymosin, affect both areas of biological investigation. Many biologists feel there will be no cure for cancer until we learn whether it is, in fact, triggered by the aging process, and how this might happen inside the body. Another interesting link: While the likelihood of getting cancer statistically doubles every nine years from 45 to 80, the likelihood of dying from any cause doubles every eight years after sexual maturation. This statistic is true for all species. It means simply that at 40 you have twice the chance of dying as you did at 32. And while the chances may start out as minimal, as you approach your 70s and 80s the odds begin to shorten. Since the same basic statistics are true with regard to one's chances of getting cancer, there may eventually prove to be some basic link between cancer cells and the aging process. To take this a step further in a provocative direction, it is possible that someday an anti-aging vaccine, composed of reprogrammed cancer cells, will be used to extend the human lifespan.

Dr. Johann Bjorksten: Cross-Linkage

One official of the National Institute on Aging said the reason so many scientists are working on longevity is because *they* don't want to die! Be that as it may, there are many reasons researchers enter this field, and many backgrounds from which they emerge. None is more interesting than the story of Johann Bjorksten. In the early 1940s, before the advent of Xerox, the major manufacturer of copying machines was Ditto, Inc. Ditto had a research biochemist named Johann Bjorksten, and Ditto also had a problem which Bjorksten set about to investigate. The problem was that special film used in making copies eventually deteriorated so that it could no longer produce copies. Bjorksten found that one major component of film, gelatin, a semisolid solution of proteins in water, was not very different in structure from collagen, the protein substance that forms human connective tissue. He found furthermore that the breakdown of the film emulsion was identical with the aging process of connective tissue and also identical with the hardening of leather during tanning. The breakdown is called cross-linkage because the collagen is protein (in fact it forms about one-third of the body's protein), and certain smaller chemicals can bond with two proteins to form a bridge, or cross-linkage. According to Bjorksten, large molecules become cross-linked through the action of smaller molecules and create an obstacle similar to the one that would be created on a football field if all the players were handcuffed together. Bjorksten also claims that cross-linkage is directly responsible for the loss of elasticity in connective tissue, one of the major effects of aging. For nearly forty years, the former industrial biochemist has been stalking possible enzymes that could circulate through the body and destroy the cross-linked connections between the protein chains. Since the human organism often produces enzymes that attack various kinds of internal deterioration, if such an adversary enzyme can be found for cross-linking, it would be possible to develop a method of rejuvenating cells and organs.

Dr. Roy Schenk: Aluminum Accumulation

I talked to biochemist Dr. Roy Schenk, Vice-President of the Bjorksten Research Foundation in Madison, Wisconsin, who told me of a whole new area of research at the foundation:

What we've been doing at the laboratory is looking at some of the polymetals and how they affect the brain. Aluminum has been a particular problem. Some people seem to be predisposed to absorb more aluminum and it seems to accumulate in the brain. If you get too much aluminum in the brain, you get things like senile dementia. There seems to be a very high correlation between the amount of aluminum in the brain and the loss of brain function. At the moment we're looking at how we can eliminate the aluminum from the brain, looking at various techniques for reextracting the aluminum. In most human beings it takes perhaps sixty or seventy years for aluminum to build up. If you can lower the aluminum levels gradually over a period of time it would be effective. I've done some work looking at lactic acid as the possible extractant for aluminum. The reason that that's interesting is that when you exert yourself strenuously, the body converts glucose to lactic acid instead of to carbon dioxide and water, and you can build up levels as high as a tenth of a percent of lactic acid in the blood. We're looking at whether we can therefore extract aluminum with lactic acid. If that's so, then exercise may have more benefits than people have already recognized.

ELECTRICAL PHENOMENA IN AGING

Dr. Schenk also described some more long-term research:

There's some work in what I describe as electrical phenomena in aging. For example, some studies involving newts. Normally, if you cut a limb off a newt it'll regrow its limb. They've found that by varying the direction of electricity, they can either speed up or slow down the regrowth. There's been a number of other studies where people are beginning to get a grasp of the electrical phenomena associated with life. I think these studies have some real potential as far as the future is concerned.

While we now know that the brain is a biochemical factory, there is also strong indication that it has some electrical properties as well. There is an energy force in the human body which has not yet been fully measured or defined. A number of physiologists feel it is bioelectrical in nature, that the body produces its own form of electricity, of internal energy. The ancient Chinese medical practice of acupuncture, for example, is really aimed at releasing blockages of human energy by stimulating various energy centers in the body. Little is known about this energy, which might be called the life force. Even Chinese practitioners of acupuncture who totally acknowledge its presence and importance admit they do not know *why* acupuncture works. It is not unreasonable to suppose that whatever this energy is, it can be affected by the brain's activities, and by an individual's emotional attitudes. Certainly, when negative emotional experiences occur, one does feel drained of energy. And when a person just gives up emotionally, that person can simply die. This is an area more and more scientists are looking into, though any real conclusions are at least several years away.

TEMPERATURE DOWN—LIFESPAN UP

Another fascinating theory about aging is that it can be slowed down simply by lowering the body's temperature. A number of respected scientists are researching this aspect of longevity, thus lending credence to Dr. Bernard Strehler's claim that lowering the body temperature as little as three degrees could add twenty years to our lives.

Dr. Roy Walford and Dr. Robert K. Kiu of UCLA Medical Center were able to extend the maximum lifespan of cold-blooded fish by 76 percent by lowering the temperature of the water in which the fish were kept. Experiments in attempting to lower the temperature of warm-blooded species have not been as successful, however. This may be due to the efficiency of our temperature control system. Part of the problem in trying to change the human organism is its powerful defense mechanisms against change; the normal body temperature of 98.6 degrees Fahrenheit (37 degrees

Celsius) is apparently an archaic leftover from the evolution of man as a warm-blooded mammal. It's a complex, remarkable system: No matter how cold or hot it is outside our bodies, there is little or no change inside. While it is true that a rise in temperature, called a fever, can be dangerous, it is only recently that scientists have been studying the possibility that lowering the temperature might be life-enhancing.

Dr. Roy Walford thinks reduced body temperature extends lifespan by depressing the autoimmune reactions that contribute to bodily deterioration. There are autoimmune diseases that occur when the immunological system mistakenly attacks the body it is trying to protect. These diseases include rheumatoid arthritis and lupus, a disabling disease which affects young women. Thymosin, with its capacity for reinforcing and correcting the immunological system, has been effective in dealing with both diseases. No extensive tests have been undertaken on whether lowering body temperature can have such a specific effect on autoimmune responses, but this offers intriguing possibilities.

In studies at Purdue University, Dr. Robert D. Myers has explored the possibility of lowering our internal thermostat. He's found that the point at which this thermostat is set in mammals may involve the balance between sodium and calcium ions in the posterior hypothalamus region of the brain. Dr. Myers found that he could lower a monkey's temperature by applying excess calcium to the posterior hypothalamus, and conversely, he could raise the base temperature by using a solution containing excess sodium. Myers is convinced that this method actually resets the body's thermostat because the temperature of the experimental animals returns to the new setting rather than back to the so-called normal level after he raises or lowers their temperatures with applications of hot or cold water. These findings offer the possibility that slightly raising the level of calcium ion concentration in the posterior hypothalamus of human beings might permanently lower our body temperature without any harmful side effects.

Dr. Richard Cutler has offered one suggestion for the future that might not be as farfetched as it sounds at first. This technique would involve inserting a tiny ceramic device into the blood vessel leading to the hypothalamus. A microwave unit would then be placed in the individual's bedroom. At night, when the body has a slower metabolic rate, the microwave unit would begin operating and the embedded device would then trick the hypothalamus into thinking the body had a one- or two-degree fever. The hypothalamus would then lower the body's temperature a degree or two. The microwave unit would switch off before the person woke up, and the temperature would then return to normal. Lowering the temperature while asleep could, according to some biologists, double our current lifespan.

This isn't the only scheme designed to insert something in the body. The Alzet Osmotic Minipump is already in existence. It's a self-powered device which is used to deliver solutions into the bodies of lab animals at controlled rates for up to two weeks. It could be used to send regulated amounts of extra calcium into the hypothalamus. These and similar devices implanted beneath the skin surface could be used to deliver calcium and other substances found to have anti-aging properties to individuals at carefully regulated rates.

It is interesting that some of this temperature control research is focused on the hypothalamus, which is considered the part of the brain in charge of hormonal secretions. Hormones help to regulate the metabolic rate. They also cause biologically programmed changes in the body at certain specific periods in life, such as puberty and menopause. There are some scientists who believe that learning exactly how the hypothalamus functions and then learning how to control it may be the answer to controlling longevity. The hypothalamus is certainly very much involved in the brain secretions Norman Cousins talks about. How this all connects up with the temperature control properties of the hypothalamus isn't yet known. But, again, while each individual research project has its specific thrust, there are many ways in which they connect. It may be that once the research is completed in many of these areas, it will somehow be correlated, and we will get a much more complete picture of the life process than has ever before been available.

HUMAN HIBERNATION

What we're really talking about in lowering the body's temperature is a form of hibernation, a slowing down of the metabolic rate. In hibernating rodents, for example, tests have shown their resistance to infection and irradiation went up steeply. Hibernation seems to have a regenerating effect on animals and always involves lowering of body temperature, known as hypothermia. Since we wouldn't want or be able to go through our daily activities in a state of hibernation, the idea expressed by Dr. Cutler of somehow lowering the temperature only while we sleep has a strong element of appeal. Some creatures, such as the hummingbird, go through a nightly rather than a seasonal hibernation. In studies of natural hibernators, those that were artificially forced to hibernate for longer than normal periods lived longer. Dr. Roy Walford reports that hibernating animals that are prevented from hibernating live a shortened life span.

This offers some interesting possibilities. Suppose we had hibernation chambers into which we could crawl for several weeks? This might restore some vigor, provide a degree of emotional/mental relaxation that could prepare us for new creative effort, and just possibly extend our lives if done on a regular basis.

Lowering of body temperature seems only to affect lifespan in later stages of life. One biologist suggests this might be true because hypothermia actually forestalls the natural aging process which only begins in later life. Whatever the case, most of the research has been done on animals, most of the success has been with cold-blooded animals, and a lot more careful investigation will be necessary, with a lot yet to be learned about temperature control and lifespan.

L-DOPA

In addition to the aforementioned experiments, there are certain drugs which affect bodily temperature. L-Dopa often has been called a wonder drug. Drs. Andrew Janoff and Barnett Rosenberg of the Department of Biophysics at Michigan State University have found that L-Dopa in combination with reserpine alters neurotransmitter levels in the brain, thus lowering body temperature. L-Dopa apparently affects the hypothalamus, and has been extremely useful in the treatment of Parkinson's disease, so much so that patients treated with L-Dopa can usually live out a normal lifespan.

Researchers came up with the L-Dopa treatment after discovering that the primary cause of Parkinson's disease is the lack of dopamine, a neurotransmitter, one of those substances that carry signals between nerve cells. L-Dopa stimulates dopamine production. In fact, L-Dopa can raise dopamine levels by 300 percent. Another major neurotransmitter is serotonin, and increasing levels of this substance are found as aging occurs. L-Dopa can reduce these levels by 30 percent. The reason the neurotransmitters may be so important has to do with the theory that one of the causes of aging is related to those programmed life stages such as puberty that are stimulated by hormones directed by the hypothalamus. The body sends signals via the neurotransmitters letting the hypothalamus know when it's time to make hormonal changes. Since dopamine levels go down with aging, while serotonin levels go up, and since L-Dopa can change both levels in the body, it's obviously why it's called a wonder drug and is the object of a lot of the longevity drug research.

Initial hints of this came when researchers realized that Parkinson's disease, which L-Dopa treats so effectively, has much in common with the symptoms of aging. Much of the initial research has been done with mice, whose brain chemistry is very similar to that of humans. In one experiment, substantial doses of L-Dopa were given to mice, who then lived 10 percent longer than their normal lifespans. The L-Dopa also seemed to bring back some youthful characteristics, including new hair growth. L-Dopa also seems to inhibit negative bodily changes due to menopause. And too it seems to effect changes in the hormone levels involving sexuality. In one case, a 76-year-old Parkinson's disease patient who had been sexually inactive for many years suddenly started to chase nurses around the hospital. Many such cases of hypersexual behavior have been reported in Parkinson's disease patients undergoing L-Dopa treatment.

Drs. Janoff and Rosenberg feel that the extension in lifespan of mice produced by L-Dopa may have been caused by the drug's ability to lower body temperature. In treating one group of rats, Janoff and Rosenberg noted a 73 percent increase in lifespan over those rats that did not receive L-Dopa. The two researchers speculate that a longevity "serum" might consist of L-Dopa, reserpine, and two enzyme inhibitors. They suggest this combination would lower body temperature and overcome the body's natural tendency to adapt to the new temperature.

It may be that the longevity of people in certain isolated areas of the world (which will be described at length in the next section) can be explained by the fact that these areas are located primarily in high altitudes, with cold mountain air helping to keep body temperature down. These long-lived people may also have hypothermic agents in their natural diets. Hypothermia might also explain the vigor and fitness of some elderly people who regularly take saunas. As it gets hotter in the sauna, the capillaries under the skin expand and the heart pumps harder, forcing more blood to the skin where it can cool off. It also might explain some of the apparently healthy aspects of running, in which individuals sweat profusely, thus allowing the body to cool down.

TEMPERATURE BIOFEEDBACK TRAINING

Perhaps the simplest way to lower body temperature would be through biofeedback training. Dr. Elmer Green at the Menninger Foundation has successfully taught many subjects to raise their skin temperature voluntarily. If you can learn to do this, then using the same internal switches can help you lower your body temperature as well. Yoga masters in the East have been voluntarily lowering their body temperatures for hundreds of years, perhaps thousands. Their efforts, plus the vast storehouse of documentation on biofeedback training, indicate that perhaps the most optimistic possibilities of all lie with teaching people self-regulation of body temperature. This is not to say we can start immediately. We still have a lot to learn about the effects of lower temperatures on warm-blooded animals, including humans. In a *Medical World News* interview, Dr. Bernard Strehler said, "There are no exceptions that I know of to the rule that animals live longer at lower temperatures." While this may be true, we humans have internal complexities unheard of in most other species, and extensive testing will have to be done before any actual temperature-lowering therapy is acceptable for general usage.

One obvious research project, which has apparently been overlooked, is the study of long-lived individuals in terms of their average body temperatures. *Do* people with lower-than-normal temperatures tend to live longer? I've done an informal, preliminary test of my own. In several cases of people in their 70s and 80s who look and act much younger and seem to have defied the normal aging process, I have found that these individuals do indeed have slightly lower temperatures than the accepted norm of 98.6. When I mentioned this to one prominent biologist studying aging, he responded, "You know, *my* temperature is below normal, and people often tell me I don't look my age, but I've never really connected the two."

It's time to do some of that connecting. Though we have just a subjective and preliminary indication, it does suggest a field ripe for further research.

IMMORTALITY IS THE GOAL

Several of the scientists interviewed for this book have admitted that the actual goal of much of their longevity research is physical immortality. One of them, a leading biochemist who asked to remain anonymous, said:

> *Look, would we spend all this money and millions of man-hours just to extend life by a few years? We already know how a sensible diet and nonstress lifestyle can accomplish the same thing. We are looking for the big breakthrough, each and every one of us. That moment when we have some positive laboratory evidence that immortality is a real possibility. And, frankly, though it may take fifty years, I think we're damn well going to do it!*

At the University of Connecticut, a first step in that direction may already have been taken. In a study financed by the Gerontology Center of the U.S. Administration on Aging, researchers there may have developed an immortal spider crab by injecting crabs with a hormone involved in the early stages of development. They ended up with a crab that shows characteristics of both youth and age. Researcher Jeanne Best says:

> *If we can keep these creatures in a "juvenile" state, coupled with their own ability to regenerate, they may never die.*

These and many other far-flung research projects are pushing at the boundaries of human knowledge about aging, death, and longevity. Some of the experiments are only in early, embryonic stages. Others, such as Johann Bjorksten's cross-linkage studies, are thirty to forty years along. Where is all this leading? No one knows for sure, but we do know this: *Human curiosity about the meaning of life is finally being transformed into action.* We know more now about the biology of human existence than at any time in human history, and what we know most of all is how little we know and how much more there is to learn. In small and large laboratories across the land modern-day alchemists are busily at work extending the frontiers and exploring unknown territory. The answers they discover will take us all into uncharted areas. How ready we are to accept their gifts will determine, finally, how successful they are. And how well we use those gifts will determine, finally, how successful we are.

Psychological attitudes will determine, to a great extent, how effectively any of these scientific discoveries are put to use. And psychological attitudes may prove to be the tool that unlocks some of the biochemical secrets of the human organism.

TIME IS NOT TOXIC

A few years ago, a conference of medical and surgical specialists was held at Cincinnati's DeCourcy Clinc. That conference issued a report which said:

TIME IS NOT TOXIC. TIME HAS NO EFFECT ON HUMAN TISSUES UNDER ANY CONDITIONS. BELIEF IN THE EFFECTS OF TIME BY THOSE WHO SUB-SCRIBE TO SUCH A BELIEF IS THE THING THAT ACTS AS A POISON.

While some biologists express doubts about the feasibility of using one's mind to substantially increase lifespan, not one of the distinguished scientists interviewed for this book had any doubt that a certain mental/emotional attitude and lifestyle could enable more people to take advantage of their current biological opportunities. When we realize that those opportunities involve a current maximum lifespan of up to 120, we can see that Psychological Immortality is not some metaphysical pipe dream.

PART
TWO

PSYCHOLOGICAL OPPORTUNITIES

MOST PEOPLE accept as an inevitable fact of life the idea that in each of us there is a biological clock ticking away. Perhaps it would be more accurate to call this a "fact of death." The belief that this clock has to run down and stop for each of us has a lot to do with our eventual physical deterioration. Before any of us can take advantage of the scientific discoveries and possibilities, we have to work on another clock, the psychological one inside our heads, the belief system that in fact eventually does us all in.

Among the minority who do not accept this "fact of death"—the idea that death and aging are certainties which cannot be tampered with—are thousands of physicians, psychologists, biologists, geneticists, biochemists, and other researchers who are actively involved in the battle against the major human disease: aging. We can choose to be active participants in this battle or passive spectators. But the spectators will not survive. In order for us to take advantage of the impending breakthroughs, we have to become actively involved and emotionally prepared.

THE MIND HAS THE POWER OF
LIFE AND DEATH

Part of that preparation is understanding that the human mind has the power of life and death over the physical body. We do not know all the whys and wherefores yet, but we now have a substantial body of proof that emotional attitudes, mental/emotional processes, have an effect, perhaps the ultimate effect, on our internal biochemistry. This section will examine the various aspects of that effect, and look at how emotional attitudes can either extend your youth and your life or age and kill you. An understanding of this impact of the mind on the body will help prepare you for effectively using the strategies presented in the following section.

In his 1950 best seller, *How to Stop Killing Yourself,* Dr. Peter Steincrohn asserts:

> *Each of us kills himself in his own fashion. The major killers—heart disease, high blood pressure, cancer, accidents—can often be conquered if the self-preservation urge is brought into play. But these killers invariably triumph if they find an ally in their victim.*

Peter Steincrohn is a living example of the self-preservation urge. At 80, he maintains a creative pace that would leave many younger individuals gasping for breath. His newspaper column is syndicated in over one hundred papers, his twenty-sixth book was recently published, and he has a high degree of what he calls "incidence of contentment."

Interviewed in his Coral Gables, Florida, home, Dr. Steincrohn reiterated what a lot of today's leading psychologists say is the foundation of an active will to live:

> *Each person has to develop an inner philosophy of what life's all about and what he wants to do with his life. If you're fortunate enough to find an interest, you can live it.*

The fact that it's an interest that absorbs you, that in itself lengthens life. You're so absorbed in that interest that you don't have time for many of the other things which so often lessen life.

An absorbing interest, a sense of purpose, something to look forward to—these seem to be the priceless factors which constitute the self-preservation urge. We all have this certain something which could be called the life force. We all have this power to live an extended life with vigor and good health *now*. We all have a maximum lifespan potential of up to 120 years *now*, without any further biological breakthroughs. But most of us are not in touch with this power, this life force. Instead, at a conscious or unconscious level, many of us are in harmony with the death force. The self-destructing mechanism permeates many lives and is strongest when it exists without awareness. Then it can emerge triumphant over the self-preservation urge. As Dr. Steincrohn says in *How to Stop Killing Yourself:*

If you say to your neighbor that he is needlessly endangering his life, he will be amazed. "Me kill myself? Now isn't that a silly statement! What normal human being would be foolish enough to do that?"

And he means it. Little does he realize that buried deep in him—as much a part of him as his arms, legs, heart, or head—is a powerful force that seeks to exterminate him. Fortunately in most of us it lies dormant. But it is there. It—the force of self-destruction—can be as strong or stronger than the great force of self-preservation.

THE DEATH FORCE

There are many ways in which we perpetuate our own mortality. Some of the negative messages we give to our subconscious minds about death and aging are contained in those seemingly innocent clichés such as:

"I'm dying to see you."

"When I die . . ."

"We all have to go sooner or later."

"It'll happen, but not in our lifetimes."

"My back is killing me."

"What do you expect at my age?"

"These tired old bones . . ."

"If I live to be a hundred, I'll never understand."

"You should live so long."

"I'm scared to death."

"I'm tickled to death."

"You look dead tired."

"You'll die laughing when you see that movie."

"When you and I are dead and buried . . ."

"We're not as young as we used to be."

These simple statements are some of the ways in which we bombard our minds with the message that we are only here for a temporary visit, that in terms of eternity, life is just a one-night stand. The media helps by glamorizing death and continuing to depict aging in stereotypical ways. Death is often depicted as noble and inevitable, while aging individuals are shown in roles that require little physical endurance or intellectual awareness. These, of course, are merely reflections of cultural myths about aging and death, but the power of modern media such as television is such that a myth often has more strength in the retelling than in its original manifestation. It is one thing to see an elderly neighbor or family member in deteriorating health, but when a famous star plays this role, feeble and senile, in a TV movie it takes on added impact and significance as a role model for limited and stereotypical thinking.

We now know that the brain triggers various secretions which affect the body's immunological system. Exactly what thoughts and what feelings, what assumptions and what attitudes trigger certain specific secretions is something yet to be discovered. But it does seem logical to assume that the brain is not going to respond in positive biochemical ways to negative thoughts and feelings. Fears and limitations we set up about death and aging are not likely to set in motion healthy biological processes.

Philosopher Leonard Orr says in his book, *Rebirthing in the New Age:*

> *The habit of affirming the power of death causes not only death but also many illnesses and states of weakness leading up to death.* **The idea that death is inevitable has killed more people than all other causes of death combined.**

I'm not saying that you, as an individual, will live forever. I *am* saying that by becoming aware of the death-consciousness programming now residing in your subconscious mind, you can start to reprogram a positive life-consciousness attitude. This is the attitude which will support your body's natural health maintenance system. With your brain having the capacity to secrete some four hundred life-enhancing substances, among which may be a number of secretions having a direct effect on your longevity, it only makes sense to adopt an attitude that will reinforce this process.

OPTIMISM THE ANSWER

The subjective evidence is clear and overwhelming: All of the scientists interviewed, all of the very long-lived people examined, everyone who has ever experienced or investigated the phenomenon of uncommon longevity has emerged with one common denominator—an optimistic attitude toward life. This has, until quite recently, seemed either an abstract or a banal concept. People have been telling us to cheer up and look on the bright side of things for many years. The difference now is that we are not talking about being optimistic merely to feel good. It goes far beyond such simplicity. What is now known is that feeling positive and hopeful about yourself and your life will biologically awaken your internal healing system. And feeling pessimistic and hopeless will kill you, will age you before your time.

And that self-destructive force Dr. Peter Steincrohn describes is manifested most strongly in the belief that death and aging are inevitable, for the subconscious mind which holds onto *that* belief also responds to optimism with the emotional reaction of: What's the use of feeling good, since the end result will be the same no matter what I do? And *that's* the great untruth which Psychological Immortality is aimed at laying to rest. The end result will *not* be the same no matter what we do. What we do and what we believe will determine how much of our individual biological opportunities we utilize.

Every time someone says "He died a natural death," the idea of death as inevitable is reinforced. A few years ago, during a class I was teaching on the psychology of emotions, I suggested that physical immortality was at least a possibility. One student, a lawyer, was aghast and proceeded to present a ten-minute argument on why death was indeed inevitable, focusing particularly on the fact that everyone ever born *has* either died or *will* die. I replied that his argument was fallacious, that all we know for a fact is that everyone *up to now* has died. Of course, even *this* is a supposition based on what we know, what we've heard from others, and what we assume from the evidence. But to go ahead and make the assumption that everyone now alive *must* eventually die is getting into beliefs instead of facts, not to mention that it presupposes that all the current research on halting the aging process is doomed to failure, or at least doomed to fall short of the ultimate goal. I brought the issue back to what I considered its proper perspective, the emotional and personal. I asked this student: "What is your personal investment in insisting on death as inevitable? What possible good can it do you to so strongly believe in your own mortality?" This stopped him cold. He later admitted to me that he didn't realize when he was making generalized statements about death that he was really talking about himself and what must be his own pessimistic outlook.

If we could picture the intricate manufacturing plant contained in our own skulls, this brain that can produce up to four hundred separate secretions, this biochemical factory, we might imagine that it is always ready for action, ready to receive the signals that will send the biological machinery into motion. Because of the nature of the brain, those signals usually have to be mental/

emotional. And we don't have to know exactly how it works, we don't have to understand all the internal complexities. What we do know now is that it responds to moods, feelings, attitudes. It's as if we had a marvelous automobile that would only operate at full efficiency when we sat in the driver's seat and *expected* it to run smoothly and take us somewhere pleasant.

There is, evidence to suggest that plants will respond to love and positive thoughts and feelings, that they will flourish if we talk to them, play joyful music for them, love them. Even people who don't quite believe this is so have reported that their plants thrived under this treatment; even people who felt silly doing it had positive results. Well, if we can talk to our plants, we can certainly talk to our brains, to our bodies, to our entire biological organisms. They *will* respond.

THE IMMORTALISTS

One group of people who have no trouble telling themselves positive things and staying optimistic are called Immortalists. Their philosophy is a simple one: They believe that physical immortality is inevitable. This group of visionaries was named after Alan Harrington's 1969 book, *The Immortalist*, which has a powerful opening passage:

> *Death is an imposition on the human race, and no longer acceptable. Men and women have all but lost their ability to accommodate themselves to personal extinction; they must now proceed physically to overcome it. In short, to kill death; to put an end to mortality as a certain consequence of being born.*

As with most visionaries, Harrington developed his idea of immortality before scientific evidence began accumulating. Before all the knowledge we now have that human life can be extended, that immortality may eventually be available, he and other Immortalists were programming themselves with the positive attitudes that could make it happen. Ridiculed at times, shunned by more cautious thinkers, this group, now numbering several thousand people in all walks of life, but usually well-educated, remains in the vanguard of the life-extension movement. And perhaps the most fascinating aspect of their strong belief in immortality is that it has had no harmful effects. While believing you are going to definitely deteriorate and die can lead to the kinds of fears, anxieties, and negative attitudes that will trigger great physiological damage, there doesn't seem to be any damage done by believing that you will live forever, or at least indefinitely, in good health.

Leonard Orr: Immortality—The Safest Belief

Leonard Orr says in *Rebirthing in the New Age:*

> *Even if death is inevitable, it won't hurt you to believe in physical immortality. It is the safest belief there is. If you are going to die anyway, the idea of physical immortality won't make a difference. So you might as well believe in it; it might have the practical benefits of making you feel healthy and wonderful while you are here. When you give up your mortal mentality, you will feel a wonderful difference.*

Do you have a mortal mentality? Chances are a part of you *has* accepted death as inevitable and natural. With this belief so strongly imbedded in our cultural conditioning, it would be difficult to avoid this. It is time to expose that belief, however, and look at whether it is accomplishing anything positive for you. Or, in fact, does this living under a death sentence hold you back in some way, in terms of long-range goals and aspirations? We might all ask ourselves how we would be living our lives differently if we did not believe our time was limited.

A. Stuart Otto: Change Your Philosophy

One of the prime forces today in the Immortalist movement is
A. Stuart Otto, chairman and founder of both the Committee for an
Extended Lifespan and the Committee for Elimination of Death.
Otto told me that he founded the extended lifespan organization
because some people were not yet ready to go so far as to consider
the elimination of death. I asked him what people could do now to
start living longer:

> *Change your philosophy. Get rid of the idea that death is
> inevitable. Before Columbus, people thought the world was
> flat. Before Galileo, they thought that falling bodies all fall at
> different rates. Before Copernicus, they thought that the sun
> revolved around the earth. And until Roger Bannister broke
> the four-minute mile, it couldn't be done. We're all captives of
> this idea that aging and death are inevitable and that they
> are part of life. Until we break that syndrome and begin
> thinking that all things are possible, we're not going to make
> too much headway, no matter what the scientists do.*

How limited and narrow and constrained is our thinking about
death and aging? Would a belief in your own biological opportunities constitute a major change in your personal philosophy? It
would if you believe now that you're only going to live until a
certain age, if you have a specific figure in mind when someone
asks you how long you expect to live. In workshops I conduct all
over the world, I often ask those attending whether they have a
specific age in mind for their own death. Inevitably they all do.

Whatever age you choose, having a preconceived notion of
when you're going to die is certain to kill you! It's certain to
inhibit the very biological functions which can keep you healthy
and alive. We now know that the cells in the body pick up
messages from the brain, from those neurotransmitters discussed
earlier. If you constantly program your mind with the idea that
you'll live to a certain age, even a supposedly generous figure, say
ninety years, then your body will constantly be fed the information

that it only has to last ninety years. The immunological system will pick up the coded messages that it doesn't have to protect you past that point. No matter how much scientists are able to extend human life—and there's every indication that *average* life expectancy will rise to at least 100 by the year 2000—we as individuals will have little or no chance of overcoming the limits we consistently program into our own biological systems.

PRECONCEIVED NOTIONS

One of my favorite quotes is from the nineteenth-century biologist and writer, Thomas Huxley:

Sit down before fact as a child, be prepared to give up every preconceived notion, follow humbly wherever nature leads, or you will learn nothing.

Though originally written some one hundred years ago, these words have particular significance in terms of Psychological Immortality. We are talking about following humbly wherever nature leads, following our natural biological tendencies. Sitting down before fact as a child means simply allowing ourselves to accept new knowledge free of the obstacles created by rigid preconceptions. Those scientists able to use effectively the knowledge revealed by Dr. Leonard Hayflick's work (see Part One), whereby he proved that cells in culture divide a limited number of times, those not paralyzed by this knowledge were the scientists who were not locked into an emotional attachment to the former belief that cells reproduced indefinitely outside the body.

While at first glance it might seem that the original disproven belief that cells reproduced indefinitely outside the body was the optimistic view, in this case optimism based on a flimsy foundation of evidence was destructive. It prevented speculation and healthy investigation and confused a lot of scientists who couldn't figure out *why* cells should reproduce indefinitely outside the body and not inside it. This didn't seem to match up with anything else they had learned about longevity and the aging process. The Hayflick Limit is an obstacle to be overcome, a challenge to all of those engaged in life-extension research, and a specific target. It is not a pessimistic view, but merely a fact which scientists can use for their optimistic research. We must look at the scientific advances discussed in the first section of this book free of the limited view that life is circumscribed, free of the *belief* that we have so many years and that's it. The successful scientists, and the successful human beings, are those most able to give up their preconceived notions.

It's fitting that a century after Thomas Huxley admonished his fellow seekers of truth and knowledge to follow nature we are now learning that the human organism is complete in and of itself in terms of repair capability, health maintenance, and longevity potential. It's not so much a question of finding new things to add to the body, but of finding out how to activate the systems and substances already there.

Psychologist and author Leo Buscaglia tells a great story about the danger of preconceived notions. A man is driving up a narrow mountain road. Just two lanes. He begins to approach a very precarious curve, when a woman comes rushing toward him in the other lane, and just as she passes him she sticks her head out the window and yells, "Pig! Pig! Pig!" As most people would, the man gets very angry, infuriated in fact, especially since the woman has already passed him and he can't yell back a suitable response. He goes around the curve getting more and more angry and frustrated, and runs right into a pig!

Preconceived notions can do you in. The more specific they are, the more damage they can do. Many people who want to live many years, mistakenly pick a specific figure, say ninety, not realizing that by the time they get there ninety may no longer be considered a generous lifespan. How much more sensible to merely say we want to stay youthful and live a long time. Or better yet, indefinitely.

F. M. Esfandiary: Psychological Breakdowns—the Software

F. M. Esfandiary, Immortalist, philosopher, lecturer at UCLA, and author of several books on future possibilities, is one of those who firmly believes in indefinite survival and indefinite lifespans. I asked him why this concept hasn't yet become more popular:

> *Some of the problems are the age-old resignation to the inevitability of death, guilt, shame, fear, self-doubt. All these, I think, stop us from hoping for or actively striving for physical immortality. Unconsciously, people say, "Live forever and ever, who me? It's too good to be true. I don't deserve it. I can't make it." I find that many of the objections to indefinite lifespans are nothing more than rationales for this age-old orientation to death or resignation to death. People will say: "Where will we put everyone?" "How will we feed everyone?" "Let's accept death with dignity." "Who wants to lie aged and infirm for centuries?" It's a basic pathological problem, the fact that people are not psychologically ready to accept this monumental breakthrough. Although we have focused quite a bit on the physiological breakdown that occurs, we have taken insufficient account of the software, the psychological breakdowns that occur, which in turn precipitate aging and death.*

It's important that we acknowledge that death consciousness is a pathological problem, that the psychological breakdowns are every bit as deadly as the most virulent organic disease. Now that we know about the biochemical significance of positive attitudes, it will be easier to reeducate people toward this new view. The biologists and gerontologists are laying the groundwork in the hope that the general public will be prepared to receive the gift of extended life. While knowledge is the gathering of information, it only becomes wisdom when it is applied. We have not been very wise so far, and have not been able to fully utilize the knowledge science has provided. As A. Stuart Otto puts it:

There has to be an intense desire for an extended life. This is something that a lot of people don't have because they are pessimists, people who, for various reasons, begin to get fed up with life and actually begin to look forward hopefully to the day of their demise.

DEATH AS AN INDIGNITY

Here's one of the most destructive ideas of modern times: Let's accept death with dignity. The popularity of Elisabeth Kübler-Ross's book *On Death and Dying* led to a whole movement designed to help people accept death as a natural event in their lives. While it is useful and healthy to stop fearing death (most of the Immortalists I talked to do not fear death, but merely refuse to accept it as inevitable), the death-and-dying movement, with its books, classes, and workshops aimed at convincing people to accept their own deaths in peace and tranquillity does its damage by insisting that in order to accept death one must believe *absolutely* that it is inevitable, unavoidable, unchangeable. I remember attending a conference in Miami several years ago at which several of us were chatting with noted anthropologist Dr. Ashley Montagu. Someone asked him if he believed there were any absolutes in life, such as indicated by the antique jibe that the only certainties in life are death and taxes. Montagu replied, "The only absolute I've ever discovered is an absolute fool!"

It's one thing, when confronted with the fact of impending death, to quietly and gracefully accept it. It's quite another thing to make a cult of it, to, as has been done in high school and college classes, have students "experience" their own deaths by lying in a coffin. All this accomplishes is to program the subconscious mind that death is definite. We don't yet know exactly what mental/emotional attitudes release all those bodily functions that protect us from disease, but the message to lie back and accept death, that it is something beautiful, natural, and the "final stage of growth" must surely be doing inestimable damage to the organism.

Dr. Arthur Falek, Professor of Psychiatry at Emory University in Atlanta, is a behavioral geneticist who says:

> *Having written about the coping mechanism and death and dying, I'm having problems myself understanding these workshops on death and dying. I wonder about the psychological impact on the individuals who start worrying about it and constructing all sorts of ways of dealing with death instead of doing something that consumes their activities while they are alive. A much healthier approach would be focusing on life rather than reflecting on their own death.*

Psychological Immortality *is* focusing on life instead of on death. One of the major psychological problems people create for themselves is focusing attention on an anticipated event rather than on what is happening to them right now. Death may or may not be in your future, but the reality is that *life* is happening for you at this moment. For this moment, at least, we are all immortal. The death-and-dying movement instead reinforces the idea that every moment is a reminder of our mortality. Dr. George Pollock, Director of the Chicago Institute for Psychoanalysis, and a psychiatrist, says:

> *There has been too much made of death and dying, and not enough of life and living. It is time for a new thrust in working with the elderly. We have been doing our people a disservice by emphasizing dying with dignity, instead of living with creativity.*

The people promoting death-and-dying educational programs mean well, operating on the premise that knowing what something is really like will allay people's fears about it. But the truth is that death is not just a gentle event akin to sleep. Maybe a healthier educational experience would be to have people encounter a corpse, and *then* introduce them to someone 90 or 100 years old who is still alert and enjoying life. This dramatic contrast between life and death would help people see that there *is* a choice, and that life is the alternative that is possible and preferable in every way. The more time one devotes to any negative experience, the more that experience becomes a part of one's consciousness. Death consciousness is the antithesis of life and the will to live. As Somerset Maugham suggested:

> *Death is a very dull, dreary affair, and my advice to you is to have nothing to do with it.*

This attitude may help explain why Somerset Maugham lived to the age of 91.

THE DOCTOR'S DEATH SENTENCE

One of the new awarenesses in medicine is that we are each unique individuals, and no two of us react exactly alike to any disease. Imagine therefore the arrogance of any physician who purports to know precisely how long an individual will survive. This has great personal significance for me, since my father was given six months to live after he was told he had lymphoma, cancer of the lymph gland. He was not told he was terminally ill, and merely thought he had a glandular condition. He gained weight, went back to work, and, except for yearly sieges of illness lasting three to six weeks, lived a happy, fulfilling, productive life for another seven years. If he had been told he had only six months to live, I'm certain he wouldn't have lasted much longer than that.

There is some argument that people have a right to know the truth about their illnesses. But since so many people are programmed with the negative belief that cancer has a hopeless prognosis, telling them they have cancer is not telling them the truth. The word itself has become too much associated with death and despair. Telling someone the truth—that cancer is often curable—will mean nothing if that person believes that cancer is the beginning of death. In such a case, the physician's truth becomes distorted by what the patient believes the truth to be.

I asked Dr. George Pollock his thoughts on the doctor's death sentence:

I don't think that anybody is able to go ahead and make that kind of an assertion. I have worked with an individual who had open-heart surgery, one of the first such patients in Chicago. When they opened him up, they closed him and did nothing because they said there was nothing that could be done. I had been working with him previously, and I've worked with him now for over twenty years. This man has now lived ten years after the surgery, and he had been told by a very eminent cardiologist that he would be dead within a year, so he should make preparations. I told this man I didn't believe it, and I thought we ought to keep working and get his tensions out, and he's still going!

It is not only arrogance but abuse of the power we give the medical "experts" for them to take upon themselves the power of life and death, and in effect to pronounce death before it happens. It is one thing to tell a patient that his illness is serious and has proven fatal in a number of cases, but to declare that this specific person has this specific amount of time left to live is practicing the most deadly deceit!

A great many physicians have to bear a great deal of the responsibility for unhealthy attitudes about death and aging. As Dr. Ron Parks, Medical Director of the Comprehensive Health Program Center in Columbia, Maryland, says:

Most traditional physicians act as support systems for the helpless-hopeless attitudes that many people have. These doctors' own attitude is that people are not able to change. Most doctors project their own ideas about themselves out to patients.

Thus, if you have a physician who believes he is going to start deteriorating at 65, he's not going to be very supportive of your determination to remain youthful and vigorous into your 90s.

Medical doctors have a lot of death consciousness. Their own death rate is slightly higher than the national average, they have shorter lifespans than most other professions, and a fairly high suicide rate. They treat most disorders of the elderly as natural occurrences which cannot be affected much one way or the other.

Dr. Robert Butler: Educating the Physician

Part of the work of the National Institute on Aging is to educate the medical profession. Director Dr. Robert Butler says:

At present, we still haven't succeeded, speaking nationally, in overcoming the traditional medical school resistance to dealing with the realities of older patients. That is changing. I'm very happy that this institute supports eighteen medical schools in developing a presence of excellence in geriatrics. That has many effects. For instance, a young, brilliant medical student who might have been intrigued to go into aging or to try to understand what happens biologically to our bodies over a period of time, if there isn't a presence in that field in the medical school, he might be attracted to cardiovascular disease, or any number of other medical areas.

We have to be an educator to the health providers to more effectively recognize, for instance, senility, and introduce immediate treatment, and not allow those conditions to become chronic. The gatekeepers are doctors, clergy, family agencies, any number of people who see older people in various stages of crisis, and who could, unfortunately, write somebody off as senile, or say, "What do you expect at your age?" or "There's nothing that can be done about that," instead of seeing that they are dispatched to effective medical care.

One of the ways in which physicians perpetuate limiting attitudes about aging is to project their own narrow expectations onto their patients by saying, "What do you expect at your age?" So many patients start believing that illness and pain are natural companions after a certain age is reached. Dr. Butler told me the following story which illustrates this:

When we first did our studies on human aging, one of our volunteers, Morris Rocklin, was 92. Morris lived to be 102. I last saw him when he was 101. He told me he had gone to see his doctor because he had pain in his right knee and he wanted some help for it. His doctor said, "Morris, what do you expect at your age? That knee is 101 years old!" Morris was not one to be acquiescent or intimidated and he said, "Doctor, my left knee is also 101, how come it doesn't hurt?"

THE LIFESPAN MYTH

On the occasion of my fortieth birthday, a well-meaning friend asked, "Does it bother you that your life is now half over?"

The mythology that we all have a limited number of years on this planet, a set figure which we might reasonably expect to reach, and after which we begin living "on borrowed time," is one of the most insidious and pervasive of all destructive human beliefs. The limit usually set by popular consensus in our Western culture is the biblical "three score years and ten." It's a startling testimonial to the potency of entrenched beliefs that we have not dramatically exceeded that limit in terms of average life expectancy. In fact, one of the great mysteries of our times is why the average human lifespan has not substantially increased in the last twenty-five years. Scientific knowledge and the conquest of disease have advanced geometrically, without corresponding leaps in life expectancy.

Are we stuck somewhere between seventy and eighty years as the amount of time most humans can expect to survive? Not on your life! The biologists, geneticists, gerontologists, and other scientists all seem to agree on one point: There is no biological reason why the body should not last at least a hundred years. And that's right now, not counting all the biomedical advances expected over the next ten or twenty years. The single most important factor, therefore, in this stagnation of average lifespans is the almost universal belief that it's natural to live to 70 or 80, but unnatural to live beyond that, especially with anything resembling youthful vigor. Thirty years ago, Clifton Webb had the title role in the movie *Mr. Belvedere Rings the Bell*. The 45-year-old Belvedere, using a stolen birth certificate to convince everyone that he is 77, enters an old-age home and tries to convert those living there to his philosophy that one can remain young through a positive attitude. Much of the first half of the film is devoted to people being surprised at his youthful vigor. What the movie does, of course, is simply perpetuate the popular myth that one cannot truthfully be vigorous at 77.

What figure do *you* have in mind when you think about the number of years you can reasonably aspire to? Ask yourself the following questions: How much energy have I invested in this personal expectation? How much thought have I given to dying at this particular date in my life? Have I planned my life with a view toward not surviving beyond this age? Have I planned my life up to and including this age, but not beyond?

The next question to ask yourself is whether you would live your life any differently if this predetermined lifespan figure were suddenly doubled. This, of course, might depend on how old you are right now. If, for example, you are 50, and picked 75 as your figure, you might be living your life based on your assumption that it is two-thirds over. You might be reluctant to start new projects. Coupled with a belief that you will soon begin to feel the degenerative effects of aging, you would not be unusual should you be living a life of caution, of limited expectations.

FEAR OF AGING

One of the prime reasons for apathy regarding the idea of life-extension is the imagery most people have of deteriorating at a certain age, in a natural downhill progression. We usually picture what it would be like at a certain age based on what as children we first encountered as that age. If you remember an aunt who was wrinkled and old at 50, then it will be hard to picture yourself as healthy and vital at that age. Can you remember, for instance, when your parents were 50, or maybe even your grandparents? They probably were not the young and vital 50-year-olds who are all around us today. But we tend to hold onto those initial images.

As F. M. Esfandiary told me:

> *Everywhere we're surrounded by this continuous programming to accept aging and to accept the inevitability of death. We're continuously told, for instance, "Act your age" or "Shame on you, you're too old for this sort of thing!" Unconsciously, we program ourselves along these lines: "I'm now 29 years old, so I'm really beginning to fall apart." "I'm now 38 years old, I'm really over the hill." "I'm now 53, I'm too old to make love more than a certain number of times every week. I should really slow down, I should take it easy."*
>
> *This kind of insidious brainwashing that goes on both within our heads and all around us precludes the fact that things have changed. That a 40-year-old today more often than not has the vigor and the stamina and the dynamism of a 30-year-old of a generation ago. A 65-year-old of today, as a rule, has the physical and psychological resiliency of a 45-year-old of a generation ago. And yet we continue playing this old programming. This brainwashing from within and without tends to incline us to accept the inevitability of aging and death. This in itself tends to accelerate the aging process. We reach a certain age and we unconsciously tell ourselves we have to begin dying, we have to begin withdrawing.*

You might check this out for yourself. With no further thought, picture in your imagination a 50-year-old man and 50-year-old woman. Next, picture a 65-year-old couple. Finally, an 80-year-old pair. How do you picture each of these couples? What are they doing? Are they active, mobile, energetic? Are they attractive? What is different about the 50-year-old couple you imagined as compared to a 30-year-old couple?

When you visualize a 75-year-old man, do you picture someone who looks like Cary Grant at 75, or someone who is wrinkled and bent and feeble?

Does the thought of a couple in their 70s making love somehow seem obscene, or joyfully romantic and hopeful to you?

There's a very beautiful woman I know who is 51 years old. She is successful in her own business, and has trouble dealing with her age, mainly because she doesn't look, act, or feel 51. She cannot relate the reality of herself at 51 with the image she's always held of that particular age. This woman looks stunning in a bikini, but when she gets the attention of younger men on a beach she finds herself thinking, "You're too old for this sort of stuff!" If she dates someone younger, she waits for the startled reaction when she tells them her age. It always comes. She's proud of how good she looks, and how good she feels, but somehow feels it's a fluke, that perhaps other people will feel uncomfortable relating to her when they know how old she is. For several years, she lied about her age, but being a basically honest person, this felt uncomfortable and she started telling the truth. But is it really the truth? A more accurate statement might be: "Chronologically, I am 51 years old, but in mind, body, and spirit, I am perhaps half that age, at least according to your beliefs of what a 51-year-old is like."

NEGATIVE VIEW OF AGING = LIMITED LIFESPAN POTENTIAL

When we hold onto fixed images of certain ages rigidly, we limit our own view of ourselves at those ages. We have to realize that people are healthier and more vigorous today in their 50s and 60s, and this youthful progression will accelerate even more for the people who will be 50 and 60 in the next ten or twenty years. Another exercise in visualization which might prove interesting is to picture yourself at 30, and then picture yourself at 60 looking pretty much the same. If you find this difficult, it may be because you are holding a very limited view of the possibilities.

There's little doubt that our view of aging and the elderly holds us back, prevents us from taking advantage of some of the life-extension opportunities now available to us.

Dr. Ken Dycktwald: The Changing View of Aging

Ken Dycktwald is a pioneer in working with the elderly. He is one of the founders of the SAGE (Senior Actualization and Growth Exploration) Project, which will be described at length later in this section. Dr. Dycktwald is also former President of the Association for Humanistic Gerontology and author of several books, including *Bodymind*. We discussed the tragedy of aging in America and the dramatic changes he sees in the near future:

> *There's been a major transition in the whole notion of respect and esteem toward knowledge. For example, one hundred years ago, John Smith had a farm. His father had the same farm and when John was growing up, he didn't know enough about farming to really run the farm. As he grew older, he learned how to run it from his father. Natural knowledge usually took time to acquire. The person who lived the longest usually knew the most and had a prominent role. Now we shift to 1950. The farm has been in John Smith's family for 150 years. All of a sudden, John Smith IV goes to agriculture college. He comes back at the age of 21 knowing more about farming than his father. This reverses the relationship between knowledge and age. It's been a profound change. Many older people no longer have positions of esteem with regard to knowledge and decision-making because younger people, either truly or falsely, feel the older ones don't know enough.*

This is a capsule explanation of one of the great sociological transformations in human history, and a phenomenon which has probably done much to prevent people from taking fuller advantage of their biological opportunities. The desire to extend life is certainly diminished in those people who see the later years as involving a loss of respect, impact, and responsibility. From John

Smith's farm, the belief that older people have less knowledge or less relevant knowledge spreads out until it becomes a part of the cultural conditioning of an entire society. As Dr. Dycktwald describes this:

During the last generation, the image-making structures of the country have placed a great deal of emphasis on youth, thereby diminishing the sense of importance and contribution and value and attractiveness in later years. This has created a cultural negative image of aging. Also, because of advances in health care, sanitation, infant mortality, and elimination of infectious diseases and plagues, there are more and more older people around. Their position in society is diminished at this point because they're not a rarity anymore. They're not the one grandfather per town, the one wise old woman per town.

Considering all of this, most older people don't feel that growing older is a positive event in their lives, they don't feel a sense of excitement about the later years, they don't have a sense of forward vision. They feel the best times in life are 20, 30, 40, and they're largely indoctrinated into that by the American media system. What they see is what they feel, which is that the country has not been set up for them. The country doesn't care a whole lot about them, and wants them out of the way. It's not surprising, therefore, to find that many, many older people have a diminished sense of respect for themselves and for their peers. They've got very little to look forward to. They imagine the later years filled with nothing but disease, deterioration, and loneliness.

Ken Dycktwald's analysis of the current situation illustrates one of the prime reasons there hasn't yet been a massive mobilization against aging and toward life-extension. If there is a sense of hopelessness among those who reach their later years, there just isn't going to be a great desire on the part of younger people to reach those years or to add to them. One of the most fascinating phenomenons of our time is the fact that a majority of the population is now either persecuting or ignoring a minority group we will all eventually join, The way we treat our elderly is doubly shocking when we realize that we are all going to be there someday! Perhaps one of the reasons many people are reluctant to think about life-extension is because they don't want to think of themselves being treated the way they are now treating and perceiving people in their 70s, 80s, and 90s. Gerontologists, sociologists, and psychologists have told me that one of the major stumbling blocks to increasing longevity is the collective guilt society feels about older Americans, the realization that these "senior citizens" really are not granted the rights of citizens at all, and that a valuable human resource has been left to rot.

Those older Americans living in our society today are caught in a major transition, one that's taken several generations to accomplish, the move from a small and appreciated segment of the population to a large and unappreciated minority. But the next change will happen much faster and be even more dramatic: the move to a majority role in American society. As Ken Dycktwald notes:

> *Obviously, we're moving into a new stage. Youth in America is shrinking very rapidly. The World War II baby boom is now approaching middle age. Continued advances in the quality of life, health, and medicine, and all kinds of biomedical technology are extending age. We're moving into an era where, in fact, America will no longer be a youthful country but a middle-aged one. I think it's not unreasonable to expect that in some strange and maybe undetermined way, the entire focus and profile of our country will shift around to begin thinking of the middle and later years as positive times, as valuable times. What will probably happen is that the American political, social, and economic structure will alter itself to accommodate the mass of the population. There'll be so many people 50 and 60 years old in the coming decades and so few people under 30, 20, and 10, that we might have a situation where it will be a privilege again to be older. It will be exciting. People will look forward to their later years: "I can't wait, look at all the fun I can have, look at all the*

friends I can make. I can still be sexual. I can still be vital. I can still work if I want. I can be wiser than I ever was. I can have a position of prominence. Society will be made for me."

This profound shift in the societal structure will likely have a dramatic impact on the degree of public support for life-extension research. If later years are happy times, those people enjoying them will want to increase them. One can conceive of a time when longevity will become a major political issue, with candidates running on a platform promising so many more millions to develop techniques for extending life. The statistics are startling, as outlined by Dr. Dycktwald:

By the coming turn of the century, every other American will be over 50. By 2020, every other American will be over 65. And you've got to remember that people who are old now are largely uneducated. They're often nonreaders, nonpolitical, and they don't know how to use media, they don't know how to advocate politically. They're not accustomed to the current pace of life. Every year that goes by, the profile of the older Americans alters. And that's hard for people to imagine, they always think of older people as being the same. There's no question in my mind that the attitudes people have about growing older influence and control how old they get to be and what they die from. We need new role models. We need to see vigorous, intelligent, creative, attractive older people.

Those reaching 50 and 60 years of age now are much different from those who reached those ages twenty years ago, and those reaching those milestones twenty years from now will be even more different. In twenty years, the rock stars, revolutionaries, astronauts, and college students of the 1960s will be reaching 50 and 60. They'll be politically active and know how to go after what they want in this media-rich society. So we're coming full circle from a hundred years ago, when the older person was a rarity and valued because of his or her wisdom and knowledge. The new older person likewise will be valued, and have the political and numerical power to back that up.

NEW OLDER ROLE MODELS

To check further on your own current role models of older people you might make a list of ten people you know over the age of 60. People you know personally, or people you've encountered through the media. Jot down their names before going on.

As you look over your list, think about each individual you named. Is this a vigorous, intelligent, creative, attractive older person? Better yet, ask yourself the question: Is this how I would like to be when I get older? And more pointedly in terms of our subject: If this is the way it will be, would I want to add twenty or thirty years to my own life?

If you can't come up with the names of ten alert, active, and interesting older people, obviously one of the first tasks in creating the psychological atmosphere necessary to extend your own life is to come up with some healthier, more attractive, and inspiring older role models.

Don't look for them in nursing homes. I've visited well-equipped, expensive nursing homes in several states and found the residents far from vigorous and happy despite a lot of planned activities. Some of the comments I got when I asked these older people how they felt about getting old:

"I wish I were dead."

"My memory keeps going, and I don't seem to want to do anything anymore."

"I can't stand all these old people they have here."

"My children dumped me here just to get rid of me."

Since most people do have negative self-images about getting older, they also project these onto other older people. Almost without exception, every coherent nursing home resident I talked to said he or she was unhappy about being surrounded by old people. When asked their opinion of the other residents, these older people referred to them as stupid, sick, crazy, dull, pesty. One 90-year-old with some life still in him told me, "They make me want to puke!"

On the other hand, I've found a number of boarding houses and apartment hotels filled with active, vigorous, creative, and very attractive and interesting people in their 70s, 80s, 90s. No statistical data is available, but common sense alone dictates that the life force would be stronger in this sort of joyful, active environment. In one such apartment hotel in Miami Beach, Florida, an old and moderately priced building decorated by the tenants themselves, I asked the manager, himself in his 70s, whether he had any problems with his tenants. He answered:

Just that damn George! He's 87 and always up on the roof painting his pictures. Can't even get him down for meals. I have to take the elevator up to the fourth floor and then the stairs to the roof and try to coax him down for lunch or dinner. You'd think someone his age would know better!

The manager then winked at me and said:

But I guess running after George and the others keeps me young!

AN AGE-INTEGRATED SOCIETY

One way to prepare ourselves emotionally for the coming biomedical breakthroughs and for a more youthful mind and body in our later years is to work toward an age-integrated society. At the beginning of this century, those people who had survived the ravages of disease and attained their senior years were part of the family environment and valued members of the total environment. Social settings and living spaces where elders mingle freely with the young and the middle-aged seem to offer the best psychological atmosphere for individual growth and support. Ashley Montagu has lamented the passing of the one-room schoolhouse, noting in one of his talks that it had taught children of all ages to relate to each other. The older children helped the younger ones; the younger children developed social graces more easily by watching the older ones. Each group benefited from the presence of the other. Perhaps we can bring the one-room schoolhouse back in an adult education model. This would allow the young, the middle-aged, and the elderly to associate in a common purpose, freely exchanging views, gaining understanding.

A special sort of aliveness seems to permeate those groups that do integrate the ages. In conducting workshops where participants range from their late teens to their eighties, I've noticed a heightened energy level. This has also been true at conferences where those attending were of varied age levels. The Association for Humanistic Psychology is a good example of this, consisting of people from all walks of life and all age groups with a common goal of increasing human potential and human dignity. It's sometimes amazing to learn the chronological ages of some of those attending AHP conferences. One lively practicing psychologist is a woman in her late 80s. Another very attractive woman, who looked to be in her late 20s, came up to a group at one AHP conference and announced with an exuberant smile on her face, "I'm 41 years old today, and I just ran 41 miles!"

Another group that is age-integrated is the National Speakers Association, consisting mainly of people who lecture and present workshops and seminars to businesses, organizations, and schools. One of the most satisfying characteristics of any National Speakers Association convention is the fact that the older members are treated with reverence, love, and genuine respect— and with good reason! These are the people who have learned how to motivate others with their words, who have traveled far and wide for many years honing their skills, and who are willing to share that information freely with the younger members. The mentor system is alive and well in this setting, with the older members sought after for their wisdom and practical knowledge. Members in their 80s, such as Norman Vincent Peale and Cavett Robert (the organization's founder), are amazingly active, sometimes maintaining schedules that would exhaust younger but less vigorous people.

All of these examples demonstrate that when any group excludes older people for fear that they are "dull" or that they will stifle the group experience, that group diminishes and stultifies itself. The group or organization that doesn't view older people as "outcasts" and judges people on what they contribute rather than on how many years they've been alive creates a life-consciousness environment for itself. This type of integrated setting also creates healthy role models for those of us determined to extend our own lives. The best role models are those who really have a role—in other words, those older people who can feel they are contributing something of value and significance. Dr. Roy M. Hamlin of the VA Hospital in Danville, Illinois, says:

> *People tend to live for as long as they feel needed. Research on aging should stress behavioral programs. The utility ceiling set by a given culture determines the age of death. If an individual has need of the years beyond 70, he will retain competence and live longer.*

A very simple concept: the utility ceiling. Do you have a utility ceiling inside your head, an age beyond which you don't think you'll be needed or useful? And how do you relate to the older people you encounter, do you put a utility ceiling on them?

As Dr. Ken Dycktwald says, our society is growing older, and older people will have greater utility roles as this occurs. But we each have a responsibility to help create an environment where the valuable resource of older people is utilized effectively. That responsibility is not so much to others as to the older person each of us will become.

STAYING YOUNG IN PRISON

One of the most provocative studies on the subject of aging is entitled *Aging in a Total Institution* by sociologists Francis Glamser and Monika Reed. The study indicates there's some truth to the belief held by convicts that prisoners don't age as fast as people on the outside. This study reveals that much of what is viewed as normal aging doesn't take place among lifers and other long-term prisoners. While patients in nursing homes and older people outside of institutions are often depressed, ineffective, and view themselves as old, docile, and submissive, the older convict is proud of his record and sees himself as vital and tough. Cell bars and security guards support this self-image on a daily basis. Almost all of the elderly prisoners Glamser and Reed interviewed said they believed they felt younger than people on the outside. The researchers reported that they indeed looked younger than their chronological years, with fewer wrinkles, less gray hair, and youthful body language.

There are several reasons for this paradox of people flourishing in an otherwise oppressive environment. First of all, as the study suggests, there is no utility ceiling on long-term convicts. If you enter prison as a murderer at 45, you have enhanced status at 75. You become a mentor and an object of respect to the younger prisoners. The rigid hierarchical system is based on seniority, much like it is in the U.S. Senate (senators, in fact, have longer-than-average lifespans). The older convicts are the ones with status and power, the wise old men of the prison society. Second, there is no retirement in prison. While the workload may lessen with advanced age, barring infirmity, every prisoner still has a job to perform and is therefore not subject to the "death sentence" of retirement. The older prisoner also has a sense of purpose—another vital factor in longevity and youthfulness. He either wants to live until the end of his sentence in order to finally enjoy freedom, or he wants to outlive his guards, or the police officer who was responsible for his arrest, or the judge who sentenced him. Finally, the older prisoner is not directly affected by the deaths of his peers and loved ones on the outside. This is an often overlooked negative factor, but one which directly relates to the role model issue. If everyone around you is sick and/or dying, it is very hard to maintain a positive attitude about your own possibilities. I talked to Dr. Harold Bloomfield, director of psychiatry at the Holistic Health Center in Del Mar, California, who told me:

The number-one cause of morbidity and mortality in the aged is losing someone close to them. Especially, of course, with widows and widowers. It has to do with the mourning process, which is both psychologically and physiologically depleting. When you lose someone you've known for thirty or forty years, it's probably the most stressful thing a human being can go through. I think, in that vulnerable state, physiologically and psychologically, out of that depression, you start to say, "Well, I'm next."

Obviously, long-term convicts, out of close touch with loved ones and friends on the outside, with their own societal structure and existence inside, are not as subject to the "Well, I'm next" syndrome.

Another factor governing older convicts' apparent youthfulness is that involving their relatively stress-free environment. Since they are removed from the outside world, they don't have to worry about survival in the highly sophisticated culture we all must cope with. They are not faced with the dramatic social and economic changes that can have such traumatic effects on people outside of prison. Once entrenched in the hierarchy of prison life, the long-term convict has little or no worries about physical danger. And the rules are all set; he doesn't have to keep deciding what the right thing to do is in a changing world. All long-term convicts "learn the ropes," learn what it takes to survive and prosper in their own world.

POCKETS OF LONGEVITY

The preceding report on convicts shows that they have a lot in common with residents of three areas of the world where people seem to live longer and younger than in most other places: the village of Vilcabamba in Ecuador; the Kashmir state of Hunza, located in the high valleys near China and Afghanistan but under the political control of Pakistan; and the Caucasus Mountains of the Soviet Union. Like prisoners, these long-lived people inhabit an age-integrated social structure, are isolated from the outside world, and have specific rules governing their everyday lives.

Dr. Sula Benet: Long-Lived People of the Caucasus

One of those devoting a lot of energy to the study of the long-lived people of the Caucasus is Dr. Sula Benet, author of *Abkhasians: The Long-Living People of the Caucasus* and *How to Live To Be 100*, Professor Emeritus of Anthropology at Hunter College, and senior researcher at the Research Institute for the Study of Man. I asked Dr. Benet what she found to be some of the factors accounting for the unusual degree of vitality and longevity found in the populations of the Caucasus:

> *Their preparedness for life. They have very few surprises. Somehow they teach the individual from the beginning of his life about the different possibilities. Teaching more by example, showing how one should act. To us, everything comes as a surprise. We just don't prepare people for* **life** *in this country. And your self-image is based very much on your conviction that you are doing the right thing.*
>
> *In these areas, parents are consistent. They don't say today you can do it and tomorrow you cannot do it. No is no. And children get used to it. I think that removes a lot of stress on parents and on children. In our culture we're very inconsistent. Today we punish for something and tomorrow we let it go and children don't know the limits. The way they do it in the Caucasus prepares children so they don't have to sit down and figure out, "Should I do it or shouldn't I do it?" It's very clear what should and shouldn't be done. I think this clarity in behavior is very important. In our culture, we have such confusion.*
>
> *The people there feel in control of their own lives because they know exactly what they should do. They know the rules. I asked one old man of 106 why he thought he was able to live so long and he said, "Because I did the right things." When I*

started to press him about what the right things were he told
me that it meant he lived by the rules.

You can see some of the similarities in terms of psychological
atmosphere between the people of the Caucasus and those long-
term convicts. They know the rules and live by them. No
surprises. And certainly in prison there is consistency in
punishment for breaking the rules.

CLARITY OF VISION

Clarity of vision is a very important factor in longevity. When
psychologist Abraham Maslow studied those super-accomplished
people he called self-actualized, most of whom lived to ripe old
ages, he noted that one of the things they all seemed to have in
common was this clarity. They knew what they wanted and had a
very clear idea of how to get it. In my workshops, I often talk
about the first thing one needs in order to achieve success in
anything: a clear vision of what you want. It seems that this clear
vision has not only psychological rewards but biochemical
significance. It certainly seems to contribute to longevity among
those populations which feature clarity instead of ambiguity,
consistency instead of constant change. And these pockets of
longevity are certainly age-integrated. As Dr. Benet says:

There are so many people with whom the youngsters grow
up. They see them quite old and yet being part of the family,
part of the community, and doing quite a bit of work.
I would spend a whole day in a village, and they were so
cheerful and optimistic. They were looking forward to the day
beginning. Some of them have radio and TV, but they never
look at it, they say people are much more interesting. The
great enjoyment is to visit each other after work and eat
together or drink together and tell stories to each other. Each
day brings something pleasant. When they have their dinner,

it's always an occasion. They never tell sad stories at the dinner table, it's just considered very boorish. You're supposed to be in good spirits, so you try not to think of anything unpleasant or disappointing.

When our interviewer was testing some of the really old people in villages, I got tired watching it. For hours they were subjected to all kinds of tests, they don't seem to get tired. They are much more relaxed than we are, especially about time. They have to do certain work, but it's not on a deadline, they are going to do it as well and as fast as they can. I know that sometimes when I get very impatient I think of them. They consider it a waste of energy to get excited about little things.

The old people in the Caucasus certainly have a high utility ceiling. And perhaps nowhere is the truth so clearly illustrated that it isn't the biological and technological advances alone that will extend our lives, but the way in which we live, the psychological environment we inhabit, the quality of our lives and the quality of our attitudes. Tests have shown that 100-year-old Caucasus residents have the vigor, mental alertness, and appearance of people of about 60 elsewhere. The fact that they look forward to getting up each morning, and anticipate with pleasure their social gatherings at mealtimes, underlines one of the major reasons people anywhere in the world have the incentive to live long: having something good to look forward to, some positive reason to continue living. In *How to Live To Be 100,* Dr. Benet talks about self-image and the expectation of long life, two of the basic concepts behind Psychological Immortality:

Social and medical attitudes toward aging are important in the self-image of the elderly. In areas of great longevity, mental and physical deterioration are not viewed as inevitable in old age. The expectation is for a long and useful life, and the old behave in accordance with that expectation. Individuals brought up in areas of high longevity expect to live far beyond the age of 100. When old persons are asked to what age they expect to live, they do not care to speculate and thus set limits. A young person will usually answer, "I will live very long, even longer than my great-grandfather."

And that young person may actually know his or her great-grandfather! Indeed, people in the Caucasus have specific linguistic expressions to describe ancestors going back six generations and who are still living.

LONGEVITY IN MAINE AND KENTUCKY

The Research Institute for the Study of Man is involved in coordinating a project which includes studies by scientists in Soviet Georgia researching the long-lived people of their region, and studies by U.S. scientists researching some long-lived people in Kentucky. These are integrated studies involving anthropologists, biologists, psychologists, etc. When the results of this joint study are in, the two groups of scientists hope to look at what (if any) similar factors exist in those long-lived citizens of two separate regions and cultures.

Sula Benet undertook a study of her own on a small island off the coast of Maine where she has vacationed for many years. She told me:

A lot of people in Maine live until a very old age and are very self-sufficient. This is what impressed me. Until the very end, they tried to be self-sufficient. Though their lives are different, I do find some similarities in attitudes between the old people in Maine and those in the Caucasus. The way they both view themselves helps a lot in their longevity. I did find it interesting that Maine fishermen and lobstermen had some similarities to people in the Caucasus who are pastoral people. Both groups are satisfied with the work they do.

Dr. Benet feels we can learn a lot from the self-sufficiency of these old people in Maine and the Caucasus. As she puts it:

We put emphasis on sending someone to help old people to move around and to do things. Many very old people get up and they don't know what to do with themselves. I have a feeling that the longer they can take care of themselves and do things by themselves the better. A lot of old people in the U.S. have a feeling of helplessness, believing that they need help for this and help for that. If one can be convinced that there are a great many things one can do oneself without demanding help, this affects enormously the person's self-image and self-respect. Because the moment one feels helpless, it isn't like a sickness that comes and goes, they project the feeling that "Now I can't do this and tomorrow I won't be able to do something else."

A few scientists seem to have made lifetime careers out of debunking the claims of longevity in the Caucasus, the Hunza, and Vilcabamba. Their main arguments are that there are no accurate birth records and that they've discovered some villagers who've added ten or twenty years to their ages. Does it really matter, however, if a vigorous 90-year-old villager claims to be 110 because he thinks advanced age will give him more status in the village? What does matter is the simple fact that advanced age does create status and respect. People in all three areas *expect* to live long and to remain healthy and active. Their bodies respond to those expectations. It seems that the rural residents of Kentucky now being studied in that joint U.S.-Soviet project and the Maine islanders studied by Sula Benet also have vigorous expectations of longevity. And in these pockets of longevity, villagers don't always *add* years. One Caucasus man of 107 denied his real age, stubbornly insisting he was only 70. When friends and witnesses who knew his true age confronted him, he said, "I want to get married. What woman wants to marry a man of over 100?"

I've talked to a number of scientists who've been to the Caucasus and feel that, if anything, the Soviet scientists have been conservative in their estimates of the longevity of their subjects. Though there are some documented cases of residents living to over 130, these are not the ones presented as evidence of longevity. Dr. Robert Butler of the National Institute on Aging told me that no claims were made for anyone being over 113, and he found no signs of exaggeration when he visited the famed Institute of Gerontology in Kiev. In fact, the Kiev facility is in the forefront of those longevity research institutions that are meticulous in their record-keeping. They've developed a 272-page manual of specific instructions for those verifying ages of long-lived villagers. Since these people rarely leave their home village, even without accurate statistical birth records it is a simple if somewhat time-consuming task to verify their advanced years by checking with other villagers, measuring the ages of their children, grandchildren, and great-grandchildren, and checking their memories of specific historical events.

PSYCHIC QUIET

Dr. Robert Butler gave me his impression of some of the long-lived people of the Caucasus:

They are not peripheral people, they're very central within the family life, and this mainstreaming is in and of itself of great healthful value. They remain physically vigorous. Their nutrition was quite moderate. It wasn't that they don't drink or don't eat or don't enjoy life, but the amount that they ate or drank was under very moderate control. I was much struck by a phrase used by a Soviet gerontologist, which he attributed to these long-lived people: psychic quiet. Frankly, it reminded me of a rather remarkable aunt of mine who lived to be about 95. I never saw her waste an ounce of time on worry. She only involved herself in something when it was an actual issue, when it directly confronted her. Otherwise, she was really psychically quiet. She wasn't full of turbulence about everyday things that some of us get so bound up in. She also had a good deal of control over her own life. She's kind of a good example as perhaps were the Soviet Caucasians in that we're not talking about big powerful industrial leaders or political figures having control, but of having control within the framework of one's particular life, where the center of gravity is within that person. There's something very important psychologically about that as it bears upon length of life.

Time and time again we hear reports that these people feel in charge of their own lives. Even in a society we Westerners regard as repressed, these people go about their daily lives feeling in complete control of their own situation. Again, that kind of feeling has to have some biochemical effect, has to have some positive impact on the body's biochemistry.

Though their lives are not easy ones—the work is hard, the terrain they inhabit is rugged—the residents of all three longevity pockets are almost entirely free of the kind of stress we face in the modern world. They are not involved, for the most part, on what goes on outside their own village. They face few of the complexities of a rapidly changing technological society. They, as Sula Benet points out, know the rules for living right. They are not competitive, other than perhaps trying to outlive one another. In our Western culture, we have what could be called a Lifespan Myth, a destructive belief that life will end at 70 or 80. If these isolated villagers have a myth at all, it's that they will easily live to be well over 100. One scientist scoffing at longevity reports in Vilcabamba told of finding out that one villager was actually 88 while claiming to be 102. What he didn't emphasize, and what may be much more important in terms of information we can all benefit from, was the fact that this 88-year-old villager was still traveling the Andean slopes to take his produce to market! There seems little doubt that all three areas have citizens nearing the 100-year mark who are far more vital and active than the average 70-year-old in the rest of the world. In fact, the Caucasus Mountains have a reputation for producing long-lived people that goes back thousands of years to reports from ancient Greek physicians.

Though some of the scientists studying these longevity areas have cited diet, climate, and lack of pollution as life-prolonging factors, attitude and expectations certainly seem important contributions. This is especially true in the Caucasus and in Vilcabamba, where the villagers smoke and drink, often to excess. One report says the Ecuadorean villagers smoke an average of forty to sixty cigarettes a day and consume up to six cups of homemade rum. Though their diets may be simple and consistent, it is certainly true that those famous TV commercials showing Caucasus villagers apparently existing mostly on yogurt are less than totally accurate.

THE SAGE PROJECT

Some of the things we've learned from studies of long-lived people in the Caucasus and other areas are that the vital ingredients for successful longevity are being actively involved in life, feeling a part of a consistent community of caring people, and having positive expectations of one's own longevity and vigor. These are also ingredients in the SAGE (Senior Actualization and Growth Exploration) Project, which was started in 1974 in the Berkeley living room of Gay Luce, whose 1979 book, *Your Second Life: Vitality in Middle and Later Age,* talks about the exciting changes in older people as a result of this innovative project. Gay Luce and her co-directors, Ken Dycktwald and Eugenia Gerrard, felt that such human potential developmental practices as yoga, T'ai Chi, biofeedback, gestalt therapy, and meditation could help "old" people grow and develop as many younger people seemed to be doing with these techniques. The core group of twelve elderly people met on a weekly basis, and evolved to a number of such groups with twelve to fifteen participants over the age of 60, who meet in weekly three-hour sessions over a nine-month period. Group members are encouraged to do various exercises at home and can also get additional individual counseling if needed. SAGE has been exported to other areas of the country, and one six-week project was federally funded in Chicago.

SAGE works on the premise that older people do not have to accept the idea that aging means deterioration and immobilization. That the later years can be times of pleasure, joy, health, and growth. That older people can be teachers, can learn new skills, make new friends, can learn to become artists, can fall in love. The results have been startling. Many remarkable transformations are part of the SAGE records. I've met some of the older people who've been through the program, and their energy and zest for life are inspiring. People who started out feeble and sickly have simply stopped being that way. Participants leave behind their loneliness and depression. Their minds and memories are rejuvenated. As Ken Dycktwald puts it:

We find that a lot of people who were diagnosed as senile aren't senile at all, they're just lonely and bored. And a lot of people who are supposed to be hard of hearing are really just alienated. It's been a long time since they've been able to talk to someone in a meaningful way. It's surprising—even shocking, sometimes—how radically people can change their condition. They can rebuild muscles that improve walking, breathing, and posture. We find that the relaxation techniques allow people to sleep better and feel more refreshed without drugs. As people pursue healthier paths, they quickly discover that they can feel more alive and happy.

Perhaps the greatest role of the SAGE Project is its refutation of the old saw: You can't teach an old dog new tricks. SAGE offers continuing proof that you can indeed become a learning, growing person at any age. As Gay Luce says:

To use an analogy, I'd say it's like alchemy. I think it is like discovering that you can transform something ordinary into something extraordinary. Here we're ordinary people and if you just put us into the crucible of a group, a jewel pops out. It's like producing a diamond from a lump of coal. You just have to know how to compress it.
It's awesome to me, because I've had the opportunity to watch people change—people over 70—and see them discover that they aren't whoever they thought they were. As they drop

their previous identities—mother, provider, executive, "doer"—they begin to discover that they are something more basic than any of these roles and, in the process, you can see their true beauty, their greatness, and their radiance shine through.

The most amazing identity-dropping of all among SAGE participants is the dropping of their identity as weak, helpless, degenerating old people.

Creating a supportive environment in which growth, vitality, and pleasure are the norm, no matter what one's age, will lead to a desire for life-extension that is essential if progress is to come. As Arnold Bennett said in 1907 in the first modern self-help book, *How To Live On 24 Hours a Day:*

> *It is always the man who has tasted life who demands more of it. And it is always the man who never gets out of bed who is the most difficult to rouse.*

Which are you? Life-extension is about to be handed out, not exactly on a silver platter, but only to those who are ready to accept it, willing to work toward it, believe they deserve it, and know they desire it.

SELF-IMAGE AS A LONGEVITY FACTOR

Interviewing long-lived people, scientists studying longevity, and going through many research reports, I keep coming up with a consistent factor: Those people who live long and healthy lives have a positive and clear image of who they are. The most destructive self-image you can have is one that involves believing you'll become old and infirm, and, inevitably, die. While people living to more than 100 have reported being surprised by their longevity, none of them ever stated something like: "I expected to be old and sick at 70."

Though the medical profession in the U.S. is often accused of being very slow in accepting innovative ideas, there has been progress in recent years, particularly in the field of holistic medicine, which dictates that doctors look at the whole person, understanding that the state of the mind has a lot to do with the state of the body. Now that we have biochemical proof of this, there is a whole new field known as behavioral medicine, which deals with the connections between health and behavior.

Dr. Ron Parks, holistic practitioner of internal medicine, says:

A person who visualizes himself as getting old doesn't give himself permission or license to do certain things and constantly sabotages himself. I see this all the time in working with the aged. Those that picture themselves as vigorous and see their life as open and interesting really are that way and have become that way. People locked into negative beliefs about themselves go that route and that route leads to degeneration and death. Any sort of technique or intervention one can make to shake loose those images can really change that course.

Dr. Lawrence Casler: Suggestion as a Longevity Factor

Self-image is the way we picture ourselves *to* ourselves. How you see yourself will determine the actions you take and the attitudes you have; in turn, this will affect the biochemistry of your body. The negative Lifespan Myth has a lot to do with negative self-image, with people who visualize themselves as aging and dying.

Dr. Lawrence Casler, Professor of Psychology at the State University of New York in Geneseo, told me:

I am more convinced than ever that the human lifespan is largely a mental rather than a physical matter. Most people die prematurely because they reach a point in their lives when

*they had expected to die. In essence, society has hypnotized us
into thinking that when we reach a certain age we're supposed
to get feeble and then just disappear.*

If you think this is an exaggeration, just consider all the images
of aging and death in books, movies, plays, on television, and in
what people talk about in social settings. Hypnosis is merely
repeated suggestion. If enough messages get through to your
subconscious mind suggesting that it is normal to grow old, lose
your vitality, and then die, your mind will absorb that information, and your neurotransmitters will then dispatch the appropriate hormonal messages to accelerate the aging process.
Remember that old folk tale in which someone is given mysterious
power to turn thoughts into reality, with the warning to be careful
because "whatever you think you will become"? In various
versions it has different endings, but always tragic, with the
person always imagining some terrible fate that then comes true.
In terms of what we now know about the brain's capacity to direct
the health and life-prolonging operations of the body, this is not so
unrealistic a premise.

Of course, once we know something is doing harm, we can take
steps to correct it. If we realize we are being hypnotized,
programmed with negative images about aging and death, we can
take positive action. Dr. Casler says:

> *If we can somehow reverse that tendency, in effect by de-
> hypnotizing, people will live who knows how long? There
> might be some limit, but I think it's silly to project that
> forward now. One hundred years ago, people said forty years
> was the limit. You just don't know.*

Dr. Casler has conducted some amazing experiments using
suggestion, visualization, and hypnosis. In 1967, he delivered a
paper to the American Psychological Association entitled "Psy-
chosomatic Aspects of Death: An Experiment with Suggestive
Therapy." This dealt with a study he had conducted among thirty
residents at the Jewish Home and Hospital for Aged in New York

City. The average age of the group was 83, and they were divided into a control group and an experimental group. Members of the experimental group were interviewed by Dr. Casler at least five times each over a period of five weeks. They were given repeated positive suggestions, such as "A person is as young as he feels"; "Advanced age need not be accompanied by debilitation, helplessness, or demoralization"; "You have many happy, healthy years ahead of you." You can imagine how rare these ideas were in an old-age home! Dr. Casler either didn't visit the control group members at all, or saw them just once to collect data. At the time the paper was written, two years after the study began, six of the control subjects had died, but only one member of the experimental group. Control subjects had been in the hospital for a total of 1,346 days, compared with just 974 days for the experimental subjects who had received the positive suggestions. The experimental group continued to do better than the control group. The last person involved in the study has died, and while Dr. Casler at this writing was still preparing the results of his follow-up research, all indications are that those people receiving the positive suggestions over that original five-week period lived longer and healthier lives than those who got no suggestions at all.

This led to a later study in which volunteer college students were divided by Dr. Casler into control and experimental groups, with members of both groups placed under hypnosis. In a single 45-minute session, members of the experimental group received forceful suggestions emphasizing that people need not die at any particular age, and that the subject will live to be at least 120 years old, retaining all his physical and mental faculties. Each was also taught a signal that he could activate at any time for added reassurance. The control group were given other suggestions not related to longevity. The ambitious project won't have final results for quite some time. In a letter to A. Stuart Otto, Lawrence Casler said:

If the results in 2070 are as anticipated, perhaps I'll pursue these matters further. But since I'll be 138 years old, I may well have developed other interests by then!

In the next section of this book, you'll have an opportunity to experiment on your own with positive self-suggestions about longevity and optimum health.

One of the tasks positive suggestion obviously can perform is to help replace some of the negative suggestions we all receive. Dr. Casler was trying through his experiments to counter negative programming with its destructive power and major impact on our attitudes toward aging:

For the elderly in our society, social expectations include the notion of gradually decreasing vitality, terminating in death. Cultural norms combine with more immediate social pressures to induce in the individual the virtually inescapable tendency to behave in a fairly stereotyped manner and the virtually inescapable expectation of dying not later than whatever age limit is culturally prescribed. These pressures begin quite early in life: Youngsters are taught to respect their "feeble" grandparents, businessmen are shown insurance tables in which their lifespans are predicted, etc. The forces are focused most strongly, however, on the aged individual himself: Seeing persons of his own age becoming enfeebled and dying, he can, perhaps, conceive of no alternative modes of behavior. A person who expects to become helpless or to die at the age of 80, 85, or 90, is likely to have his expectation confirmed.

Our self-image is often the result of the suggestions we give ourselves. If we give ourselves negative suggestions, unhealthy messages, our self-image and self-esteem will suffer. Self-image can be described as how we picture ourselves. Self-esteem is how valuable and good we think we are. Self-image does not exist in a vacuum. If, as Lawrence Casler suggests, someone sees persons of his own age getting feeble and dying one after another, it takes a strong act of will to overcome this negative impact.

Dr. William J. McGrane: Self-Esteem to Live Longer

Dr. William J. McGrane is Director of the McGrane Self-Esteem Institute and a professor at the University of Cincinnati. He feels that self-esteem is the answer to living longer. Bill McGrane notes that people without self-esteem keep their feelings buried, not trusting others enough to let them out, not valuing themselves enough to consider those feelings worth expressing. Feelings buried will emerge eventually some other way, often in illnesses connected with aging. As McGrane says:

> *The level of someone's self-esteem will determine the amount of actions he or she will take. You hold onto your personal power only when your self-esteem is sound, when you feel good about yourself.*

Someone with negative self-esteem will often be immobilized by indecision and inaction. Obviously, someone with low self-esteem will have neither the capacity nor the desire to extend his life by taking advantage of the biological and psychological opportunities.

This issue of personal power is an important one. In a conversation with Dr. McGrane, Dr. Robert Butler noted:

> *Personal power is one of the least talked about factors in living long, having control over one's life.*

This is one of the factors mentioned often in studies on the long-lived citizens of the Caucasus—that in fact they have control over their own lives, have personal power. If someone doesn't think he is in charge of his own life, he'll have little or no desire to continue that life indefinitely. And if someone thinks he's worthless, incompetent, unlovable, he's not going to want to inflict himself on the world for any great length of time.

Bill McGrane often gives his students the following formula:

> *What the mind attends to,*
> *   the mind considers.*

What the mind does not consider,
                    the mind dismisses.
What the mind continually considers,
                    the mind believes!
What the mind believes,
                    the mind eventually does!

Reverend Terry Cole-Whittaker: Eternally 28

One person who believes this strongly is the Reverend Terry Cole-Whittaker, author and minister of the Church of Religious Science in La Jolla, California. Terry says:

I have the idea that I'm eternally 28, which means I choose to have the cells of my body at 28, and that I'm eternally youthful and the cells of my body are always replacing themselves in a youthful manner, and that my body is alive. I praise all the parts of my body and praise my youthfulness, and don't talk about, "Oh, I'm getting old, look at this wrinkle." Giving up all words and all statements of old age and sickness and death. People are constantly affirming the negative: "Well, at this age I'm losing my memory." If I find myself saying something like this, I'll stop immediately and put a positive statement in, such as: "I'm younger than I've ever been and every day I'm feeling more alive and my life is better!

THE BODY RESPONDS

The body already responds to the indirect negative messages we give it—the beliefs that we deteriorate as we get older, the limits we place on our own capacities. Why not, therefore, start talking directly to it, start visualizing positive changes taking place? This is so much related to the work of Norman Cousins that in addition to the interview quoted earlier in this book, I wanted to share as well some of the far-reaching comments from a speech he gave to the Santa Barbara Writers' Conference in June of 1980:

> *The emotions can make you sick. All you have to do is live in a condition of tension or apprehension or despair and you'll become sick. Now, if the negative emotions produce sickness by changing the body chemistry, and this is demonstrable, then it stands to reason that the positive emotions can have a role to play in making you well, in keeping you well. When you're talking about the positive emotions, you're talking about love, hope, faith, the will to live, laughter, creativity, any of the things that give you robust expectations and make you want to get up in the morning.*

Notice how some of the basic ideas run through all of the research, all of the speculations about longevity. *Robust expectations*. Now there is a term to conjure up visions of vigorous people of whatever age being cheerfully active! And the idea of really wanting to get up in the morning—each day can be considered a microcosm of one's entire life, with the awakening period as birth. The attitude one has toward a single day is a reflection of the attitude one has toward life itself. In order to have the desire to continue and extend life, one would have to enjoy getting up, one would have to look forward to a new day. Strong desire always precedes positive action. Sublimating or denying that desire will create frustration. Lack of desire creates boredom, which Norman Cousins calls the greatest disease of all. Someone once described boredom as hostility without passion. It was once thought that such emotions as boredom, fear, frustration, anger, and apathy merely created unpleasant psychological states, but we now know that they have an impact on the body. As Norman Cousins goes on to say:

> *There is a difference in body chemistry as a result of what happens in the brain. The brain as Richard Berglund has said is the most prolific gland in the human body. We're used to*

thinking of the brain as the seat of consciousness, which, of
course, it is. We're used to thinking of the brain as a factory
for the manufacture of thoughts and for the warehousing of
ideas, which it is, too. But basically, the brain is much more.
The brain is a prolific gland which produces all sorts of
chemicals that the body needs. The future, it seems to me, of
medicine, is directly tied to the future of brain research.

What we're talking about is the simple truth that psychological opportunities create biological opportunities. There is no separating the two. You cannot have a healthy body without some sort of positive psychological approach.

THE PLACEBO EFFECT

One of the psychological factors carefully studied by medical researchers is the placebo effect: people getting well by taking an inactive pill or powder which they believe is a new medicine. In his book, *Anatomy of An Illness*, Norman Cousins has a chapter on "The Mysterious Placebo," in which he describes a test undertaken by the National Institute of Geriatrics in Bucharest, Rumania. They were testing a new drug designed to activate the endocrine system and increase longevity. A group of fifty people given the placebo showed a measurably lower death rate than a group of fifty who weren't given anything.

A third group of fifty given the new drug showed about the same improvement over the placebo group as the placebo group showed over those not given anything. In his Santa Barbara talk, Cousins said:

The placebo is a valuable key to the understanding of the
human healing system. If we understand how the placebo
works, we can understand how the human healing system
works, and a great deal more about how the brain works.
About 60 percent of the time a patient will react to a placebo,
an inactive substance, the same way as the patient would react

to a new drug being tested, **but only if the patient understands what the new drug was supposed to do.** *Therefore, if the mind, by anticipating something, can produce very profound changes inside the body, why can't we use the knowledge to prevent disease or to overcome disease when it occurs?*

This same power of the mind to heal the body is the basis for the suggestion experiments of Dr. Lawrence Casler mentioned earlier. If we can take control of the body's healing process by directing the mind to have "robust expectations" of health, vitality, and longevity, then this is true Psychological Immortality. And the evidence clearly indicates this is a very strong possibility. Norman Cousins talked in further detail about an experiment also mentioned briefly in his book, and I think it strikingly illustrates the placebo potential and the power of psychological beliefs to influence bodily functions.

Is the mind that powerful? Can the mind actually make things happen just because it believes that they will happen? Let me give you an example. They brought about 200 medical students together. They were testing a new tranquilizer, but they also wanted to test a new stimulant. The researchers conducting the test held up a red pill, the stimulant, in front of the students and said, "Those of you who want to volunteer to take this new stimulant in the red capsule should know that it will give you a high. So much so, you'll have no desire to go to sleep, and also, in a certain number of cases, it will make you so stimulated that it will nauseate you—but the nausea will pass after about fifteen minutes. You'll be able to work almost through the night and the next day you'll have no feeling of fatigue."

Then the researchers held up the blue pill, the new tranquilizer. "This is a super-tranquilizer," they said, "and, as is the case with most tranquilizers, this is going to make you very lethargic, but it also will make you very forgetful. Sometimes you won't remember what you did fifteen minutes ago, or what you started out to do. If you go into the bathroom to comb your hair, you may forget why you went in there, that's how severe it is. If what you want is sleep, then this is just perfect because you'll sleep fourteen hours without any difficulty."

So the students volunteered to take these new pills. There was just one thing the researchers did that was different. They did not tell the students who volunteered for the stimulant in the red capsule that they had instead filled the red capsule with the tranquilizer. And they did not tell the students who volunteered for the tranquilizer in the blue capsule that they were actually taking the stimulant. Not only did the mind expect to be stimulated by the red pill and to have all the effects that the students were told they were going to have, it had to punch its way through the tranquilizing effects of the drug really given. And what the students expected to happen did happen. Sixty percent of the students who took the red pill thinking it was a stimulant became nauseated, became high, and did everything the mind told the body would happen, and the same thing happened with the blue pill!

This kind of experiment has profound significance in our quest for a longer and younger life. For this placebo effect, this proof that the body responds to *expectations* more than to the actual substances taken, shows us that we are indeed in charge of the biochemical functions of our own bodies. If we therefore believe strongly enough that we will go beyond average lifespan figures, that we will live beyond 100, and that we will stay youthful, healthy, and active for as long as we want, then the body *can* respond and release the chemicals necessary to make it happen. As Norman Cousins says:

If, therefore, the mind creates chemical changes in the body as a result of expectations, how do we use this knowledge for good? We use it by understanding how the mind works. We use it by understanding that the mind is a chemical factory. We use it by having confidence in our ability to make changes in ourselves. We have this magic chemistry inside us and we

*can put it to work by knowing that we are in command, we do
have control.*

Again, here is the issue of personal power, of taking charge of
one's own life—the quality so often cited in studies of long-lived
residents of the world's longevity pockets. We *are* in command.
That realization will help us put that magic chemistry to work
inside us. We are just beginning to learn about these internal
processes and how to activate them. The future is limitless. No
one has dared venture an opinion as to the final limitations, if any,
on this kind of personal power. But we do have to begin, and, as
Cousins advises, we have to have confidence in our ability to
make changes in ourselves. Psychological changes, followed by
biochemical changes. I remember a psychologist saying, "How
you feel is who you are." We can now take that a step further and
say: How you feel is how your body functions. This is a whole new
approach to health, and it's no doubt going to take some getting
used to. Norman Cousins believes it's a tremendous and dramatic
transformation:

> *A whole new concept of disease is emerging. This new
> concept is not one that regards disease as being caused by
> specific germs. This new concept of disease is that your
> regulating system isn't functioning properly. Something has
> gone wrong with the thermostat. Something has gone wrong
> with that beautiful control mechanism. Also involved in this
> new concept is the fact that you can control that control
> mechanism. If you're in a condition of despair or depression or
> profound anxiety, your immunological system will not be
> working as it was intended to work. Your defenses will be
> down. And this is something you have control over.*

Here is another key concept in Psychological Immortality:
something you have control over. One can easily imagine a time
when future civilizations will look back and wonder at how naive
we were about having control over our own bodies and minds.
There are many moments throughout our lives when we have to

make decisions about how much control to take over our own lives, when we have to decide whether to take the power of life in our own hands or give it up to others, others who may have been programming us with negative beliefs about our own potential. It's interesting that this concept often is used negatively: "He's crazy, he's taking his life in his own hands." But can anything be saner, healthier, more sensible than taking charge of your own processes?

BIOFEEDBACK TRAINING

A powerful tool for taking charge of our own bodily processes is biofeedback training. Perhaps the major scientific accomplishment of the last decade has been the development of biofeedback as a science, art, and medical tool. As a part of the biofeedback community during its infancy in the early 1970s and editor-publisher of the first newsletter on the subject, I had occasion to work with and interview the pioneering researchers of this technique. Throughout the hundreds of research projects and training programs one conclusion emerged, shattering basic concepts about physiology and the role of the conscious mind. This was that individuals could learn to control bodily functions that were heretofore thought to operate automatically and without volition. In the initial experiments, by being wired up to measuring instruments that gave moment-to-moment indications of physiological changes, subjects were able to exercise voluntary control over their own brain waves, blood pressure, body temperature, muscle firings, heart rate, skin surface moisture, and other processes thought to be beyond the realm of conscious control.

It was difficult to get biofeedback accepted by the medical establishment and considered as a valid science. Many researchers were determined to hold onto their old belief that the autonomic nervous system could not be affected by voluntary effort. They all, of course, had eventually to accept the changes wrought by biofeedback, thanks to the overwhelming body of meticulous research in the field.

In addition to its usefulness as a medical tool, now widespread in its acceptance, biofeedback training offered those people working with the instruments an opportunity to sense their own power over their bodies. If we are to believe that we can control the aging process by using our minds, then biofeedback has paved the way by showing us how very possible it is to start exercising psychological control over our own physiology. As Norman Cousins puts it: "We are in command, we do have control."

Dr. Elmer Green: The Psychophysiological Principle

Some of the most impressive early biofeedback work was that of Dr. Elmer Green and Alyce Green, his wife and colleague. At the Menninger Foundation in Topeka, Kansas, they teach individuals to raise bodily temperature voluntarily. This work is discussed in their book, *Beyond Biofeedback*. I was involved in bringing the Greens to New York in 1971 for a series of workshops. As a participant in one of these workshops, I was astounded to learn I could raise the temperature in one of my hands by 9 to 12 degrees. This training had led to the Greens' now famous treatment program for migraine headaches. At that time, Elmer Green shared with me what he called his Psychophysiological Principle. This is simply that for every psychological change in an individual, there is a corresponding and appropriate physiological change, and, conversely, that for every physiological change, there is a corresponding psychological change. In other words, nothing can happen to your mind without something also happening in your body, and nothing can happen to your body without it having a conscious or unconscious effect on your mind.

For example, if you were 72 years old and started to have some difficulty walking, your mind might very well tell you that you were getting senile and death was approaching. This can have a spiraling effect, in that your mind telling you these negative things will then cause your body to respond with more of the same. In psychology, this is known as a self-fulfilling prophecy. If you constantly yell at a child that he or she is clumsy, that psychological input is certain to affect the child's motor responses, and clumsy he or she will be. If you're in the hospital and your doctor shows up with a glum expression on his face, no matter what he tells you, part of your physiological processes will respond to his expression. And if you constantly tell yourself that you are only going to live to be 75, and that you will start to go downhill at 50, your body will respond with appropriate deterioration.

Elmer Green is now head of the Voluntary Controls Program at the Menninger Foundation, and I talked to him about the Lifespan Myth, the limited view people have of their own potential. He says:

To a large extent it's pessimism and negative visualization that is connected with aging, with aging prematurely. If people think they're done for by 70 or 75, then probably that negative visualization sets the stage—the same way that positive visualization sets the stage for health. Most people begin dying about twenty years before they die. They begin decomposing and degenerating. What we're really interested in is self-regulation of the autonomic nervous system and other physiological processes so that a person can live fully.

Positive visualization is one of the most powerful ways to take charge of the psychological opportunities and affect the biological opportunities. The Psychological Immortality Strategies in the next section include a number of visualization exercises.

Can biofeedback help extend life? Well, simply by helping people understand that they can take charge of their own bodies it is already affecting attitudes and abilities in this area. Dr. Green says:

I would imagine that the lifespan will be expanded merely because of the fact that, if people stay healthy, whatever they do die from would have to be a whole lot more acute. A lot of people die gradually until finally the whole body gives up. If they keep themselves healthier all along, there ought to be a life expectancy increase. If a person stays healthy and they're 70, why should they die at 71? If they're healthy at 71, why should they die at 72? What we're concerned with is staying healthy one day at a time. How far can that be pushed? I really don't know, but I can't imagine a situation in which the life expectancy won't be increased.

Elmer Green's statement about dying gradually reminds me of the saying "Old age creeps up on you" and that the gradualism of the aging process can resemble a sneak attack on the human organism. Paying more attention to what is happening inside one's body can prevent this kind of sneak attack. Taking control can build up the natural defense system so that any such effect will be reversed.

Bogomolets on Longevity

In 1946 there appeared in English a book that had sold over one million copies in Russia. *The Prolongation of Life* by Alexander A. Bogomolets, often considered the father of modern longevity research, was inspired by investigations into the longevity of the people of the Caucasus in Soviet Georgia. Dr. Bogomolets was founder and Director of the Kiev Institute of Experimental Biology and Pathology, President of the Ukrainian Academy of Sciences, and Vice-President of the Academy of Sciences of the USSR. The book itself was not limited to the Caucasus region, but looked at longevity and long-living persons all through the Soviet Union and elsewhere in the world. He also wrote of the gradualism of old age:

Old age creeps upon a healthy man in stealthy manner. He readily agrees that he looks ten years younger than his actual age—the age of his contemporaries. And then, suddenly, he begins to suspect the advent of old age. This may be caused by an accidental remark he overhears about himself, by an unusual expression on his face observed in the mirror, or by a charming girl, much to his surprise, offering him her seat on a crowded bus. When he takes a stroll, he notices that he is not as tireless as he used to be, but has to stop to catch his breath or to ease a pain caused by movement.

After having used and abused our body during a certain number of years, we are pleased thereupon to declare it old and decrepit, and worn out. We then neglect it with a carelessness which completes its ruin. After having suffered for long years for our excesses and our follies, it succumbs under the weight of our gratuitous contempt.

Throughout literature and art death is depicted as sneaky, a vague, and stalking, shape. What really seems to be happening, however, is not so much the arrival of death suddenly, but the letting go of a belief in life. Our life-force can be very fragile indeed. One interesting aspect of this is that when someone reaches a really advanced age, say 90 or 100, that belief in life returns, as if to say, "We made it this far, so let's keep going." This is why people in their 90s sometimes seem more lively than those in their 70s, approaching the limits they've set by focusing on the average lifespan figures. And there's little doubt that when life expectancy figures loom large in the consciousness, each little pain becomes magnified in the imagination. Something that might have been dismissed at 30 or 40 becomes a major milestone, an indication that deterioration is steadily progressing, that death is near. This attitude, of course, reinforces any biological decline in the body's defense system. The immunological substances now have not only to fight physical incursions, but psychological ones as well. If one's positive beliefs can enhance the physiological well-being of the organism, then negative beliefs, or merely lack of positive ones, can expand and accelerate the aging process. As Dr. Bogomolets puts it:

Man arrived at a certain age, or even at a certain mental state, undergoes a sort of auto-suggestion of death. He then believes himself to have reached the end of his days, and feeds as much on the fear of death as on bodily foods. From this

*moment onwards death fascinates him. He hears its call with
terror everywhere and always. The victim feeds upon this fear,
intoxicates himself with it, and dies of it.*

*The scorn of death is, then, one of the methods of
prolonging life. The best way not to die too soon is to cultivate
the duties of life and the scorn of death.*

THE SCORN OF DEATH

To scorn death, to hold it in contempt or derision, is the
attitude that can prolong your life. Psychological Immortality is
based on such scorn, rather than fear or terror. Peter Sellers, the
late actor, is said to have had an obsessive fear of death. He
would not work on a movie set containing the color purple because
he associated that color with death. This lifelong obsession as well
as his weak heart may have been responsible for his death at 54.

There are those who suggest that an awareness of one's own
mortality creates an appreciation for life. This is as ridiculous as
saying that one must starve before being able to enjoy a good
meal, or that one must be exhausted with overwork before being
able to savor a vacation. Life can be appreciated on its own terms,
without having a constant awareness that time is running out.
While it's true that some people use this awareness of their
mortality to intensify their day-by-day living, this is merely an
excuse, an unnecessary and perhaps a fatal one. It would be much
more sensible to enjoy a day fully because that particular *day* is
limited than because the total number of days are limited. And
any benefits to be gained by an awareness of mortality are more
than offset by the psychological damage this does and the
biological-biochemical breakdowns it promotes.

If you're *not* scorning death, then you may very well be
embracing it. Embrace life instead, or as Dr. Bogomolets says,
"Cultivate the duties of life." The greatest of these duties is to *not*
let go listlessly, to *not* fade away with grace and dignity, but, if
you have to go at all, to go out kicking and screaming. A

successful life doesn't end at 75 by dying with a smile on one's lips. How much more triumphant to depart at 120 with a curse on one's lips!

F. M. Esfandiary says:

If it is natural to die, then the hell with nature! We must rise above nature. We must refuse to die.

There are those, even in the scientific community, who claim it is foolish to battle the inevitable, that we should leap into our coffins with a dignified attitude of resignation. That our expectations should be limited. That nature shouldn't be tampered with. Much more in keeping with the basic premise of Psychological Immortality are the comments by philosopher-scientist, Dr. William Marias Malisoff, whose 1937 book, *The Span of Life*, offered the following advice:

There are those who are ready to argue against the prolongation of life for the sheer deviltry of it. Among their specious premises are the contentions that "there would be nothing but masses of old idiots after a while, the country would go bankrupt on old-age pensions, how will you do this, that, or the other thing? Will anyone be happier? We ought to take death nobly. Death, properly conceived, is but part of life. One should not tamper with God's or Nature's order."

Poor, foolish humanity! If it were enlightened, would it not bend every effort toward systematic victory over the abyss which swallows it? "Time and tide," said Sir Walter Scott, "wait for no man." For generations those words have been considered a statement of eternal truth. Not so. Man is supreme; he has the potential for dominion over all. I therefore propose a slogan for those who are determined to achieve that dominion and exercise it: Time and tide **will** *wait.*

TIME AND TIDE *WILL* WAIT

Most of the objections cited by Dr. Malisoff as often-heard negative comments about prolonged life stem from the fear which Dr. Bogomolets claims most people feed upon at a certain age. These are emotionally charged objections rather than rational views. The willingness to accept the ideas, concepts, and suggestions of Psychological Immortality indicates a letting go of some of those intoxicating fears, and eliminating fear as a motivating force will enable us to make clear and positive choices. If one is paralyzed with the fear of death and deterioration, then one is not free to make the personal decisions necessary to prolong youthfulness and life itself. For instance, a well-known literary figure on the West Coast who died in 1980 was obsessed with death, often using it as a theme for his fiction and literary criticism. As soon as he was told he had cancer he assumed the worst. He started withdrawing from relationships, he stopped work on several projects, he made little or no effort to mobilize his system against the cancer. In effect, he gave up, preferring to prepare for death rather than fight it. His fear immobilized him and distorted his sense of reality. When he died in his early 50s, many of his friends and colleagues were saddened but few were surprised. One told me that he always knew this man would kill himself and it was only a question of how he would eventually manage to do it. It's really an ability to see alternatives, rather than just one dismal choice. Dr. Malisoff says:

> *There are minds that can face possibilities. They are the philosophic minds, since philosophy is the analysis of possibility. And there are minds that cannot face possibilities. They are content to drift about on a raft of what seem to them to be actualities.*

One of those common denominators which seem to link those people who remain youthful and alive well past the statistical norm is this ability to face possibilities, this willingness to wait and see what happens rather than allowing fear and doubt to rule one's expectations. One reason so many people in their 80s and 90s seem feisty and even cantankerous is the fact that they have the spirit and the energy not to buy into everyone else's expectations that they should have died at 70 or 75. Those who refuse to see the possibilities are always those with the narrowest vision, those to whom each new scientific achievement is a shock calling for a total reevaluation of their core views of the ways things are. And when some of the longevity research starts paying off, they will still be emotionally locked into those core views of aging and death, and not be as able as the rest of us to take advantage of the new emerging possibilities. Malisoff writes:

> *As to the familiar argument that no one ever has conquered death, all swans were white, millions upon millions of them, till a black one was discovered in Australia. The "impossible"—a black swan on the evidence of a long history of white swans—suddenly becomes possible, nay, actual! Thus, too, it is advisable, when someone in a frenzy of inductive generalization states that women cannot be great poets, to mention quietly Sappho. It is an old fallacy, called the fallacy of enumeration. The story of science is full of these fallacies. A sincere scientist is always looking for the exceptions, and for extenuating circumstances. And that is precisely what we have to do with the problem of increasing the lifespan.*

Today's exceptions will always prove to be tomorrow's norm, as long as looking for these exceptions is a desirable goal which engages minds that can face possibilities. It might be interesting to ask ourselves whether we have minds that can face possibilities, particularly the possibility of our own life being extended. Or is openmindedness sabotaged by such negative beliefs as the fallacy of enumeration? Thomas Troward wrote in his 1945 book, *The Law and the Word:*

> *To say that the inevitability of death is proved by the past experience of the race is the same argument which our grandfathers would have used against aerial navigation—no*

*one had ever traveled in the air, and that proved that no one
ever could.*

A similar analogy would be to say that because, before biofeedback, no one could control his or her autonomic functions, these functions were irrevocably involuntary. Of course, for hundreds of years there had been reports from the East of spiritual masters who could control these bodily functions, of yogis who had mastery of their own physiology. But few accepted these as accurate reports until modern technology provided the machines that could measure the changes, could measure the control being exerted. And *even now,* with biofeedback training an accepted fact in every major medical research center, with thousands of magazine articles, newspaper articles, television documentaries, and several dozen books reporting on the success of this breakthrough, there are probably still millions of Americans who have never heard of biofeedback, who have never thought about its application to their lives, and who still accept the now disproven belief that the autonomic nervous system is involuntary and not subject to conscious control. Likewise, tens of millions will not accept the possibility of life-extension, even when its actuality is proven time and time again in the laboratory. They will not be able to accept this possibility even when they see people taking advantage of these new opportunities and actually living longer! Old beliefs are not easily surrendered. Many people *would rather surrender their lives than their beliefs!*

DEATH AND AGING AS VOODOO

The belief in death and aging is as archaic as the belief in voodoo, and as deadly. Dr. Joseph W. Still, author of *Science and Education at the Crossroads—A View from the Laboratory,* noted:

When people say, "You can't live forever," they are really saying, "Science can't discover and learn to prevent the cause of aging."

Dr. Still felt that this sort of fixed and rigid belief got in the way of scientific research and public support for that research.

Most people are living in the dark ages in terms of their beliefs about death. These fixed beliefs are handed down intact from generation to generation with no allowance for the amazing biomedical achievements of this century and certainly no faith in the coming breakthroughs. The biological opportunities are there now, but until people take advantage of their psychological opportunities, until these fixed beliefs are modified, no real progress can be made. These archaic beliefs not only hurt laboratory research, but are a massive stumbling block for any individual who might desire a longer life. There are many obstacles on the road to increased lifespan, but none so threatening as those fixed beliefs in the inevitability of death and aging.

Dr. Still called the idea that once one has reached seventy he is living on borrowed time a "false notion." He was concerned that such false notions are often buried deep in people's subconscious minds, and he said:

They act as a sort of voodoo curse.

Over and over again, throughout this book, we've heard about the dangers of believing in a fixed and limited lifespan. The reason for this is simple: the more deeply ingrained an idea is in our subconscious minds, the more difficult it is to remove it. When that idea or belief is destructive and negative, the only way to change it is by constantly reinforcing the mind with positive information to counter that fixed belief. Repetition is an important tool in this regard, as is hearing new and healthier ideas from as many different sources as possible. If you were sick and believed it was serious and your doctor told you it wasn't, you might not believe him. But if, one by one, twenty respected specialists paraded in front of you to announce that your illness was minor and would soon pass, your subconscious mind would be more likely to accept that information as true, *and then be able to affect the release of substances in your body to help make it true.*

Psychological Immortality and the strategies contained in the next section must be reinforced by positive beliefs on the part of anyone using them—just as voodoo and other primitive threats must have as an ally the victim's belief. In a conversation with Norman Cousins, we talked about the Australian aboriginal medicine man who points a "death bone" at someone who has broken tribal laws. Quite often, that person actually dies. As Cousins describes it:

> *It's the will to die. This is the way a hex works. There's no doubt about the fact that people who expect to die at a certain age generally fulfill those expectations. Conversely, you can have people who are ill with malignancies which might be expected to claim their lives after three or four months, but these people are determined to live through, let's say a fortieth wedding anniversary, or a seventieth birthday, or whatever . . . and they do.*

The negative beliefs handed down about death and aging are just as much superstition as that "death bone," and can be just as fatal if supported by the victim's fears. And that aboriginal medicine man has something else in common with people who hold onto the belief in the inevitability of death and aging: There are always plenty of people around willing to reinforce the hex. There are always people who will immediately write off anyone at whom the bone is pointed, just as there are many in our culture who write off anyone over 70.

EMOTIONALLY INVESTED DEADLINES

Norman Cousins mentions another fascinating example of the power of the mind: People do seem to live beyond normal expectations when an important event is approaching. Dr. Philip R. Kunz of Brigham Young University conducted a study of 747 subjects. He got their names from obituary columns of newspapers in a large city over a period of one year. He then got the birth date of each subject and compared it with their death date. Dr. Kunz found that 46 percent of the deaths occurred in the three-month period following birthdays, indicating that these people waited at least until their birthdays to die. Only 8 percent died within the three months preceding their birthdays. Obviously, a large proportion of these people wanted to live to celebrate another birthday, and that desire kept them alive! Dr. H. Keith Fischer, Clinical Professor of Psychiatry at Temple University, believes that will power is very much involved with the time arrangements people choose unconsciously to become sick and die. His theory is that people set up "emotionally invested deadlines"—special dates they want to live to observe, special events they want to participate in, such as a grandchild's birth or wedding or a long-planned vacation trip. How many times have we heard a grandparent say, "I want to live to see you married"?

Though scientists are only recently testing out this theory, the idea is certainly not new, nor is the evidence: John Adams and Thomas Jefferson, both signers of the Declaration of Independence, died on the fiftieth anniversary of its adoption.

One prominent physician told me that the best way to support and increase longevity is to give people something important to look forward to. It certainly seems that those people with an important date coming up, an "emotionally invested deadline," seem to defy death itself. Several doctors have reported that patients have held on against tremendous odds waiting for the arrival of a loved one from a far distance. In fact, this was true in the case of my own father, who not only stayed alive an extra day awaiting my arrival from out-of-state, but snapped out of a comatose state just long enough to exchange a few words with me.

PARENTAL REPETITION URGE

Our greatest role models are our parents, and we do tend to lock into their lifespans in terms of our personal belief in a specific amount of time allotted to us. One of the most popular folk myths, and one of the most dangerous, is the belief that you can tell how long you will live by looking at how long your parents lived. Leonard Orr believes that the most dangerous time an individual faces is immediately following a parent's death, when one's own unconscious death urge is brought to the surface. And he goes on to say:

Death does not occur at random, but seems to occur statistically according to family tradition. The time of death is not controlled by God or Nature or the Devil, but is determined by a family pattern: Parents sell death to their children, consciously or not, generation after generation, without questioning it. Insurance companies make a profit on the fact that, statistically, family members tend to die, generation after generation, of the same symptoms and at about the same age. If you wish to attribute this to genetic factors, why are there any exceptions to family tradition? Charles Dickens died at age 58; his son, Charles Culliford Dickens, died at age 59; his grandson, Charles Walter Dickens, died at 58. However, dozens of other descendants lived ten to fifty years longer than that. These divergent tendencies seem to indicate that family tradition may be passed on as a mechanical pattern unless the individual becomes conscious of his own programming and takes responsibility for it.

While there is little doubt that certain genetic characteristics are handed down through the generations, these do not seem to include a fixed biological clock that will determine the age of death. And even should the genes pass down a susceptibility to one disease or another, or a weakness in some part of the immunological system, these could be called negative biological opportunities, which could either be taken advantage of or circumvented. Since most people do not take advantage of their full list of positive biological opportunities, or else we would all now live to over 100, there seems little reason to suppose we must take advantage of all our *negative* biological opportunities passed down by parents.

Dr. Robert J. Samp of the University of Wisconsin Medical School says simply:

Life expectancy isn't hereditary, and that's a very good thing.

While life expectancy isn't hereditary, there *is* this Parental Repetition Urge, and it must be overcome or it will do us in. The first line of attack is awareness. Once we are aware that this urge, this negative psychological belief system, exists, we have already diluted its power. As F. M. Esfandiary told me:

> *We have taken insufficient account of the impact of this on the aging process. We know, for instance, that there are individuals very physically healthy and suddenly when they get to a certain age,* **bang,** *they start falling apart. On closer examination we realize these are people who somewhere along the way have programmed themselves to begin falling apart. Either they have plugged into a certain time when their own parents have died, or some other symbol that plays in their head. For instance, a very healthy, robust, vigorous man, whose father, let's say, had died at the age of 56, such a person may unconsciously carry that image. When he reaches the age of 56, suddenly he begins to die.*

One simple reason insufficient account has been taken of this Parental Repetition Urge is that when someone dies at or about the same age as one or both of their parents, it's considered normal, part of a continuing pattern. Scientists have done us a disservice by not refuting this myth once and for all. Unfortunately, a number of the scientists and physicians themselves carry this same subconscious urge.

If one or both of your parents are dead, understand that a part of your subconscious may be attached to the age at which they died. When you reach that age, you can make a special effort to affirm life and keep vigorously involved and excited about things. In the next section, we'll have a specific visualization tool for this purpose.

In a conversation I had with prominent Gestalt therapist Nancy Bristol, she suggested:

Just as parental messages are imprinted on the subconscious mind, forming Life Scripts which determine our behavior, so can parental role models create expectations which have a profound effect on individual lifespans.

REWRITING THE DEATH SCRIPT

Let's call these expectations Death Scripts. We all have them, and just as some people can make the most of their biological opportunities, some can rewrite their Death Scripts by activating their will to live.

One person who did so is psychotherapist Dolly Lavenson of Philadelphia. Dolly is one of those exceptional, beautiful women who enjoys the fact that people are shocked to find out her true age. At 50, she has the figure, skin tone, and energy of someone at least twenty years younger. When we discussed the psychological factors which might account for her youthfulness, she told the following powerful story:

When I was 6, my mother died at 26, during childbirth. I always had the idea that I was going to die when I was 26 years old. I didn't understand it, but I had that feeling. When I was 26, I was pregnant and I had absolutely no problems with the pregnancy. All of a sudden, on the delivery table, I started exactly the way my mother had. They just couldn't stop the bleeding. It was my will to be with her. My muscles wouldn't contract. There was nothing they could do to stop the bleeding. I had to have a partial hysterectomy. Nobody could ever figure out what caused it. But afterwards, when I went into therapy, my doctor said it was an identification with my mother, an unconscious desire to be with her and go the same way. The thing that seemed to pull me out of it at the time was the fact that they showed me the baby. While I was bleeding, they held my son up to me. After the operation I had all sorts of bottles attached to my arms, my leg up in the air, I was a wreck. A week later I was together and walked out of the hospital. That's how I decided to become a therapist. I realized the will that a person has can determine anything. I decided from then on, since I had had such a rough experience at 26, that was it, and I was going to have a new life. I decided that if I wasn't going to die at 26, I wasn't going to get any older either. Not physically, not any way! And that's the way it is.

Dolly Lavenson managed to conquer the Death Script implanted by the circumstances and early age of her mother's death. Also, since she wasn't exposed to her mother's aging process, that very visible model was removed from her conscious experiencing of life. In her memory, that mother is perpetually young. This isn't to suggest that we encourage children to kill off their parents at a young age so that they will avoid the role model of aging parents, but merely to illustrate the potent effect parents have on their children's attitudes toward aging and death!

One of the major prerequisites in conquering the Death Script is for each of us to realize what our own specific script is. Look at the circumstances of the deaths of parents and other significant people in your life. If one or more of these people died in their 50s, then this can be a potentially dangerous time for you, but one in which certain countermeasures can be taken. In the coming section on strategies, we'll examine some of these measures.

It is also true that long-lived and youthful parents can provide a positive role model. But even here it would be more productive for an individual to take responsibility for his or her own lifespan rather than saying, "My parents are healthy and in their 80s, so I've got a long life ahead of me." Much better, in terms of Psychological Immortality, to say, "I am in charge of my own life and am choosing to live a long and youthful life!" Part of the process of growing up, no matter what our age, is letting go of the belief that our parents are to blame for our limitations or should be given all the credit for our triumphs.

We each have that core of strength within us, that core that came to Dolly Lavenson's rescue when all indications were that she would repeat her mother's Death Script. Passive or active, we all exercise choice when we follow such a script. To *not* follow the script, however, we always have to make an active choice. Doing nothing will enable that negative programming to gain strength in our subconscious minds. It's significant that Dolly Lavenson believes being shown her newborn son pulled her out of it, that being exposed to new life pulled her away from death. This is why nursing homes, filled with hopelessness and pain and boredom, are so often responsible for activating individual Death Scripts.

One of the best supportive tools for overcoming Death Scripts is to associate with people who are not actively engaged in living theirs—another powerful reason for promoting age-integrated environments. The original thought behind segregating people according to age was that people of similar ages have similar interests, capabilities, and talents. This could be said to be encouraged by the concept of life stages, the idea that emerged in the 1970s, that human beings go through various predictable stages of growth and development. This, of course, was widely communicated by Gail Sheehy's bestselling book, *Passages*. The basic premise is that we all go through very similar stages of life at similar chronological ages.

LIFESPAN DEVELOPMENT

There is, however, a new view of human growth and development called Lifespan Development, a concept more in harmony with the philosophical thrust of Psychological Immortality. This 1980s view is that we do go through change all our lives, *but that this change is not necessarily tied to our ages*, and that these changes do not occur in any particular sequential order. The assumption is that age is not an indication of how people feel and what they do with their lives. As gerontologist Bernice Neugarten of the University of Chicago said in a *Newsweek* interview:

Our society is becoming accustomed to the 28-year-old mayor, the 50-year-old retiree, the 65-year-old father of a preschooler, and the 70-year-old student. We are evolving into an age-irrelevant society.

Lifespan Development looks at people as unique and therefore different from each other. Each person ages at his or her own pace. Trying to toss everyone into the same mixing bowl has just created a lot of confusion about the process of aging. Developmental psychologist Dr. Paul Baltes of Penn State says:

As people grow older, they become more and more different from one another, so that age means less and less as a determinant of character and behavior.

AGE-IRRELEVANCE

Psychological Immortality is aimed at producing age-irrelevance: a society in which men and women would not start to feel unattractive at 45 or 50, in which no one saw enforced retirement leisure as a punishment for anyone unlucky enough to stay alive past 65, and in which the major activity after 70 would not be waiting for the grim reaper.

Age-irrelevance will shake up some of our basic concepts about life. It would be more comfortable to just stick to the old belief that life begins to end from the moment of birth and that it's downhill from then on. Many people live their lives as though some doctor slapped them on the bottom at birth and announced, "You have 75 years. Use them well, that's all there is. And whatever you do, when you pass 50, start acting your age!"

Going back to the citizens of the Caucasus, Hunza, and Vilcabamba, we see that they do not accept life stages as most of the so-called civilized world accepts them. Their work continues indefinitely and keeps them occupied unless accident or very severe disease intervenes. Their sex lives are active throughout their lifespans, and most of all the old person is important in their society. Everyone aspires to a long life, many can't wait to *be* old, even to the point of sometimes lying about their ages. No one in those cultures tells a person to "act your age." Doctors do not use that asinine remark, "Considering your age, you're in good shape." In fact, removal of "considering your age" from our vocabularies would go a long way toward eliminating the Lifespan Myth and taking greater advantage of the biological and psychological opportunities.

GROWING YOUNGER

The people of the Caucasus and other long-lived areas could be described as "growing younger" as they reach old age. They often seem more alert and vital in their later years, and this certainly has to do with the supportive psychological process which views aging as a positive achievement in those cultures. In Western culture, we often refer to someone entering his or her "second childhood," usually meaning they are acting immature and foolish. If someone starts acting youthful and skips down the block at the age of 80, we accuse him of being senile and attempt to repress that behavior, perhaps by sending him to a nursing home where no one would dare act youthful.

SENILITY AS PRIMAL THERAPY

The pioneering American psychologist William James said that in order to change any behavior or belief system you had to go about it flamboyantly. The Immortalists as a group have some flamboyant beliefs and convictions, and none of them have more outrageous ideas than Leonard Orr. He says:

I believe that senility is a natural form of primal therapy. I believe that senior citizens who unravel their death urge will discover the fountain of youth within their own minds and bodies. The basic question is why did they not discover it already in sixty or seventy years? I believe the answer is to be found in the way children are treated in our society. Most people have experienced their divine child being suppressed at an early age.

The tragedy of convalescent hospitals is that senior citizens die in the middle of the youthing process. This tragedy is caused by the gloom and doom of deathist mentality. So a practical way to save our society from prophecies of doom is to eliminate mortal mentality in senior citizens' homes and include people who are experiencing senility in the mainstream of society. Senility is the process of rediscovering the natural divine child within. When it becomes safe for senior citizens to act like children and be childish, then the magic of the fountain of youth will become ordinary. It is a fact that most senior citizens would rather die than suppress their divine child any longer. Suppressing our natural divinity is so painful and takes so much effort that it leads to mental and physical illnesses and death.

This concept, of course, can boggle most minds—the idea that senility is a stage we have to pass through in order to become youthful again. The idea that repression of youthfulness is what kills us. While this goes against everything we've been taught to believe about aging, it is important to remember that we really know next to nothing about the aging process. Each year many distinguished scientists come up with new theories and new biological evidence that dispels earlier beliefs about this mysterious process. It would be very arrogant indeed for anyone to dismiss Leonard Orr's theory as nonsense. We just don't know. One thing we do know, however, is that repression itself kills people. Any natural feeling or inclination that is consistently held back will turn to inner frustration and hostility and is almost guaranteed to produce a stress-related disorder. If someone were 75 and had an urge to do something youthful and silly, but repressed that urge because it would be an action viewed as "inappropriate behavior for someone your age," that act of repression could produce the physical and psychological deterioration that would lead to degeneration and death.

At the very heart of Leonard Orr's flamboyant statement and also at the core of this mental/emotional approach we are calling Psychological Immortality lies a basic undeniable conclusion: *It is possible to grow younger instead of older.* Acceptance of this conclusion is the key to effective rejection of the belief that death and aging are inevitable.

The simple but deadly belief that with every passing year we grow a year older will eventually kill us. If it doesn't kill us, we'll probably wish we were dead no matter what the scientists come up with. If someone believes that he or she is slowly rotting away, then there will be little or no desire to spend even more time in the process. When addressing audiences on the subject of life-extension, I invariably hear the robot-like response: "But who wants to be *old* for another twenty, thirty, or forty years?" It's as if, once having expanded the imagination by considering increased longevity, the consciousness stops short and refuses to accept the next logical step. But scientists all agree that they are working toward extending *youth,* not just extending life.

There is a very deeply imbedded part of all of us that will resist this idea that one can grow more youthful as the years pass. Once we recognize that a part of us is holding onto the idea that we *must* grow old, that we must senesce, then we can move around that immovable mental object and start trying on for size the idea that we can juvenesce instead. That we can grow younger instead of older. In Edgar Allen Poe's short story, "The Pit and the Pendulum," the author used the slowly descending scythelike movements of the deadly blade as a metaphor for aging and death. It was belief in that knifelike pendulum that did Poe's hero in, and it is the belief in slowly increasing deterioration that does many people in today. No one has ever calculated what the human imagination can do once it lets go of that voodoo curse. We can't even begin to know what limits we've placed on ourselves by believing that growing older is natural and inevitable.

The belief that time marches on like some indestructible warrior ready to do battle with our living cells is the very belief that creates a supportive environment for the aging process. We've been programmed since infancy to lie back and passively accept growing older:

"No use trying to change what can't be changed."

"You can't hold back the clock."

"We're all going to end up in the same place."

"These old bones are beginning to slow me down."

"As your doctor, I want to tell you that there are some things you just can't do anymore."

"We're all getting older."

The programming is so subtle and insidious that we even laugh at the fact that comic-strip characters never seem to age. As if this were the one quality that prevents us from believing in them! It's as though we're saying that Charlie Brown and Dagwood Bumstead would be more *believable* if they would only begin doddering. We hear statements such as: "Little Orphan Annie? Don't make me laugh! She's 60 if she's a day!"

An interesting mental exercise would be to picture all the psychological reinforcement we receive in a lifetime of the idea that we steadily grow more feeble and less capable as the years advance. The books, the movies, the jokes, the attention paid to someone who does seem to be youthful at an advanced age, as if that person were some strange aberration. When we look at where all these very rigid images of aging come from, we see that the sources are all outside ourselves. Again, self-esteem comes into the picture: The more we trust our own view of the world, the more we are willing to discard what others have told us and form our own opinions and make our own decisions based on our personal experience of the way things are.

HEALTHY DENIAL

We sometimes hear the cliché "I'm not getting older, I'm getting better!" That is probably a very healthy thing to believe, but many people saying it don't really believe it. Is it denying reality to say to one's self that old age is *not* creeping up, that one can feel as good at 70 as at 40? The view of this book and my own personal view is that the inevitability of death and aging is not the way things *are* so much as they way things *apparently* are. Many people believe that a wrinkle is the beginning of the end, relating this physical loosening of the skin with degeneration and death. But many very wrinkled people are amazingly fit and active, so this is only an apparent conclusion. The fact is that unless you are experiencing real physical incapacity, aging is a fantasy for you. It doesn't exist in personal terms except as a future fear, an image of impending deterioration, a negative expectation. To deny this seems the only course open to someone with a realistic view. It used to be thought that denial was always unhealthy. This too has come tumbling down in the minds of all but the most archaic psychologists and psychiatrists. Psychiatrist Dr. Harold Bloomfield emphasized this in a conversation with me:

> *Recent research shows that people who deny getting older do very well. It used to be said that you have to accept getting older and all that goes with it, the deterioration, loss of function. It used to be a psychological view that was accepted and seen as part of the role of working with people in middle-age crisis. There's now evidence to suggest that people who are now out to stay young and vigorous do themselves a lot of good.*

We're not talking here about the desperate craving for youth of some people who have every wrinkle attended to by a plastic surgeon and practically kill themselves trying to recapture their youth. These people are obviously trying to stave off the aging that they believe is inevitable, thereby reinforcing this negative belief by seeking extraordinary solutions outside themselves. Just as their cosmetic surgery offers only superficial changes, their denial too is superficial, in that they really do believe death and aging are rapidly approaching. Healthy denial involves a quiet acceptance of possibilities, an understanding that just because *other* people may age and deteriorate is no reason to assume *you* must do the same. Dr. Bloomfield underscores the healthy transformation in professional therapeutic attitudes toward denial:

Denial is no longer considered the pathological state it once was thought to be. In people who are determined to stay young, intentionality is very important. People who buy the programming that with age comes deterioration will deteriorate. Now certainly with age comes change, no one would deny that, but you don't have to buy the feeling that "I will come down with a chronic illness, which one will it be?" Having a sense of optimism and hopefulness and looking forward, and even denial of what used to be thought of as the inevitability of the aging process, actually works for you rather than against you.

Can there be an unhealthy denial of age? Of course! I remember one counseling client who was paranoic at the approach of her thirty-fifth birthday. An extremely attractive woman, she dated younger men and lied to them about her age. She was not saying that age didn't matter, she *was* saying that it mattered so much that she wasn't willing to acknowledge her own belief that she was indeed getting older. Many people put so much energy into fighting age that they have no time to grow younger.

The way in which we use language also holds us back. There is nothing "growing" about getting older. Growth has to do with youth and life and possibilities. Aging has more to do with stagnation. We age when we *stop* growing. It would be much more accurate to say "ungrowing older" or "shrinking older" to describe what most people really believe about the later years. People who defy the aging process all seem to have one quality in common: They *haven't* stopped growing, learning, doing.

ACTIVE ENJOYMENT VERSUS PASSIVE APATHY

Those people who survive longer than most, whether in our society or in far-flung simpler cultures, are always active participants in their own lives, rather than passive, noncaring observers. While human consciousness is multitalented, it does seem to have one limitation: Only one major idea can be activated at any given moment. If the idea being activated is that life is worth living, then that is the whole thrust of a person's existence. If, on the other hand, the idea is firmly implanted that there's no use trying, that the end is approaching and one may as well accept it, then this is what gets nourished and supported and becomes real. Now that we know that attitudes affect the actual biochemistry of the body, we can see that the human organism is powerfully responsive to suggestion. A belief in active participation will set off the secretion of those substances necessary to maintaining that role; a belief in resignation will suppress certain natural rejuvenating processes.

REJUVENATION AS A POSSIBILITY

Some people do seem, as Leonard Orr suggests, to pass through senility and old age. Of course, the dream of a magic formula to restore lost youth is universal. People spend tens of thousands of dollars and travel thousands of miles to try out this or that treatment purported to restore vitality and youthfulness. A remarkable man by the name of Dr. J. A. S. Sage wrote a book at the age of 84 entitled *Live To Be 100 and Enjoy It—Without Looking or Feeling It*. In it, he describes how he was falling apart at 76. He reports that he transformed himself from a doddering old man rapidly failing in health to the picture of health by programming his body's cells to rejuvenate themselves through auto-suggestion. He remarried at the age of 95, and at last report was alive and well on his farm in South Africa, inviting people to join in celebrating his 250th birthday in the twenty-second century! It doesn't matter whether or not he actually lives to 250— what does matter is that the belief in a long and healthy life reinforces *current* vitality.

Worden McDonald had his book, *An Old Guy Who Feels Good*, published at the age of 76. In 1973, "Mac" McDonald was walking around with a plastic hip and a crutch in a senior-citizen apartment complex in Berkeley, California. He says:

Mostly we talked about our insides, which were worn out.

Then McDonald joined the SAGE Project, mentioned earlier, and is now a youthful lecturer at local universities on current aging issues. He describes the philosophy that helped him grow younger:

The whole idea of SAGE is to refuse to be old, scared, pushed around, or told that you're too old or can't do anything.

Again, we see the value of healthy denial. Just writing a book entitled *An Old Guy Who Feels Good* reinforced that internal attitude, with McDonald making a psychological commitment to life instead of to death—his personal mental/emotional statement to the effect that "I'm fed up with the way everybody says it has to be, and from now on I'm going to live my life the way I *want* it to be!"

PREFERENCE VERSUS ADDICTION

In the teachings of Ken Keyes, Jr., author of *Handbook to Higher Consciousness*, one of the primary causes of healthy growth is the transformation of one's addictions into preferences. An addiction is described as anything whose absence will upset, anger, or sadden an individual. By upgrading these addictions to preferences, one can still prefer things being a certain way, but won't go to pieces when they aren't. This seems also to be the deciding factor in healthy versus unhealthy denial. If someone is addicted to being young, so that any indication of the absence of youth sends him into panic, so that the appearance of one gray hair convinces him that death is approaching, then that person will be feeding the aging process, adding energy to his death consciousness. But if you *prefer* being young, you are making a *choice*. Not because you can't stand the thought of getting older, but simply because you prefer the idea of getting younger, then you are harnessing the unlimited resources of your brain, which will then probably activate those very life-enhancing substances to turn your preference into your actual experience.

The fictional cliché of the multimillionaire fighting old age with desperation, having goat- and monkey-gland operations, seeing soothsayers, devoting all his money and time to fighting the ravages of age, is an example of death consciousness. This is someone who deep down believes that aging is inevitable and who really doesn't expect to win. Psychological Immortality is really a matter of *preferring* life over death, of *preferring* vitality over deterioration.

Dr. Barton Knapp: Moving Sideways Through Time

Preferences make good sense. When Abraham Maslow revolutionized psychology by deciding that he preferred studying superhealthy people rather than emotionally disturbed ones, and came up with the concept of self-actualization (fully realizing one's own potential), his approach provided us with a body of information heretofore unavailable. Likewise, when Dr. Richard Cutler says we should study longevity rather than aging, this *preference* makes good sense, and provides us with a different perspective on the issue of life-extension. When interviewing people for this book, I did not choose to talk to people who were senile, feeble, hopeless. Those who seemed to have the most to offer, and those whom I preferred talking to, were the ones who were apparently overcoming their negative conditioning and defying preconceived notions about getting older. One of these people happens to be a highly respected clinical psychologist, Dr. Barton Knapp of Philadelphia, now an adjunct faculty member at Rutgers Medical School. I first met Bart in 1971 and was amazed at his energy and zest for life then, when he was 50. At 60, he looks even younger. We talked about this recently:

Someone just said to me, "You don't seem to get any older, you just move sideways through time." I'm aware of not **feeling** *my age. Most of the people I have contact with are in their 30s or 40s—I don't really have a model of what it's like to be 60. If I went to a retirement village, I'd be surrounded by models of people who have retired and are into an entirely different scene.*

Again, we see the importance of an age-irrelevant environment. Perhaps it's a sad commentary on our age-segregated society that Dr. Knapp has to associate with younger people in order to have models of vitality. His comment on being told that he moves sideways through time is indicative of one factor in continuing vitality: the belief that time is not the enemy. As in the medical report mentioned at the end of the first section which stated that time was not toxic, it is the belief in the effects of time which are poisonous. Rather than accepting Einstein's conclusion that time is relative, that it changes under certain circumstances and conditions, people still adhere to the ancient belief that time is immutable, relentless. One's attitude toward time has a lot to do with the basic attitude one has toward death and aging. For instance, the more valuable one considers one's time, the more desire there is to extend it and to use it well. Negative ideas and feelings about time are passed on. As Bart Knapp puts it:

I have a hunch that there's also a lot of learning how to be your age. There's a lot of that social pressure: "This is the way you should be." Look at so many of the commercials and ads. What do you see older people doing if you see them at all? Some of those traditional stereotypical things that are the "role" of the older person. Because I don't have that model, my expectation of myself is that I'm going to continue doing either similar things or new things for the rest of my life. I can't imagine retiring, and this is such a change for me— fourteen years ago that was all I was focusing on. Now I expect to continue to increase my earnings. Why not?

"Why not?" seems to be a very healthy question for people to ask. Why not feel good? Why not live longer? Why not continue to expand creative horizons and increase earnings? In the coming section on specific strategies, we'll look at ways of fostering the idea of newness in one's life, the idea that good and enjoyable things always are coming. This is again the attitude of the long-lived people of the Caucasus: They expect each day to bring something good into their lives, and this one-day-at-a-time approach becomes a many-years-at-a-time reality in terms of the ages they attain.

When we talk about the stereotypes of aging, the fact that older people on TV are never as quick or as successful or as romantic as younger people, we must also realize that it is the individual observing a stereotype who has the power either to accept or reject it. If people are aware how ridiculous these images are, they will remain merely images and have no negative effect.

Instead of focusing energy on what others tell us it's like to grow old, we can choose to pay attention to all the alternatives we have for staying youthful and involved. As Dr. Knapp puts it:

> *People stay young when they find things to become excited about. It's not that they wait for exciting things to happen, they* **create** *the excitement. That's one of the reasons I feel so good about myself. I create the excitement, I create the opportunities. So something miserable can be happening, and rather than* **feel** *miserable about it, I'll change my perspective, feel better, and* **then** *deal with whatever is happening. I don't feel helpless.*

Though it sounds simple, that one sentence of Bart Knapp's is really the basic solution to staying motivated and taking advantage of the biological and psychological opportunities: "People stay young when they find things to become excited about."

Ray Bradbury

In October of 1980, *Time* Magazine reported, "Most people lose the capacity for wonder as they grow older. Not Bradbury." Ray

Bradbury is not only one of the most gifted fantasy writers of our time, but a true visionary as well. His views on all sorts of subjects are filled with common sense as well as a very special mind-expanding insight. We talked about the changes that would be brought about by extending the human lifespan and motivating people to take advantage of it:

> *The problem is making sure as we move ahead and give these gifts to people that we do the educational job along the way, to stimulate them and make them want to have not just one career but three or four. Now that's a big order for any society, because most people today, even with their short lifespan, are not filling it up, and they're boring to themselves and to others.*
>
> *The mystery of unmotivated people boggles a lot of us. We look at them and say, "How the hell can we excite them?" What's the use of being alive if you are not excited by life? I would love to have three additional lifetimes because there's a lot I won't be able to do. There are areas I would like to go into where I will never be able to move. I'd like to be a full-time actor. I'd like to be a full-time minister. I'd like to be a full-time poet. I'd like to be a full-time painter. The problem with extra life is the boredom that will go with it and the possible insanity if we don't train people well to their own potentials.*

It may never really come to that, for those people who are not able to find excitement in life are unlikely to seek extension of that life. What *is* the use of being alive if we are not excited by life? Part of that excitement is keeping actively involved, actively engaged physically, intellectually, emotionally. Keeping busy, not to fill time, but because the act of doing is exciting and fulfilling in itself. Ray Bradbury says:

> *I think busyness is everything—I don't care what you do as long as you're busy and as long as you **love** doing it. Orchestra conductors live to be 90 because they're vigorous and curious. Curiosity is another important factor—if it takes*

long to achieve and still offers challenges. Busyness connected
to curiosity. Whether you're a horticulturist, or a police
detective, or an orchestra conductor, the curiosity about
finding out **yet more** *about the field you're in. Because you*
haven't learned it all. There's so much that we haven't found
out yet. Look at the record of most of the great artists of the
last one hundred years—almost without exception they lived
to be 80, 90, 95. Look at Picasso, still producing so late in
life. The whole thing is the fun of living!

At 61, Ray Bradbury has the vitality and curiosity of a child.
His eyes sparkle with wonder and excitement. And his attitude is
exactly why he is so alive.

Ray Bradbury's comments illustrate several of the very significant factors in living longer and younger. First, the idea, also
expressed by Dr. Barton Knapp, that you stay young when you are
excited by life. Linked to this is another vital factor: having a wide
variety of alternatives to choose from. When Ray Bradbury
described to me his desire to be an actor, or a painter, or a
minister, his whole face lit up with enthusiasm, touched perhaps
with a wistful perception that he wouldn't get to live *all* of his
dreams. But he is living more than most, and this may indicate
another strong formula for longevity: always having more desires
than can possibly be filled, so that there is always more to urge
you on, more to live for.

This factor was also emphasized in a conversation I had with
former astronaut Wally Schirra, who said:

> *As a child, one thing I learned from my father: If you have*
> *a goal, get a new one when you get near that goal. Otherwise,*
> *you're going to stall out. I've lived that one all along and*
> *that's probably why I could adapt to doing something else*
> *after doing what many think was the ultimate, the space*
> *flights. After those flights, my goal was to go into a whole*
> *different area. I rejected aerospace and got into the free*
> *enterprise world.*

This ability to go beyond merely coping with change and

actually to embrace it, welcoming new alternatives as they emerge, seems to keep people young. While the long-lived peoples in the world's longevity pockets seem to have simple and consistent lives, perhaps we in more complicated societies can only find consistency in the realization that everything changes. Enjoying the new things that are coming along is a way of keeping mind and body alert. Ray Bradbury, Bart Knapp, and Wally Schirra all have this in common, this savoring of possibilities, creating their own excitement. And all three are youthful beyond the norm for their years.

STAYING YOUNG AND ALIVE

One evening in the fall of 1979 I had the pleasure of being at The Cookery, a restaurant/night club in New York, when pianist Eubie Blake came in to see his old friend, Rose "Chi-Chi" Murphy perform. Eubie, then 95, sat down and hypnotized the audience with his mastery of the piano, his youthful charisma and charm. Nowhere was this more evident than when Rose Murphy kissed him on the cheek and he said, "I'm not going to wash my face for twenty years!" How's that for growing young! And need anyone, after hearing those words, have any questions about what kind of attitude has kept Eubie Blake young and alive while most of his contemporaries have long since departed?

A man of 101 was interviewed on one of the TV network talk shows. The interview took place in his greenhouse, where he was cultivating orchids. The interviewer kept asking this gentleman the secret of his longevity, while never hearing the greatest secret of all: This 101-year-old man kept pointing with pride to his orchids; they were all he wanted to talk about. At one point, he showed off the plants in a cross-breeding experiment, and announced, "This project will take about six years to complete." Not being afraid to start something new, having something to look forward to, can keep us young as well as alive.

Having continuing projects can provide us with a number of what were described earlier as "emotionally invested deadlines"—events we are so looking forward to that we will hold back disease and death to make sure we are alive to meet those deadlines. One question we might ask ourselves is this: How many events coming up are we really looking forward to? This also has to do with the degree of excitement in our lives, and how much energy we have for living.

William Eaton, who lived to the age of 101 in Des Moines, Iowa, was interviewed around his 100th birthday and asked his secret. He answered that he had farmed until the age of 58, then went to work for the Maytag Company, where he remained until he retired 30 years later, at the age of 88. Eaton said he never even thought about retiring, and gave no thought to the fact that he might receive Social Security benefits someday. His advice:

> *Keep working as long as you can. Better to wear out than rust out!*

Monsignor Charles Finn of Boston didn't retire from the priesthood until he was 91. At 101, he still walked a half hour every day and was alert and active.

William H. Starratt of Woburn, Massachusetts, said at the age of 103:

> *I've always had something to do.*

Gay Farwell Steele, 101 years old, keeps busy at several hobbies, still participates in spelling bees, and advocates this as the secret of longevity:

> *There is no substitute for hard work. Practice makes perfect.*

Practice makes perfect. It does take a long time to learn how to live well. The more practice one has, the better one should get at it. It doesn't really make much sense to fail at something because you've had a lot of experience doing it. Yet this is what our old programming about death and aging tells us: The more you live, the less aliveness you will have. To accept this as so is to deny all hope for the fulfillment of the human species. Those long-lived villagers of the Caucasus, the Hunza, and Ecuador all keep actively engaged in their life's work. Some of them don't even have a word for retirement.

Dora Spangler of Wichita, Kansas, a sprightly 101-year-old, golfs, and belonged to a bowling team until an unusual obstacle got in her way:

> *When I was 80 I started to play golf; when I was 81 I started to bowl. I could still be bowling, but my daughter got what they call tennis elbow and had to quit.*

Ikutura Imamura, the 84-year-old principal of a Yokohama school for the blind, pitched his two hundredth victory against strong semipro baseball teams. His youthful energy derives from his love of baseball, having that emotionally invested deadline of the next game, the next scoring crisis.

RETIREMENT AS A DEATH SENTENCE

The advice Wally Schirra's father gave him always to have a new goal once you get near to achieving a previous one is very relevant to the issue of retirement. For those people who have spent years with retirement as their goal, and then have chosen no next step, retirement is a death sentence. The average retiree lives only six years after retiring! Psychiatrist Dr. Harold Bloomfield told me:

> *There's a lot of documented research to the effect that retirement is one of the worst things you can do for your health, and that we really need to have a sense of meaning and purpose to our lives. The kind of person who spends their life straining to make a million so they can retire is impairing their health, happiness, and well-being both in the straining and in the retiring. Straining to retire just doesn't work. What*

that person is doing, working at a strain pace, is developing
certain emotional and physical habits. It's not as if you
suddenly retire and learn to become a relaxed person. It
doesn't work that way. In fact, many of these people
experience a very serious depression because they're used to
that excitation, that tension as a way of being. Rather than
get relaxed when they retire, they go to boredom and to
restlessness, and are caught on the stress cycle.

Other than the strain of getting there, there are two other major
reasons retirement is a killer. One is simply that the worst
possible thing someone can do at 65 or 70 is dramatically curtail
mental and physical activity, and yet this is exactly how most
people see retirement! To take a mind and body used to a certain
level of activity for forty or fifty years and then drastically change
that pattern gives an unmeasurable shock to the entire organism.
The most difficult thing any of us have to deal with is change, and
one of the most effective ways of coping with change is to plunge
into activity with a passion. In the case of the major change of
retirement, we create the trauma and simultaneously remove one
of the best cures by no longer having work that can absorb us. The
second reason retirement is a killer is because of what it tells us
about the years spent working and what it delivers in unrealized
expectations. In order to strongly desire retirement, as most
people do, one has to be working in a job, profession, or business
that is less than joyful, challenging, absorbing, and satisfying.
Those people doing work that totally absorbs and excites them
would never think of retiring. The desire for retirement in and of
itself indicates that dissatisfaction exists. Added to this is the
constant programming that whatever dissatisfactions now exist, all
will be well once retirement is achieved. Perhaps no other entity
is so heavily burdened with unrealistic expectations. Most people
have only a vague idea of what they will do after retiring, and the
question which comes up time and again is, "Is this what I've
been working all my life for?" The payoff almost never justifies the
effort.

As longevity levels increase, there will be continued relaxation of the mandatory retirement rules, but in the meantime a lot more attention can be paid by those approaching this danger point, more attention to a specific plan of action, more attention to re-creating the sense of aliveness and excitement present in whatever work is being left behind. Best of all is to have work that can continue indefinitely. As Harold Bloomfield says:

> *It's important to find some kind of work in an ongoing fashion that we look forward to getting up in the morning and doing, rather than retiring, which can cut our lives short. It's also very important to develop habits of relaxation, habits of stress reduction all along, so that you can meet the challenges of activity as well as the challenges of a new and dynamic lifestyle should you decide to leave one line of work and get into other forms of activity.*

One of the great American myths is that working hard for forty years, nine to five, forty hours a week, will earn one the right to a secure and pleasurable retirement for the last few years of life. This is a poor bargain on any terms, and merely serves to reinforce the idea that there aren't too many years left once retirement is reached—an idea that all too quickly becomes reality for most. A large proportion of those retiring actually are dependent on others for their survival, and the average cash assets of those retiring at 65 are two hundred dollars (on South Miami Beach and other retirement "paradises" many people are subsisting on diets largely based on cat food). A very poor bargain indeed, and not the sort of supportive environment designed to promote a long and youthful life.

We have to get away from the notion that retirement is the cessation of activity. The dictionary definition of retirement is "to withdraw from active life." We can easily eliminate the word "active" and would then be painting an accurate picture of what retirement means for most people. If life is unpleasant, retirement is not going to solve that issue. It is no better a solution than suicide, and in fact can be considered an indirect form of suicide. How much better to look at a new approach as suggested by

Harold Bloomfield, to see that period of time not as retirement but as a time to switch to a new and dynamic lifestyle in which you leave one line of work and get into other forms of activity. And the more specific those plans, the more successful they will be. It's never too early to start reprogramming the old concepts about retirement, to have a clear vision of what that life will be like, and how it will work.

We can help to change perceptions about the danger of retirement by consistently being aware that withdrawing from active life is synonymous with death.

A SENSE OF PURPOSE

The power of this emotional attitude cannot be overestimated, and the idea that a sense of purpose will keep one youthful and alive is certainly backed up by substantial evidence. Those creative people who don't ever really retire all have a surging momentum in their lives, a vivid sense of purpose. The far-flung villagers of those longevity pockets have a lifestyle which generates a sense of purpose and belonging. The self-actualized super-healthy people studied by Dr. Abraham Maslow had very strong and clear senses of purpose.

Maslow described self-actualization as "the full use and exploitation of talent, capacities, potentialities, etc. Such people seem to be fulfilling themselves and doing the best that they are capable of doing." One fascinating thing most of these self-actualized people had in common: They were usually 60 years of age or older when they reached the peak of their success. And most of them kept going to the very end. They definitely did not fit the concept of predictable life stages, but were more inclined toward age-irrelevance. These people Maslow studied included Walt Whitman, Pablo Casals, George Washington Carver, Robert Benchley, Harriet Tubman, Sholom Aleichem, Goethe, Thomas More, John Muir, Albert Einstein, William James, Spinoza, Albert Schweitzer, Aldous Huxley, and Helen Keller.

All of the self-actualized people studied by Maslow had a sense of purpose involving the personal belief that they were performing an important and worthwhile task and were definitely contributing something of value to the world. This sense of purpose seems to have a life of its own in that the energy and momentum created by this inner belief keep those possessing it on a positive forward track. There were certainly setbacks and disappointments; those self-actualized people were not "perfect specimens" but rather people who were using the most of what they had. But where many people get confused and feel rudderless when something doesn't work out, this sense of purpose, this sense that what they are doing is worthwhile and important seems to quickly allow self-actualizers to get back on a productive path.

Dr. Harold Bloomfield feels that a sense of what he calls "eternal purpose" is the inner fountain of youth we all can tap. In my observations of those who survived longer than most and with a youthfulness beyond the norm this is certainly evident. It makes simple sense: Desire is a major factor in staying youthful and living long. As Harold Bloomfield told me:

If there's one thing that stands out from the people I see as a psychiatrist and who have difficulties from mid-life onward, it's the failure to really have a sense of purpose and meaning. And it's not just keeping active—it's keeping active with a sense of service, and a sense of contributing. I think that really reflects people's need to transcend, to become a part of a larger whole, to not just survive in a biological sense. And yet, when we contribute to that larger whole and feel a part of that larger purpose, we also notice that there's biological survival as well. Quality and quantity of life go together.

There's a lot of talk about the importance of the quality of life, but when we see it as so sharply connected to the quantity of life it becomes more clearly defined as something which requires more attention. And now that we know that this sense of purpose, this feeling that life is aimed in a worthwhile direction, has biochemical significance, we can see that improving the quality of our lives is an integral part of extending our lives.

When Abraham Maslow charted human needs he found that

among the basic needs we all have, in addition to food, shelter, and security from attack, is the need to belong, a sense of being part of that whole mentioned by Dr. Bloomfield. For some, this involves a spiritual belief. Most of the self-actualized people were reported as having some deep spiritual belief, not necessarily related to any of the organized religions. Throughout the world, a high proportion of centenarians are devout believers. They believe in something higher and larger than the human experience.

Dr. Joseph Freedman of the Gerontological Society comes up with the provocative view that a sense of purpose may be much more important than freedom from stress. He says:

> *Being totally involved with things, even when that means taking on stupendous burdens, can lengthen your life. A great deal of fanciful data claims that people who live very long lives are free from worry, tension, strain, and responsibility, living simple lives in relative isolation. Actually, our studies show that people in high stations involving heavy responsibilities tend to live longer than the general population. Executives live longer than unskilled workers. Presidents of the United States, even with all the pressures of their executive duties, have a longer average lifespan than vice-presidents and defeated candidates for presidential office. Through 2,000 years of documented history, only the eminent Greek philosophers, as a group, have outlived U.S. presidents.*

I do take some issue with Freedman's contention that stress and strain somehow increase longevity. What really seems to emerge from these statistics is the fact that people with a strong sense of purpose—the only type who would seek high public office in the first place—have an attitude that helps them deal with stress. And they may be just too busy to experience many of the negative effects of worry or strain. The physiological and psychological damage caused by stress often occurs when intense stimulation isn't followed by action, when action is somehow frustrated. People who are in positions of heavy responsibility are active participants in life rather than passive observers. And while they may be surrounded by stressful situations, they are often immune to negative effects of this just by virtue of the fact that they are deeply and intensely involved in so many activities simultaneously and successfully. These people often seem to have youthful energy to spare. It's as if the body provides the energy required when one has a compelling direction in life which would be enhanced by more youthful vitality. This overwhelming body of evidence and professional opinion leads us to one inescapable formula:

ACTIVE PURSUIT OF PURPOSE = LONG AND
YOUTHFUL LIFE

STRESS VERSUS THE LIFE-FORCE

In sophisticated, "civilized" societies, the biggest threat to life is stress. Stress-related disorders certainly kill more people than any other combination of diseases. Dr. Hans Selye, whose pioneering book *The Stress of Life*, originally published a quarter of a century ago, changed the minds of the entire medical profession about disease and its causes, still maintains at 74 a youthful vitality and an exhausting speaking and writing schedule. His basic premise that vulnerability to disease and physical deterioration was directly related to stress revolutionized our perceptions of how and why the human organism breaks down. Selye's work led to the creation of an entire new profession known as stress management. One of the things he pointed out was that there was productive and healthy stress as well as the destructive type. It all started in 1925, when the 18-year-old Prague medical student wondered why sick people seemed to be so much alike, whether this was a result of being sick or indicated some factor responsible for their sickness. At McGill University and the University of Montreal he found that rats developed certain similar ulcers and glandular disorders when exposed to stress. He called this reaction the General Adaptation Syndrome, and it is now considered the basic experience of all species under stress. The General Adaptation Syndrome comes in three stages. First, the organism is activated suddenly and dramatically. This is the famous "fight or flight response," whereupon a creature faced with danger finds the body coming to its rescue by enabling it to have the added burst of energy necessary to either fight for its life or run for its life. The second stage of the syndrome involves endurance, the actual stamina needed to fight or flee, to keep up one's energy until the danger or stress has subsided. The third stage is ushered in by exhaustion, the body's natural reaction to that overwhelming burst of energy.

Biofeedback researchers and psychophysiologists studying stress feel that what does human beings in nowadays is the fact that we don't often get a chance to fight or run for our lives, even though our bodies activate in the same ways as did those of our prehistoric ancestors when they were faced with the danger of immediate extinction at the hands of ferocious animals. When we don't get to use it, all that energy gets cut off and turns to frustration and hostility. It begins to eat away at our insides, and thus produces stress-related disorders. The modern business executive whose fight-or-flight mechanism gets activated by a stressful situation at work cannot release that energy by running or fighting for his or her life. Another factor in the negative aspects of stress is that we human beings retain the original stimulus in our memories, and relive it over and over again. So that the executive might stew for a week or two over an issue that took only a few minutes to occur. Someone once said that the difference between a human being and other animals is that a deer, for instance, when confronted by a lion, will run for its life. The next day, it will return to that same field, careful but not worrying about that lion or any other lion unless one actually shows up again. A man, just hearing there is the possibility of a lion in a certain field will fear that field for the rest of his life, even if he has never personally experienced being chased by a lion. This capacity to retain and repeat fears is called "modeling." It is the same ability that enables humans to be the most creative species, by creating thoughts and ideas in our heads that haven't actually happened—

the basis of most art, music, writing, etc. It is also this same modeling capacity that enables people to fear death when they obviously haven't died themselves, to experience the fear of old age when it is nowhere near.

A QUICK RECOVERY TIME

The real issue is not the elimination of stress, for that would involve a total withdrawal from day-to-day living, in itself a destructive emotional act. What seems to determine a person's success at overcoming the ill effects of stress is his ability to go quickly through the various stages of the stress cycle, to experience the stress but quickly recover. As Dr. Arthur Falek of the Georgia Mental Health Institute told me, this type of person is the one who may have the best chance to live a long and vital life:

> *They have the capability of dealing with stresses so that they develop a psychological homeostatic mechanism that will deal with that kind of response in a very rapid fashion—in other words, a quick recovery time from the stressful event. Not only at the intellectual level, but, equally important, at the emotional level as well. I think some of the training programs that are around now, training people to modify behavior by looking at how they deal with things and teaching them to respond to stressful events in a more pragmatic fashion, could certainly help an individual function better, and I'm sure, in the long term, could help him to survive longer.*

It does appear that people who have spent some time and effort working on personal emotional growth, in whatever form, remain unusually youthful. Many of the skills taught by stress management specialists, biofeedback trainers, and human potential developers are those which could very well help someone cope more effectively with stress and thus escape the debilitating organic breakdowns tension can cause. Dr. Falek says:

Some of these psychological skills, learning how to deal with problems in a positive manner and in rapid fashion, and then moving on to the next situation, enable the individual not to be so caught up in his own demise. So he deals with his own biology, utilizing it for his own greatest good. I have seen individuals utilizing these psychological skills to the point of, instead of reflecting upon their own problems all the time and having great difficulties in facing crisis kinds of events, they use their skills to overcome those kinds of events and deal with it, so that life is not a constant stress. I think those people are at a tremendous advantage for utilizing their biological opportunities for survival.

TEACHABLE SURVIVAL SKILLS

The fascinating factor here is that these survival skills are *teachable*. Dr. Richard Cutler talked in our first section about the fact that those species which require more learned behavior for survival are exactly the ones that last the longest. Part of learned behavior can consist of the kinds of awarenesses taught in workshops and groups aimed at expanding human potential and training people in understanding their own minds and bodies. Building self-esteem also helps, since the more self-esteem one has, as we've said, the more willing one will be to communicate feelings and not allow them to build up tension and hostility. Gerontologist Dr. Bernard Strehler described in the first section how he sees the quickness of the organism's response to attack as a determining factor in whether a person is going to stay young and live longer. It is not unreasonable to suppose, therefore, that someone who has developed skills to cope with stress would develop an immunological system that would likewise respond faster than normal. If, as we now know, certain emotional attitudes affect the biochemical productivity of the brain, and if some of those brain secretions enable the body to respond to attack, it does seem logical to assume that those skills which help someone to deal with stress and everyday problems effectively would be the same skills that could lead to the attitudes which would help release those secretions.

One of the most stressful situations in life is loss, whether of a loved one, a job, a home, money, whatever. Dr. George Pollock, Director of the Chicago Institute for Psychoanalysis, is now working, as he has been for the past twenty-five years, in an area he calls Mourning Liberation. He says:

I think if people are able to appreciate appropriately what is past, and have been able to put their house in order, they're able to go on to the present and the future. The reason I call it the Mourning Liberation Process is because I think once you go through this mourning process, you are liberated. I have found that those people who can successfully age are the ones who are able to appreciate current reality and make plans for the future, and who do not get bogged down in what they could have been, or what they should have been, or what was.

This is definitely the sort of skill being taught in many awareness and psychology groups and classes across the country, many of which focus on teaching people to be alive in the "here-and-now" rather than dwell on the past or worry about the future. This is congruent with the idea that being excited about life can extend life. Excitement certainly is most powerful as a current event, and almost never occurs while remembering the past. Letting go of losses is the only way to prepare for upcoming gains. *If you hold onto your last breath, you won't be able to take in the next one.* Dr. Pollock goes on to say:

Essentially, I am now doing psychoanalytic work with people in their 50s, 60s, 70s, and 80s. I feel that they can be helped to have a different kind of orientation to life. A group of investigators at the National Institute of Mental Health found that there are concomitant biological changes in the various stages of mourning. So that initially one gets alterations in the cortical steroids and things, and as one comes to terms with the stress and strain, then there is a biological reorientation and the individual then has the capacity to have energy, and we move on.

This is closely related to a concept in Gestalt therapy, explained to me by noted therapist Maria Fenton, Director of the Bucks County Institute. The concept involves a circular pattern wherein sensory stimulus starts the cycle.

This sensory stimulus leads to energy.

The energy leads to a desire or want.

The desire or want leads to movement or action.

The movement leads to a feeling of completion.

The completion leads to a feeling of openness.

The openness means we are ready for more sensory stimulus.

Often we don't complete the cycle. For example, building up the energy and then the desire without making any movement leads to the internal buildup of tension. What a therapist trains clients to do is flow through this cycle as rapidly and smoothly as possible.

If we see a member of the opposite sex whom we find very attractive, this visual sensory stimulus builds up energy, which in turn leads to a desire to get to know the person. If we stifle that desire, because we're shy, or it's inappropriate to take any action under the circumstances, then frustration builds to the point where we are less open to new incoming sensory information. Another example: If hearing about Psychological Immortality excites you, and the desire you build up is to live longer, and then you don't take any action in this regard, the flow gets shut down. Most chronic tension is due to this type of shutdown.

Dr. Pollock also talked about the type of results teaching these psychological skills can produce:

I saw a man who is 92 and he is doing fabulously well. He plays golf, goes on excursions, has been to Europe. Sure, his memory gets a little hazy, he's got some arthritis, but he's got an orientation that says he's going to do all that he possibly can, and it's a very healthy and positive orientation. I find in my own therapeutic work with patients, that this is what is possible using psychological methods. To help people remove some of the blocks that impede their ability to live more fully. I feel that there is ultimately some kind of biological mechanism or a series of mechanisms, but I find that doing psychological counseling and therapy is very, very helpful. I see people who I worked with twenty years ago who are still moving along and doing things very creatively. I think we have to introduce this into courses for doctors. To only have a death orientation is not very helpful, because it tells somebody to get ready to die. And I'm saying I think you have to help people get ready to live!

This death orientation Dr. Pollock talks about is all around us. When something is physically wrong with us, we often concentrate our energy on that, complaining and worrying about it, rather than paying attention to everything else in our lives that is working nicely. The human organism is composed of literally millions of separate functions, and when any one or two of them are not working properly, all the others still go about their business. Just as newscasts focus on bad news, so do most people. When people talk about older relatives it's usually their illnesses that are discussed rather than any good health they may be enjoying.

But basically life is like most other skills: The better you do it, the longer it can last. Being good at life means being excited and absorbed by it. I talked to an Olympic skating trainer who told me about one student he had who was the best natural skater he had ever worked with. But she hated to practice, wasn't particularly excited about performing, and only did it because her mother pushed her into it. Strangely enough, this young girl was an excellent performer, but her lack of enthusiasm began to affect her development and she stayed stuck at one level of performing skill. The trainer told me that she would never be good Olympic material, she just didn't care enough.

In one sense, life can be compared to an athletic competition, or individual sport, in which mental/emotional attitudes cannot be divorced from physical condition and natural talent. Living and enjoying one's life is the greatest skill of all, but one that won't earn you a Ph.D., and one that won't be taught in any school. Psychological Immortality is a personal reeducation process.

A LIFE-ENHANCING PATTERN

A life-enhancing pattern evolves when one appreciates life, thus creating a supportive environment for growing young and living long. Life is a gift and how well that gift is used determines how long it lasts. Negative expectations come when we aren't using our lives well, and at some deep subconscious level people know when this is so. If someone were the president of a company and doing a fantastic job and winning the love and respect of his or her employees, that person wouldn't expect to be replaced. So it is with life. Ordinarily, you don't die prematurely by living well and taking care of yourself. Those people who reach advanced ages displaying a youthful exuberance are those who have created a pattern of exuberance throughout their lives. Those lives are lived in balance and moderation. Moderation is a word that often appears in descriptions of the lifestyles of centenarians. When one is living a life filled with excitement and joy there is little or no desire to do anything to excess. Moderation in food, drink, exercise, etc., seems to slow down the aging process. This may also involve a decrease in total daily oxygen consumption, which as Dr. Richard Cutler described in our first section, would result in a longer lifespan.

REBIRTHING

Leonard Orr has popularized a spiritual breathing and relaxation process known as Rebirthing. This involves learning to connect one's inhale and exhale breaths in a circular breathing rhythm. The process, he feels, helps release certain stored-up traumas, including the birth trauma itself. The lessons involve relaxing and receiving instructions from a person trained in Rebirthing techniques. At the very least, Rebirthing is a method for more efficient use of oxygen, which in and of itself can extend life. The more efficient our breathing, the less oxygen we need. Rebirthing is an important part of Leonard Orr's basic approach to immortality. Several hundred physicians and health professionals have undergone this process and report positive results. A number are using the breathing process as a tool in their own healing work.

During the writing of this book, I experienced a rebirthing under the direction of Dr. Sonya Herman of La Jolla, California, a spiritual healer, college professor, and former psychotherapist who teaches many physicians and nurses the Rebirthing process. Under Dr. Herman's direction, I started slowly pulling my breathing up into my chest, making sure my exhalations were deep, and eventually moving into a rhythmic, deep, but gentle breathing pattern. After some fifteen to twenty minutes of this, I felt my arms go numb with paralysis, and the same thing happened to my legs. I kept breathing. Sonya Herman said the paralysis was the releasing of some negative emotional experiences and that I shouldn't worry about it. The breathing kept me relaxed. I soon felt a deep vibrating sensation from my chest to my abdomen. This was a very powerful feeling of energy and relaxation. The whole process took just over an hour, and as the paralysis left my arms and legs, I felt a sense of peace and deep contentment sweep over my body. My mind felt extremely alert and alive. The paralysis is part of something called the hyperventilation syndrome. Rebirthers say this is the memory of the fear of being born—the emotional memory of contractions being physically relived. Some people faint during the process, which Leonard Orr says is caused by the anesthesia stored in the body at birth or at some later time in the person's life. It is often true, in fact, that an odor of ether escapes from the rebirthed person's lips. This was true in my case, and medical research is now underway to determine whether the breathing rhythm involved in Rebirthing does in some way release anesthesia stored in the body, or whether the body is actually manufacturing some etherlike substance that is activated by the Rebirthing breaths.

The Rebirthing movement is dedicated to teaching everyone how to breathe properly. Dr. Sonya Herman says that this educational process is particularly important with all the negative beliefs being perpetuated about death and aging. As she told me:

> *When a whole group consciousness supports aging and death, you've got to be breathing really well and be very conscious to decide what you're going to do. If you hang out with people who are reinforcing their death consciousness, then you have a tendency to repeat that whether you consciously realize it or not.*

Part of the reinforcement for death and aging, according to Dr. Herman, comes from such ordinary actions as making a will, having life insurance or medical insurance. While one can argue that these are prudent and responsible things to do, it is true that they tend to focus emotional energy on the idea of death, aging, and sickness. Those things we feed with emotional energy, even if that energy is aimed at avoiding them, are exactly the things that get nourished and reinforced in our lives. If someone is placing bets, via insurance, and the only way to collect on those bets is to get sick or die, then some part of the consciousness becomes permanently focused on sickness and death. Of course, sometimes it's a case of choosing the lesser of two evils, since some of us would focus more worry and attention on sickness and death if we were not insured.

CANCER AS A SELF-DESTRUCT MECHANISM

If most people, in effect, kill themselves by focusing energy on death, then cancer is one of the most frequently used tools for this. It has been suggested by a number of specialists working with cancer patients that the disease is triggered by a certain state of mind, and there is documented evidence to support the hypothesis that a cancer patient's prognosis is largely dependent on that patient's attitude—the attitude toward cancer itself and the attitude toward life in general. In the second century A.D., Claudius Galen, a Greek physician and medical writer, noticed that depressed women were more susceptible to cancer than were contented women. Galen, perhaps the first holistic doctor and the father of what is now called behavioral medicine, was apparently the first person to see the connection between the mind and the body, and that certain types of behavior are related to health while certain other types of behavior are related to disease.

One of the possibilities some physicians and therapists are now exploring is that cancer may be a way the body has of destroying itself when the mind no longer has a strong commitment to life, or when a certain degree of personal satisfaction is missing.

Dr. Gary Schwartz of Yale, one of the major forces in the development of behavioral medicine, says the current research is aimed not only at discovering the cause of disease, but going a step further and finding ways to modify people's behavior so as to make them less receptive to disease and better equipped to fight it.

THE SIMONTONS AND VISUALIZATION

Whatever progress is made in this field, some of the credit has to go to the team of Dr. O. Carl Simonton and his wife, Stephanie Matthews-Simonton, of the Cancer Counseling and Research Center in Fort Worth, Texas. By using a behavioral approach in addition to conventional treatment, they have had remarkable results. Twice as many of their cancer patients show dramatic recovery results as compared with the national average. Their patients also seem to survive twice as long as average with certain types of cancer. Terry Cole-Whittaker's telling her body that its cells are eternally 28 and always replacing themselves in a youthful manner may be a very effective methodology in light of what the Simontons have been doing with cancer patients. One of their most effective and dramatic techniques is to teach the patient to put himself in a relaxed, meditative state and then imagine his body's own healing system doing battle successfully with the cancer cells. The immunological system does seem to respond to this type of suggestion. Again we go back to the work of Norman Cousins in exploring the brain's secretions, and see that a number of healing processes can be activated in the body through positive mobilization of the mind.

Psychologist Barton Knapp has been focusing a lot of his clinical work on cancer patients. He deplores the fact that while we've known of the connection between attitude and cancer for nearly two thousand years, since Galen, there is still a great deal of resistance to incorporating this knowledge into the treatment of the disease. He describes his own work:

One of the things I do within the realm of normal psychotherapy is helping people change their belief systems about themselves and the nature of their relationships with the world, looking at the nature of the cancer, exploring what options are open to them, and examining specific stress areas in their lives. I want to look at secondary gains involving the cancer: What does the illness do for them? I just had a patient in and when I asked him what he was getting out of having cancer, he said: "For the first time, I can go the office and I don't have to work as hard because people are concerned about my health, whereas before it was work, work, work." I find this sort of thing very quickly among cancer patients. They can identify what needs are being met by the illness. One of the things I help them with is to find other ways they can get those same needs met. What is it within themselves that has necessitated their moving in the direction of being ill to meet those needs? It's a very expensive price to pay, to get that sick in order to get taken care of, or in order to take it easy, to rest, relax.

Another factor in the onset of cancer seems to be resignation, a feeling that peak achievements have already been experienced and that there's nothing terribly exciting to live for. When considering famous people who have died of cancer, one almost always finds that they had already passed their periods of highest creative production—or at least felt that they had. Hardly anyone in show business has ever died *during* their greatest performance. Even film comedian Peter Sellers, apparently haunted by the fear of death for many years, seems to have waited to die until the reviews were in for *Being There,* his greatest critical success. Director Gower Champion succumbed at 61 on the day his musical *42nd Street* opened on Broadway, after attending to many of the problems that had plagued the show out of town. No one seems to die in the midst of a comeback, but quite a few celebrities drop off following the failure of such an attempt. Again, while life surges on, creating its own momentum, it's as if the organism doesn't have the time to die. It does take a tremendous focusing of energy on sickness and death to kill off a human being, and if instead that person is focusing powerful amounts of energy on some activity that absorbs and excites them, then death just has to wait.

Dr. Knapp was trained by the Simontons in their methods and has also developed his own approach. One fascinating ability he's acquired is often to be able to predict the course of cancer by looking at the patient's emotional state. His experience reflects the opinion of many researchers that the docile, self-sacrificing person can often become a cancer victim. Again, this attitude of resignation comes up:

One patient was referred to me by a physician. She was in a hospital, a fairly young woman. She was lying in bed, and her husband asked her, "Would you like the bed raised or would you like it left the way it is?" She answered, "Oh, it doesn't make any difference." On the basis of that and some other talking we did, I recommended to her that she begin to identify specifically what she wanted. A short time later, I went to her funeral. She was eulogized as a self-sacrificing woman who always took care of everybody else and never asked a thing for herself. I was so uncomfortable with this that I wanted to stand up and scream!

It's interesting that those professionals trained to look at human emotions and behavior can easily see the connections between attitude and disease. This certainly supports the need to train physicians in this area, so that we may have a greater understanding of the potent effect the mind has on the body. One question it would be interesting to ask patients is this: "Just before your heart attack, or just before you discovered you had cancer, was your life satisfying enough so that you looked forward to getting up in the morning?"

More and more we see that it is the person with the victim mentality who gets attacked, the person who builds up negative expectations or has a real lack of positive ones. As Dr. Knapp says:

What does people in is the belief system that says, "I'm not worth anything." Or: "I'm worthwhile only if . . . only if I do this, only if I do that." I think this kind of belief contributes to a psychological inability to cope with stress and make the kinds of changes necessary.

While it is true that people with naturally healthy attitudes toward life and with robust expectations will have the best all-around chance for youthful survival, negative belief systems can be changed. After all, that is the purpose of this book. Certain strategies can help us overcome the self-destructive tendencies we all have. Since attitudes do have biochemical significance, we now have a much stronger incentive to replace unhealthy ones with life-enhancing ones. Bart Knapp relates one of his successful cases:

One patient I've been seeing for over a year now had had cancer twice. This patient has been coming to me not because he had cancer but because he wanted to be sure that he didn't get it again. He's been willing to work on his belief system and recently said to me, "You know, Bart, I won't get cancer again." And I believe him. He's made changes in the way he's seeing himself. He's taking care of himself. He's self-reliant now, whereas he wasn't in the past.

Taking care of oneself—another factor reported by individuals who've lived long and active lives. Most who have lived at least a hundred years report that this is something they've done most of their lives. The conclusion is a simple and direct one: The desire to take care of yourself leads to the action which leads to prevention of disease, which leads to the prolonging of life beyond the accepted norm.

A lot of the research now devoted to cancer may eventually be very important in prolonging life. Much of the DNA and hormonal knowledge is coming to light at cancer research centers. When we learn about the running amok of cancer cells, we also learn something about healthy cells. And the subjective experience of both patients and doctors can be equally valuable, especially in relation to behavior and attitude. As more doctors are willing to look at this aspect of the disease, more knowledge will become available and we'll have a more definitive model of what it takes to avoid cancer or successfully fight it. Dr. Ron Parks of the Comprehensive Health Program Center told me of one patient he had who was doing very nicely in recovering from cancer. She then got involved in a nasty divorce; her cancer "took her over" and she very rapidly deteriorated and died. As we discover that a calm emotional environment is just as important as other forms of treatment, more attention will be paid to educating patients and their doctors in this area.

The visualization techniques used by the Simontons to combat cancer can easily be adapted to focus on longevity and staying youthfully vigorous. We'll explore some of this in Part Three.

LEARNING AS A REJUVENATING PROCESS

If disease is the negative side of the human coin, then growing and learning are the positive sides. When we stop learning, we die—it's as simple as that. Abraham Maslow considered growth one of the higher needs humans develop after survival needs are met. Some people never grow, others never stop growing in terms of learning new things, expanding their own awareness of themselves and the world around them. Again, that comment by Dr. Richard Cutler has relevance: that there is a correlation between the need of a species for learned behavior and that species' longevity. Those species which require more learned behavior for their survival do tend to live longer. This could be turned around to say that those species *capable* of higher levels of learned behavior have the longest lifespans. And to go a step further: Those individuals who utilize most effectively that capacity for increased learned behavior can also utilize more effectively their built-in biological opportunities.

Those people who live long and stay vital are those who keep learning all their lives. Perhaps the deadliest thing we do is perpetuate the myth that learning ends at an early age with the end of formal education. If we can keep learning new things, new skills, new behavior during our later years, we might be stretching the evolutionary process as well as our individual lives, moving toward expanding human consciousness.

One of the major reasons for continued learning is that nothing so efficiently engages and activates the mind. Dr. Bernard Strehler of U.S.C. says:

> *Something that's challenging maintains mental vigor. People who go into mental inactivity tend to deteriorate mentally much more rapidly than people who keep an interest in a variety of things. Mental activity is very important in preserving memory, which is essential to efficient functioning. I think when you use your brain for one thing, you're also rehearsing a lot of other memories simultaneously. It's known*

that people who go into a deep depression, and stay there for a long time, deteriorate rather rapidly. By withdrawing from the world of thought and activity, they are not rehearsing things that are ordinarily rehearsed when one uses one's brain. When I am talking to you, I am actually reinforcing the stability of memories that I am not even eliciting at that time, because every time one searches through memory for a particular set of items that are related to, say, these questions you are now asking me, one searches through a great deal of stuff and that's rehearsal. You then reject the stuff that's not relevant, but in the process of looking for it, you're reinforcing other memories. This comes out of a theory I'm working on of how memory is stored in coded form on an anatomical/ biochemical basis. Every time you activate the brain for anything, you exercise all those things that are even remotely related to what you're working on.

This theory seems particularly appropriate when applied to the subject of continued learning. To start with, whenever you learn something new, that scanning of your memory has to reinforce some things you learned in the past, so that you are not only absorbing new material but keeping alive already learned knowledge. The loss of memory in advancing years is often not organic at all, but merely the failing of the memory from disuse. Learning, whatever form it takes, will stimulate the mind and thereby affect the body.

TEACHING OTHERS

People growing older can counteract negative social changes that have occurred, such as older people no longer being models and mentors to younger people. If those in their 70s, 80s, and 90s are willing to share their wisdom with much younger people, the stereotypes about aging will start to fade. One of the major factors in longevity and keeping youthful is a sense of service to others and of making a worthwhile contribution. What we've lost sight of in our society is the wisdom and practical knowledge that older people can offer. If they are given the opportunity to offer it, and decide to make that sort of contribution, they won't stay "older" people, but will become, as they have been throughout history in numerous cultures, "the wise ones."

In the conversation I had with behavioral geneticist Dr. Arthur Falek, I noticed—though we talked about a variety of subjects from DNA to the coping mechanism—that he seemed most animated and alive when telling the following story:

I remember interviewing a lady in her 80s on a Sunday morning in upstate New York. She was a quite remarkable woman and I interviewed her in the field while she was teaching her great-granddaughter how to ride a horse. To me, this was the most remarkable event one could possibly consider. There she was at the age of 80-plus, teaching this girl how to get on and off the horse, how to get the horse and the human body into unison with one another to ride. Quite an unusual experience.

Sadly, it is all too unusual to see this sort of natural connection, this very powerful handing down of knowledge from one generation to another. And no doubt that woman was much younger than others her age, because she had a purpose, a function. As Dr. Peter Steincrohn puts it, "The fact that it's an interest that absorbs you, that in itself lengthens life." During a visit to the Steincrohn home in Coral Gables, Florida, I saw another example of this phenomenon, and the kind of taking advantage of biological and psychological opportunities that keeps both Peter Steincrohn and his wife Patti youthfully involved in life. Patti Chapin Steincrohn, a former 1930s radio musical star, was teaching her granddaughter Jenny some piano techniques and they were singing together. At the same time, Dr. Steincrohn was showing his grandson, Joel, some boxing moves as they playfully sparred.

Of course, these examples involve something just as life-enhancing as the mere fact of keeping active by teaching others—the sharing of love.

The energy shared between the teacher and the student, whether in a classroom or in a home, is vital and enduring. We all remember an older teacher who had something valuable to share with us in our youth. By not making use of this priceless resource we cheat the young by eliminating a powerful source of knowledge and wisdom, and we punish the old by relegating finely tuned minds to an inactive limbo. One of the happy side effects of increasing longevity will be the fact that great minds will be able to continue their contributions that much longer, but only if someone is willing to listen, and it has to start now with ever-increasing dialogues between the old and young. This will open up new opportunities for keeping older people actively involved in the future, actively absorbed in the present.

LOVE AS THE ANSWER

When I talked with Dr. Bernard Strehler, famed biologist and gerontologist at U.S.C., we discussed the potent effect of thoughts and feelings on the body, and he suggested that perhaps none was more potent than love.

> *What is it that happens to a man, for instance, what generates that wonderful aura that goes with falling in love at a particular time? Obviously, there is some kind of chemical transformation: It's not just stimulation of the secretion of sex hormones, it's a whole transformation of one's attitude toward life. A deep romantic involvement with somebody is certainly one of the more uplifting and invigorating experiences one can have. One forgets about all unpleasantries and goes on.*

It may sound simple and silly to suggest that one way to keep youthful and live long is to fall in love, but that certainly seems to happen to people. There are many instances of dramatic changes in residents of a nursing home when romance brings them together. They not only look and feel younger, but quite often their energy positively affects other residents. There is little or no research on the feeling of love as an energy force, and none as yet on what brain secretions love might release and what effect these might have on health and longevity. We all know that love feels good, but little has been done to find out why.

One of the pioneering efforts to explore the phenomenon of love and its effect on our physical/emotional states was a paper entitled "The Experience of Love," originally delivered at the California State Psychological Convention in January of 1975 by clinical psychologist Dr. Marjorie Toomim and her scientist husband, Hershel Toomim. Here are some excerpts from that paper:

> *Love is a feeling that arises from within us. It grows only when nourished by the same qualities that are essential to participation in the flow of life. To love, as to live, requires an exchange of energy—a flow. I am aware that I feel good when I am with you. I feel life-energies flow through me when I talk to you and touch you.*
>
> *We all feel energized and alive in a relationship where good feelings, trust, and acceptance are experienced and communicated in a way which is meaningful and acceptable. We feel energized and alive when ideas and emotions arise easily within us and are freely given, received, and returned, enriched by the other's experience and expression. We feel energized and alive in a relationship in which our needs may be expressed and respected, and where enough care exists that needs are gratified.*

In line with this, it is interesting to note that many of the longest-lived peoples of the world are those still actively engaged in love relationships and sexual activity in their 70s, 80s, and 90s. If there is a life-force, some biochemical or bioelectrical energy pattern that has been measured but not yet clearly defined, then it certainly is related to the emotions, and none more strongly can affect our biochemistry than the force of love. "Dying of a broken heart" may not be as farfetched as it sounds, for suddenly being deprived of loving feelings can indeed cause severe physiological changes. In terms of psychological skills, perhaps those most useful would be the ones that teach people to focus their loving energy inward, creating love within themselves, a love that isn't dependent on being in a romantic involvement. Since love is a feeling, it can be created by the mind, with or without a suitable romantic partner. One can love one's friends or relatives or activities. That same sense of energized excitement can happen in any number of circumstances.

Gestalt therapist Vicki Johnson told me:

> *When you feel you're in love, you feel really young. I know a 64-year-old woman who's now in love after being widowed some years ago, and she feels like an adolescent. The state of being "in love" is that of youthfulness. As I grow, loving myself and loving others and feeling love from other people, I feel younger. When I was an adolescent, feeling "in love" was always connected with a member of the opposite sex, as it still is for most people. But love can happen in many different ways between many different people, and it all has the power of making us feel young.*

The strange and ironic truth is that many people are too busy feeling sick and old to allow love into their lives, or too busy looking for other obscure, even unsafe "cures," to try out this simple and effective solution. It is almost impossible to be resigned to death and aging when one is feeling love. An important factor in the longevity found so often in the people of the Caucasus is the warm and loving feelings between neighbors, the nourishing companionship of friends gathered around for the evening meal. And while it may seem simplistic to suggest love as a prescription for longevity, the continued work in behavioral medicine, as well as the research into those secretions produced by the brain, is likely to turn up increasing evidence of the profound biological impact of the feelings we associate with love.

VOLUNTARY LONGEVITY

Since it goes without saying that each individual has the most direct control over his or her own psychological state, and we now know how important this is to our physical well-being, what we are seeing is the validation of a prediction made sixty years ago by George Bernard Shaw. Shaw first published his play, *Back to Methuselah*, in 1921 at the age of 63. In his preface, a wonderful philosophical treatise, there was a segment entitled "Voluntary Longevity," in which Shaw stated:

> *Among matters apparently changeable at will is the duration of individual life. Even our oldest men do not live long enough: They are, for all the purposes of high civilization, mere children when they die. Conceivably, however, the same power that has taken us thus far can take us farther. If Man now fixes the term of his life at three score and ten years he can fix it at three hundred or three thousand, or even until a sooner-or-later inevitable accident makes an end.*

With this attitude, it is not surprising that Shaw himself lived a long and robust life, dying in 1950 at the age of 94. Voluntary longevity really means that once we accept the possibilities of a longer life, we can then *choose* to extend our own life. Cary Grant, at 77 still youthful and handsome, says he doesn't have any longevity secret but doesn't do the things he's observed as making other people grow older sooner. He doesn't smoke, drinks in moderation, gets plenty of rest, and eats a balanced diet. He also stays relaxed and keeps active, but doesn't worry about keeping in shape. Perhaps most important of all, in terms of Psychological Immortality and life-enhancing attitudes, is the fact that Grant enjoys his life (have you ever seen him without a big smile on his face?) and says he wouldn't mind living two hundred years. His mother lived to 95 and Cary Grant sees no reason he shouldn't do far better. So here is a living example of the kind of voluntary longevity Shaw talked about and lived.

Holistic physician and author Dr. Irving Oyle also believes it's a matter of choice:

I plan to live to 150 myself. The brain runs the body. If we correctly program the brain, the body will respond. If you can control your thoughts and look at life as a happy experience, your body will be healthier. But if you view the world and life as a series of ongoing catastrophes, calamities, and crises, those beliefs put your body in a fight-or-flight state, in which your body is constantly geared to defend itself against hostilities. If you presume that you live in a hostile universe, the reaction to that presumption takes its toll on your body.

We are not isolated from the rest of the world, and each individual's view of that world is a reflection of his view of himself. If we are having a good time, we view the world as a place of great beauty, love, and opportunity. If we are miserable, then the world is a dark and gloomy place filled with crime, deprivation, and hopelessness. One of my favorite Sufi stories concerns the great old wise man who lived in a faraway land. One day a new arrival made his way to this wise man and said to him, "Oh great and wise teacher, they tell me you know all there is to know. I am just coming from across the ocean and am looking for a new home, can you tell me what this land of yours is like? Will I enjoy it here?" The wise man looked at the traveler and replied, "What was the place you just left like? Did you enjoy that?" The visitor replied, "Oh no, it was a difficult place, filled with unfriendly people, filthy streets, lots of turmoil. I definitely did not have a good time there or I wouldn't be here." The wise man looked at him and said, "That is exactly what this land of mine is like, so perhaps you had better move on." The next day, by the kind of coincidence which happens so regularly in a Sufi tale, another traveler arrived from the very same country as the first stranger. He also made his way to the wise old man and asked, "Pray tell me, kind and wise sir, is this a country I might be happy living in?" The wise man answered with, "What was it like in the country you just left?" The stranger replied, "It was wonderful! Filled with love and joy and dancing in the streets and good friends and good times." The wise man then answered, "Then you will find this land just the same."

Our perception of the world is carried within us and colors our perception of the value of life. The more we do value that life, the easier it becomes to maintain it. Taking advantage of one's psychological opportunities also means creating a personal environment which will give one a pleasant and nourishing view of the world. Those people who choose to live in conflict, turmoil, and ongoing crisis are committing long-term suicide. It's been said that suicide is the sincerest form of self-criticism, and living in a nonsupportive personal environment is one of the most unpleasant and most self-loathing ways to go.

The future has never more surely been in our hands.

LIFESPANS ARE CHANGING

One of the important awarenesses we must all hold onto is that we do live in a world in which life-extension seems to be happening quite naturally, though more slowly than it has to. Paying attention to those exceptional people who remain young indefinitely is one way to reinforce our own determination.

In the late seventeenth century, Edmund Halley (discoverer of Halley's Comet) first charted lifespans. He figured out that human beings lived to an average age of 34. This remained fairly static until the late eighteenth century, when expansion due to medical advances, increased awareness of the importance of sanitation, and a reduction of infant mortality boosted the average lifespan statistics. While a lot of the credit for a longer lifespan was due to decreased infant mortality (thus not actually reflecting the fact that people lived longer, but that there were more of them to reach maturity and old age), the lifespan statistics did become common knowledge, thus perpetuating the idea that a specific age was what people could expect to attain. The lifespan finally reached 47 in 1900. This was the average age a person might expect to live to. By 1930, the lifespan increased to 59 years, and it is now in the low 70s, moving toward the mid-70s.

This isn't to say that people haven't lived beyond those "average" figures all along. And indeed, certain groups seem to have their own, more attractive, statistics. U.S. senators, for example, elected between 1789 and 1860, when the average lifespan was under 40, lived an average of 68½ years. Of course, one of the factors in this is the psychological opportunities provided by the seniority system, which, though watered down a bit in recent years, still provides status and increased responsibility with increasing age. Supreme Court justices also do well in the aging sweepstakes. Oliver Wendell Holmes was born in 1841, when he might reasonably have expected to live to 40, but he survived to make valuable contributions until the age of 94. The artists and musicians who seem to survive longer also illustrate the simple point: We almost always exceed our life expectancy by being actively and positively engaged in living.

While scientists tell us that most people between the ages of 30 and 45 today can look forward to lifespans well beyond one hundred years, individuals in that age group often consider their lifespan to be the current statistical average, which is some thirty to forty years short of the real possibilities. This arbitrary limit on life is ridiculous, inaccurate, and potentially fatal. The Lifespan Myth has got to be discarded by any individual who wants to live long and grow young.

One unfortunate side effect of our tremendous progress in communications technology is the fact that a lot more people have been provided with the damaging information that they are expected to reach a certain age and then drop dead. It may very well be that the long-lived residents of those pockets of longevity in isolated villages survived at least partially because they have been shut off from more sophisticated civilizations and from the media with its stereotyped images of aging and death. What we don't know is the damage that may already have been done by revealing to them exactly how unusual they are, and exposing them to the amazed reactions of the outside world.

Along with the psychologically sound attitudes necessary for life-extension, and the vision to seek it, we need to accept the responsibility for passing on the knowledge that the Lifespan Myth is no longer valid. Beliefs *can* be changed with positive communication, reinforcement, and healthy examples. We're fortunate in that each passing year provides us with healthier examples of people defying the myth. There's a fable about a peasant who makes his old father eat out of a small wooden trough at mealtimes, apart from the rest of the family. One day he finds his son fitting little boards together. "It's for you when you are old," the child tells his father. Immediately, the grandfather is given back his place at the family table.

We have to recognize not only the amazing possibilities for the future, but also that we have already made fantastic strides in expanding the possibilities of the present. The visionary Ray Bradbury certainly realizes this:

When I was born in 1920, 50 percent of everyone died by the age of 12. Every family, just about, had to face the fact that two out of four of their children would be dead in a few years. It was true in my family. My little brother died before I was born, my sister died when I was 7. We accepted that. Plays were even written about it. A couple of years ago, George Cukor, the director, wanted me to write The Bluebird *for the screen. I said, "No, I can't, because science fiction has become science fact." The science fictional dreamers in medicine have done away with death in our society and children no longer die. Occasionally, yes, and it's a terrible thing—a single death is terrible. The play,* The Bluebird, *is all about the fact of disease and death in 1905. When you wanted to visit your family in 1905 on a Sunday, where did you go? You went to the graveyard, because most of them were there. I have four daughters. They have grown up, the oldest is 30 now. They have yet to go to their first funeral! That's incredible! The only way that their friends can die in our society is through the automobile, but not with disease anymore. It's amazing, this science fictional thing that has occurred to us. And we don't notice it. You don't notice that you're not dead. You're so busy living, you don't notice it and you don't celebrate it.*

As Ray Bradbury says, we *don't* notice that we're not dead. We don't notice "this science fictional thing." What is science fiction, after all, but a leap of the imagination to anticipate the coming fact? All scientists are engaging in science fiction until the moment their efforts and experiments bear fruit. It's often deemed some miraculous feat that some of our great science fiction writers of the 1920s and 1930s, along with Jules Verne in the nineteenth century, actually predicted science fact. What does this mean? Is it some kind of magic? No, it's merely that once we expand our horizons, once we lift the lid off our narrow expectations, we come up with all sorts of wonderful and *possible* ideas. Is living to 150 any less possible than space travel was when Jules Verne described it? It is time to start enjoying the science fictional possibilities.

Paying attention to the very fact of our aliveness can reinforce just the attitudes we need to keep up the momentum. Life itself is a "science fictional thing." And the truth is that you are already practicing Psychological Immortality. Right now you are putting more energy into life consciousness than into death consciousness. Otherwise, you'd be dead. We can now start fortifying and nourishing this life-force. It is, quite literally, the only thing worth living for!

PART

THREE

PSYCHOLOGICAL IMMORTALITY STRATEGIES

THE ONLY way to change negative belief systems and destructive conditioning is by experimenting with new beliefs and new behaviors. William James said the first step in changing any behavior is to start immediately. Reading this book involves action, and is certainly a first step. But as astronaut Wally Schirra's father told him, it's important to have your next step in mind as you approach any goal. So, as you finish this book, it's vital that you have an idea of what comes next for you in terms of working toward extending your own life and youthfulness. The purpose of this section of the book is to provide some tools with which to activate your will to live. A strategy is the means by which we can put an idea into action. Thinking about living long is not enough. You can think positive from now until 2050 and not actually experience any changes, not to mention the fact that you'd probably not last that long just passively thinking about change. The mind is not an entity separate and apart from the rest of the organism. It is directly and indirectly linked to every life process. In order to enlist its aid in the fight against aging and death, certain actions have to be taken.

207

THREE STEPS FOR SUCCESS

In order to achieve success in any endeavor, three basic steps are required:

1. A CLEAR VISION OF WHAT YOU WANT.

This involves really seeing how you want your life to turn out, with specific ideas of how you want to enjoy it and what you would do with the extra time you received through increased longevity. The more clearly your mind can see how you want something to be, the easier it will be for the subconscious to activate and accelerate the physical and mental/emotional processes that can support your vision.

2. THE BELIEF THAT YOU CAN GET WHAT YOU WANT.

The first two sections of this book were devoted to reinforcing the belief that it is indeed possible to prolong your youth and your life. The more things you do to nourish such a positive belief, the more automatic the process will become, so that you can develop a belief system which will act in tandem with the robust expectations you have. Nothing is quite so futile as a goal or direction which is not supported by a person's basic belief system.

3. PRACTICAL SKILLS TO PUT YOUR BELIEF INTO ACTION.

Practical skills are those you can start using immediately. The various strategies and experiments in this section are designed to give you some new perspectives and new tools for changing old habits, patterns, beliefs, and actions concerning aging and death, to help you move toward the idea of growing youthful and living indefinitely.

The success of this part of the book depends largely on you. If you choose to just read through it, then little will happen. If you follow William James's admonition to start immediately, and actually begin trying on some of the strategies for size, then they will surely begin to affect your belief system. What that actually will do to your internal processes and your brain secretions no one really knows yet, but we do know that positive emotional experiences and habits create positive biochemical experiences. Dr. Bernard Strehler says:

> *Since the activity of the brain has a large influence on the endocrine system, the muscular system, and on the cardiovascular system, I think that a healthy attitude toward aging will have a healthy effect, but particularly activity, something creative, something that's challenging.*

This comment from a leading molecular biologist underscores the increasing awareness of scientists that the final stages of the great longevity breakthrough will occur inside the human mind. How much you allow the following strategies to activate you, challenge you, and help you create a new perspective on your own lifespan will determine how effective they are.

THE PRIMARY RELAXATION EXPERIENCE

This is not a new exercise created for this book, but a time-tested approach to producing what one Soviet gerontologist calls "psychic quiet."

Having led literally thousands of people through this particular relaxation technique since its introduction in 1971 at the Biofeedback Institute, I have found it to be the single most effective and easily applied relaxation tool possible. It originally was suggested by Drs. Tom Budzynski and Johann Stoyva of the University of Colorado Medical Center, among the pioneering biofeedback researchers and clinicians. They used it, as I did, in conjunction with various biofeedback instruments, including electromyographic units which measure muscle firings. It's proven equally effective minus the biofeedback units. The Primary Relaxation Experience involves a combining of two much older techniques: Dr. Edmund Jacobson's Progressive Relaxation (described earlier), which focuses on more efficient awareness and utilization of the muscles, and Autogenic training, developed some sixty years ago by German psychiatrist and neurologist Dr. Johannes Schultz, and consisting of a series of auto-suggestions. This is not to imply that the Primary Relaxation Experience will do more than provide a sample of these two different and long-term techniques, but in this brief combined version they do provide a valuable tool against stress, and create the sort of relaxed but alert state that can be ideal for positive programming.

This is an expansion of the same exercise I used in training executives for a number of major corporations in the early 1970s, when there was an increased corporate awareness of the dangers of stress. The Primary Relaxation Experience was easily learned by executives, took very little time to use, and was a tool which could be brought into play even during stressful situations.

I suggest that you lie down in as comfortable a position as possible for this experience, with your eyes closed. You may want to either record the entire exercise on tape, or have someone read it to you. Perhaps the most valuable feature of this particular technique is that it's cumulative, meaning that each time you experience it you become more adept at relaxing your mind and your body. Eventually, you'll be able to just suggest the word "relax" to yourself and achieve the same state without going through the exercise.

PART ONE.
   ALLOW YOUR BODY TO SETTLE DOWN INTO THE MOST COMFORTABLE POSITION POSSIBLE.
   CHECK YOUR BREATHING WITHOUT FORCING IT. BE AWARE OF YOUR OWN BREATHING RHYTHM WITHOUT TRYING TO CHANGE IT. BE AWARE OF HOW YOUR BODY FEELS RIGHT NOW. SILENTLY FINISH THE FOLLOWING SENTENCE TO YOURSELF: "RIGHT NOW, MY BODY FEELS_____."
   YOU'RE GOING TO PROGRESSIVELY TIGHTEN AND THEN RELAX MOST OF THE MUSCLES IN YOUR BODY.

   START WITH YOUR FEET AND YOUR TOES. TIGHTEN

THEM UP AS MUCH AS POSSIBLE. TIGHTEN THEM STILL MORE. AND EVEN TIGHTER. FEEL THEM VIBRATE WITH TENSION. NOW, LET GO. LET ALL THE TENSION FLOW OUT OF YOUR FEET.

NEXT, YOUR LOWER LEGS AND CALVES.

TIGHT. TIGHTER. TIGHTER. AND LET GO. WITH THE LETTING GO, IMAGINE A WARM TIDE OF RELAXATION WASHING OVER THOSE MUSCLES.

YOUR UPPER LEGS AND THIGHS NOW.

TIGHT. TIGHTER. AND EVEN TIGHTER. LET GO.

YOUR GENITALS.

TIGHT. TIGHTER. TIGHTER. LET GO OF ALL THAT TENSION.

KEEP BREATHING.

YOUR BUTTOCKS.

TIGHT. TIGHTER. TIGHTER. LET GO AND RELAX.

YOUR ABDOMEN.

TIGHT. TIGHTER. TIGHTER. FEEL THE TENSION, AND LET GO.

YOUR CHEST.

TIGHT. TIGHTER. TIGHTER. HOLD . . . AND LET GO.

YOUR SHOULDERS.

TIGHT. TIGHTER. TIGHTER. FEEL THE TENSION, AND LET GO.

YOUR UPPER ARMS.

TIGHT. TIGHTER. TIGHTER. NOW LET GO. RELAX. BREATHE.

YOUR LOWER ARMS.

TIGHT. TIGHTER. STILL TIGHTER. EXHALE AND LET GO.

JUST YOUR HANDS AND FINGERS.

TIGHTEN THEM UP. TIGHTER. TIGHTER. AND LET GO.

YOUR ENTIRE ARM. TIGHTEN BOTH ARMS FROM FIN-GERTIPS TO SHOULDERS.

TIGHTER. TIGHTER. AND LET GO AND RELAX.

YOUR NECK.

TIGHTEN IT. TIGHTER. TIGHTER. NOW LET GO.

YOUR FACE.

SCRUNCH IT UP TIGHT. STILL TIGHTER. AND TIGHTER. LET GO.

YOUR ENTIRE BODY FROM HEAD TO TOE.

TIGHTEN IT ALL UP. TIGHTER. TIGHTER AND FEEL IT VIBRATE WITH TENSION.

NOW LET IT ALL GO. FEEL YOUR ENTIRE BODY RELAX.

TAKE A DEEP BREATH AND LET IT OUT. STRETCH ANY PART OF YOUR BODY THAT WANTS TO STRETCH. SILENTLY FINISH THE FOLLOWING SENTENCE TO YOURSELF: "RIGHT NOW, MY BODY FEELS _____."

KEEP BREATHING FOR A MINUTE OR SO, JUST LYING QUIETLY, AND PREPARING FOR PART TWO.

PART TWO.

THIS AUTOGENIC PART OF THE PRIMARY RELAXATION EXPERIENCE INVOLVES MAKING A SERIES OF SUGGESTIONS TO YOURSELF. YOU DO NOT HAVE TO BE CONCERNED WITH WHETHER OR NOT YOU FEEL ANY OF THE CHANGES YOU SUGGEST. JUST RELAX AND MAKE THE SUGGESTIONS AND WAIT UNTIL IT'S OVER BEFORE THINKING ABOUT WHETHER IT'S WORKING FOR YOU. SILENTLY ASK YOURSELF TO EXPERIENCE EACH SUGGESTION, WITHOUT WORRYING ABOUT WHETHER IT'S HAPPENING OR HOW IT MIGHT BE AFFECTING YOUR BODY. PAUSE BRIEFLY AFTER EACH SUGGESTION.

MY RIGHT ARM IS HEAVY.

MY LEFT ARM IS HEAVY.

MY RIGHT LEG IS HEAVY.

MY LEFT LEG IS HEAVY.

MY RIGHT ARM IS WARM.

MY LEFT ARM IS WARM.

MY RIGHT LEG IS WARM.

MY LEFT LEG IS WARM.

MY RIGHT ARM IS HEAVY AND WARM.

MY LEFT ARM IS HEAVY AND WARM.

MY RIGHT LEG IS HEAVY AND WARM.
MY LEFT LEG IS HEAVY AND WARM.

MY FOREHEAD IS COOL AND CALM.
MY HEART IS CALM AND RELAXED.
IN THE CENTER OF MY BODY, MY SOLAR PLEXUS IS WARM.
IT BREATHES ME.

SILENTLY FINISH THE FOLLOWING SENTENCE TO YOURSELF: "RIGHT NOW, MY BODY FEELS _____."

As you experiment with this exercise initially, check out how many actual physiological changes you can notice after it is all over. What you are doing is taking more active control of some involuntary processes. Being fully aware of those changes and that you are directing them can give you the confidence and desire to go on.

At the end of the Primary Relaxation Experience, you may choose to program into your subconscious mind some life-affirming suggestions. One possibility is to follow the series with the following self-suggestions:

IN ITS RELAXED STATE, MY BODY IS REGENERATING AND REJUVENATING ITSELF. I AM GROWING YOUNGER AND MORE VITAL. MY ENERGY IS INCREASING. I AM IN CHARGE OF MY OWN LIFE AND IT WILL GO ON AS LONG AS I WANT IT TO.

MY BODY FEELS RELAXED AND YOUNG. I AM LETTING GO OF ALL DEATH CONSCIOUSNESS. EVERY BREATH I TAKE RESTORES MORE OF MY YOUTHFUL VITALITY.

MY CONSCIOUS MIND IS RELAXED AND CALM. I AM ALLOWING MY SUBCONSCIOUS MIND TO ACTIVATE IT-SELF AND RELEASE ALL THE SUBSTANCES AND PRO-

CESSES THAT WILL KEEP ME YOUNG AND ALIVE NOW
AND FOR THE INDEFINITE FUTURE.

I AM RELAXED AND LIVING AN EXCITING, FULFILLING
LIFE WHICH KEEPS ME INVOLVED, HEALTHY, AND
MENTALLY AND PHYSICALLY FIT.

Of course it's true that the Primary Relaxation Experience itself
can keep one young and vital by acting as a powerful antistress
tool. Whenever we are confronted by a stressful situation, the
body reacts in negative ways. Having a technique for counteracting that negative physiological and biochemical reaction, and one
that may be put into action immediately, can substantially reduce
the harmful effect of stress in our lives.

It's also important during any of these exercises to calm the
restless scanning of your conscious mind, which may be telling
you things such as, "This is silly. How can I know whether it's
working? Why am I doing this?" Remember Thomas Huxley's
good advice to let go of all preconceived notions.

WHAT WE KNOW AND WHAT
WE CAN ASSUME

We know right now that built into the human organism is the
capacity to fight disease and prolong life. We also know that the
brain is a complex chemical factory which produces a number of
substances to promote health and longevity. We know that even
without the impending biological breakthroughs, some people
manage to live much longer and stay much more youthful than
others. These people seem to have some basic attitudes about
themselves and life in general, some common attitudes that
presumably create the kind of brain activity which galvanizes their
own body mechanisms. We may assume that the closer we can get
to those kinds of healthy attitudes, the closer we can get to a
healthier state of mind and body. We may assume one thing

further: Holding onto old beliefs about the inevitability of aging and death will eventually kill us.

The suggestions and exercises contained in this series of Psychological Immortality Strategies are aimed at helping the mind let go of those old beliefs. The best way to use these strategies is to experiment with them without prejudging, but carefully paying attention to how you feel after doing them.

THE LIFE-AFFIRMING JUMP

This is a rather simple and seemingly silly exercise, but it can act as a powerful, instant stress-reducer and consciousness-changer. All it involves is jumping in the air and yelling at the top of your lungs. When you land, just focus your attention on your breathing and what is happening inside your body. You might feel light-headed or some tingling, but don't worry about that—it's just the release of some energy. If you do the jump several times a day, it will help activate your energy and stimulate your breathing. When you land, always check out whatever bodily sensations you feel.

A number of primitive tribes use jumping in their ritual ceremonies and dances. This jumping tends to lift the spirits and prepare one for whatever activity is coming up. As Ray Bradbury suggested, we do not usually celebrate the fact that we are not dead. Jumping can be such a celebration, and it's certainly not something you can do without conscious awareness. Many of our negative, death-affirming habits are done without awareness. Once we do something as a conscious act of will it no longer is a habit, but a choice, which is in itself a life-affirming event.

THE LEARNING STRATEGY

Leo Buscaglia often tells his audiences about his parents' rule that each member of the family learn something new each day and announce it at the dinner table. Sometimes there was a mad scramble for the encyclopedia as dinner approached, but it instilled a lifelong dedication to learning in Leo. In our culture, we tend to take learning and knowledge for granted. When Leo Buscaglia grew up in Italy, it was considered a privilege to be allowed to learn. This is why so many of our immigrants accomplished so much; they were enthralled by the wonder of learning itself.

This is an easily adopted strategy and a good opportunity to keep our minds alive and to make a strong personal commitment to life-extension. The strategy is so simple that there would be no reason to consider changing it: Just make an agreement with yourself to learn one new thing each day. It doesn't matter whether it's a skill, a piece of information, or a new way of looking at something already in your life.

If you want an additional or alternative learning process, Ray Bradbury suggests a potent one: Each night before retiring, read one essay, one poem, and one short story. Certainly, at the end of a week, a month, a year, you have substantially expanded your knowledge and exercised your brain. Imagine how the mood in a nursing home might change if every resident made this commitment to learning!

Again, the biologists and psychologists agree on this cardinal point: When we stop learning, we stop living.

YOUR LIFEBOARD

When starting on any new path of personal development, the more reinforcement we can get the more effective our efforts. The following strategy is deceptively simple. Obtain an empty bulletin board, which you will call your LIFEBOARD from now on. On this board, tack up all the positive items you can find about longevity and growing young. Cut out pictures of older people who defy their age, put up souvenirs of particularly alive moments you have experienced, cut out inspirational words or phrases from ads, such as "Longest Lasting." Put your own picture in the middle of the lifeboard. Arrange it so that it is easily visible on a daily basis, providing you with data that will make you feel good. If you can really participate in this multifaceted strategy, and get into the fun of putting together this visual reminder of life-affirming items, it can have a potent effect on your attitudes, which in turn will help the brain release those powerful substances which can stimulate health and long life.

THE UNBIRTHDAY PARTY

We all imagine that we get older each and every year, which isn't really true unless we make it true. There is nothing so ludicrous as celebrating getting older, and this is usually the focus of ordinary birthday parties. Instead of celebrating the fact of aliveness, birthdays usually are events reminding us of our own mortality, even down to the humorous birthday greeting cards which exaggerate the idea of our falling into decrepitude and senility. Vicki Johnson has a better idea. In Boca Raton, Florida, this holistic Gestalt therapist is one of those people who deny aging in healthy, wholesome ways. She is rarely assumed to be out of her 20s, when in fact that's where her oldest daughter is, and in her attitude are the obvious seeds of her youthfulness. Vicki Johnson conducts a workshop she calls the Unbirthday Party, an anti-aging experience:

> *At a birthday party, someone always gets older. At an Unbirthday Party, everyone gets younger. Everyone takes a candle from the Unbirthday Cake and blows it out, concentrating on the feeling that they are blowing age itself away. We choose to be the age we are and if we want to blow away the years, we can do it!*

You might want to experiment with this strategy alone or with some friends or loved ones. Reinforcing the idea that you are in charge of your age can be a healthy self-affirming and life-affirming practice. If each day, as we wake up, we suggest to ourselves that it will be a wonderful day and we will go to bed younger than when we got up, the body will have to respond eventually. Subconsciously, we are already telling ourselves that we are getting older each day, so this is merely replacing those negative messages with positive ones. Have yourself a daily Unbirthday Party, in which you celebrate your aliveness and your growing younger!

The most destructive fact about birthdays is that we somehow seem to identify *as* the age we are. If someone is 55, he or she sees whatever early image was implanted of a 55-year-old person. A much healthier attitude would be to say to oneself: "I just happen to be 55, but that doesn't have anything to do with how young I feel or how young I am."

THE POWER OF PRETEND

Psychologists have known for a long time that fantasy is an important part of the human experience, and that it can be a powerful and highly useful instrument for change. Two psychologists, Dr. Claude Nolte and Dr. Maurice Rapkin, have worked extensively with a system originally developed by Dr. Rapkin and called the Power of Pretend. In attending an intensive weekend workshop conducted by Dr. Nolte and his wife and colleague, Dr. Dorothy Nolte, some of the real potency of this type of fantasy work emerged. As Claude Nolte describes it, we all pretend much more than we think. All of the emotional material we use in making choices usually involves pretending, what we might imagine will happen if we make a choice, what we imagine other people's reactions to be in the face of such choices. On top of the original fantasy, quite often someone will have another fantasy: that the original belief is real. If, for instance, you were pretending that you were going to die at the age of 75, you might pretend on top of that that it was really already beginning to happen, and in still more pretending, you might assume that you were becoming susceptible to certain debilitating diseases. Pretends often occur in multiple layers: Some people pretend they are accident-prone, and then establish a whole array of other pretends to make that come true, such as pretending that they can't lift their feet when stepping over a threshold—which causes them to trip and hurt themselves. The Power of Pretend work is aimed at establishing some skills in deliberately pretending, so that people can learn consciously to choose whether or not to pretend under certain circumstances. Once we become adept at switching fantasies on and off, we can come closer to operating in reality most of the time. Once we realize that most of our beliefs and attitudes are basically pretends, we can choose to continue or to change them. Quite often during a Power of Pretend workshop, someone will say, "Wow, I pretend a lot more than I thought!"

Part of the layering of one pretend on top of another involves the process of changing focus. During a Power of Pretend exercise, for example, when someone is visualizing a dog and is then instructed to stop pretending that dog, he or she might very well replace the dog with a cat. This is normal, but involves a pretend on top of a pretend. Once the skills are learned, that person can just shut off the dog without inventing something to replace it.

Pretends get us in trouble when we don't examine them in the light of our realistic experience. You might have a friend, for instance, who you pretend is your best friend, and who you visit often and call on the phone daily. That "friend" might be bored stiff by your attention, and be himself pretending that by being honest he would hurt your feelings. Thus two people might be stuck in a nonproductive and non-nourishing relationship because of their rigid pretend systems. If someone pretends that she can't resist chocolate cake, and then on top of that pretends that the cake will damage her health, then that is probably what will happen.

Let's try some pretend strategies now. For these, the best position will be for you to sit in a comfortable chair. At first, you will probably find it easier to keep your eyes closed. After some practice, the exercises can be done with your eyes open. Keep in mind that these are mental practice sessions designed to give you the ability to turn your pretends on and off. You may find that they are tiring, since they're using a part of your brain not often exercised. Don't overdo it. Take your time.

Again, you might want to record these on tape, or have someone read them through for you. The pace should be slow and deliberate.

FIRST, WE ARE GOING TO FIRMLY ROOT OUR AWARENESS IN REALITY. BECOME AWARE OF WHAT IT FEELS LIKE TO SIT IN THIS CHAIR. WHAT ARE YOUR SENSES TELLING YOU ABOUT THIS MOMENT'S EXPERIENCE? NOTICE HOW THE CHAIR FEELS AGAINST YOUR BACK. HOW THE CLOTH OF YOUR CLOTHES FEELS AGAINST YOUR SKIN. WHAT CAN YOUR EARS TELL YOU ABOUT THE SOUNDS COMING IN RIGHT NOW? NOTICE ANY TASTE YOU CAN SENSE IN YOUR MOUTH. NOTICE ANY SMELLS PRESENT IN THE AIR AROUND YOU. NOTICE IF THERE IS ANY TENSION ANYWHERE IN YOUR BODY, AND WHETHER THE AIR IS WARM OR COLD. REMEMBER THAT YOUR BODY IS CONSTANTLY GIVING YOU SIGNALS AS TO WHAT IS HAPPENING INSIDE AND ALL AROUND YOU. PAYING ATTENTION TO THOSE SIGNALS IS THE WAY TO UNDERSTAND WHAT IS REAL VERSUS WHAT IS NOT.

PRETEND THAT YOU ARE HOLDING YOUR FAVORITE SANDWICH IN YOUR HAND. NOTICE ITS COLOR, TEXTURE. PRETEND TASTING IT. STOP PRETENDING THE SANDWICH. BE AWARE THAT YOU'VE STOPPED PRETENDING THE SANDWICH AND EXACTLY HOW YOU STOPPED PRETENDING. NOTICE WHETHER YOU JUST SHUT OFF THE IMAGE OF THE SANDWICH OR HAD TO REPLACE IT WITH THE VISUAL IMAGE OF SOMETHING ELSE.

PRETEND THAT YOU ARE YOU AT THE AGE OF 8 OR 9, ATTENDING A BIRTHDAY PARTY. PRETEND YOU ARE UPSET BECAUSE YOU FORGOT TO BRING THE GIFT. PRETEND EVERYONE WILL BE UPSET WITH YOU. NOW PRETEND THAT NO ONE NOTICES. YOU ARE WARMLY GREETED BY ALL YOUR FRIENDS AND HAVE A WONDERFUL TIME. PRETEND YOU REALIZE IT DOESN'T MATTER THAT YOU DIDN'T BRING A GIFT. STOP PRETENDING THE PARTY AND ALL YOUR FRIENDS. STOP PRETENDING ANYTHING YOU'VE BEEN PRETENDING UP TO NOW.

PRETEND YOU ARE RUNNING ALONG A TRACK. PRETEND YOU ARE

RUNNING BECAUSE YOU BELIEVE IT WILL KEEP YOU HEALTHY. PRETEND YOU ARE NOT ENJOYING RUNNING. PRETEND THE SUN IS BEATING DOWN ON YOU. PRETEND YOU WOULD LIKE TO STOP RUNNING, BUT YOU DON'T WANT TO ADMIT DEFEAT. PRETEND THAT YOU SUDDENLY UNDERSTAND THAT IT'S OK FOR YOU TO STOP RUNNING. PRETEND YOU WANT TO STOP RUNNING NOW, BUT YOUR LEGS WON'T STOP. STOP PRETENDING YOU'RE RUNNING. STOP PRETENDING THE TRACK. STOP PRETENDING ALL THE PRETENDING YOU'VE DONE SINCE THE BEGINNING OF THIS EXERCISE.

PRETEND YOU ARE 100 YEARS OLD, AND STOOPED OVER IN A ROCKING CHAIR. STOP PRETENDING YOU ARE STOOPED OVER. PRETEND YOU ARE PLAYING VOLLEYBALL WITH A BUNCH OF CHILDREN AND KEEPING UP WITH THEM. PRETEND THEY ARE SURPRISED YOU ARE DOING SO WELL. PRETEND THE VOLLEYBALL IS GOING BACK AND FORTH OVER THE NET. PRETEND THE CHILDREN ARE NO LONGER SURPRISED YOU ARE DOING SO WELL. PRETEND YOU ARE NO LONGER 100, BUT YOUR CURRENT AGE. PRETEND THE GAME SLOWS DOWN BECAUSE YOU ARE NOT AS SKILLED NOW AS YOU WILL BE AT 100. STOP PRETENDING THE BALL. STOP PRETENDING THE CHILDREN. STOP PRETENDING YOU ARE PLAYING. STOP ALL THE PRETENDING YOU'VE BEEN DOING.

PRETEND THAT WITH EVERY BREATH YOU TAKE YOU ARE GETTING YOUNGER. PRETEND THIS PROCESS SPEEDS UP SO THAT YOU CAN FEEL YOURSELF GROWING YOUNGER BY THE MINUTE. PRETEND YOU START HOLDING YOUR BREATH FOR FEAR YOU WILL DISAP-PEAR. STOP PRETENDING YOU ARE GROWING YOUNGER. STOP PRETENDING HOLDING YOUR BREATH. PRETEND YOU ARE GROWING YOUNGER WHETHER YOU BREATHE OR NOT. PRETEND YOU ARE BEGINNING TO FEEL PANIC. STOP PRETENDING THE PANIC. STOP PRETENDING GROWING YOUNGER. STOP PRETENDING YOU ARE BREATHING. STOP ALL THE PRETENDING YOU ARE NOW DOING.

PRETEND YOU REALLY WANT TO LIVE A LONG, LONG TIME. PRETEND YOU ARE DOING SOMETHING ABOUT IT. PRETEND YOUR FRIENDS ARE ENVIOUS OF YOUR INCREASING YOUTHFULNESS. STOP PRETENDING YOUR FRIENDS ARE ENVIOUS. PRETEND YOUR FRIENDS ARE EXCITED AND HAPPY FOR YOU. PRETEND YOU KNOW YOU WILL LIVE TO AT LEAST 150. PRETEND THAT IT IS GOING TO CREATE A LOT

OF PROBLEMS. STOP PRETENDING THE PROBLEMS. STOP PRETENDING YOU WILL LIVE TO 150. STOP PRETENDING YOUR FRIENDS. STOP PRETENDING YOU ARE DOING SOMETHING TO LIVE LONG. STOP PRETENDING YOU REALLY WANT TO LIVE LONG.

As you can see, these pretend exercises can get very intricate. They are supposed to stimulate your imagination, and help you understand the differences between fantasy and reality. Fantasy can give you a new perspective on various situations in your life, but only if you learn to control its use.

PRETENDING WITH OTHERS

Children get to experiment with all sorts of behavior under the guise of pretending. They get to try on different roles, and experiment with new parts of themselves. You might try the same thing. The next time you meet a stranger and get into a conversation, and the other person asks you your age, add ten years to it. Do it just to see what the other person's reaction will be to someone looking as you do but claiming to being ten years older. You might get a compliment on how young you look. Absorb that compliment. This is a way of exploring our fixed notions of what people are like at certain ages. Some other time you might claim that you are ten years younger, to see whether this will be accepted as true. Through such pretending exercises you will be playing with changing your perceptions about age.

CHILD'S PLAY

One way to experience a more youthful feeling is to play some children's games. Also, you might pay a visit to a toy store—just for yourself, not to buy presents for any actual children. Buy a children's record containing games. See if you can keep up with the level of activity of a child. Seek out children to play with once in a while. If you have young relatives, and haven't played with them, romped on the floor with them, ask them if they've ever thought of playing with *you*. Perhaps they think you are too old. Try playing with them, see if they're right.

Tell some children about your own childhood. As vividly as possible, describe what you used to do, including the mischief you may have gotten into. Notice the expressions on their faces. Are they absorbed in what you are telling them, or is it boring them? Is it interesting to you? Are you talking about it with youthful exuberance?

When Leonard Orr said that people would die rather than act childish, he was reiterating a fact known by anyone studying human behavior: People would rather do almost anything than appear foolish. Are you too old to appear foolish? If you had to stand up in front of a group right now and do something foolish, something everyone would agree was foolish, what would it be? Picture yourself actually doing this. And, if you are willing to take a risk for your own growing younger efforts, go ahead and do it!

YOUR 100TH ANNIVERSARY CELEBRATION

This is a strategy that can be a lot of fun and that can have real value in providing you with an emotionally invested deadline to look forward to and to aim at surviving. Start planning a gigantic 100th anniversary celebration. Not a birthday party, but a celebration of how alive you will have been for all the years up to and including your 100th year. Imagine how you will look, and who you will invite, and what will be served, and where the celebration will be held. Plan a real treat for yourself, something that will actually make it worthwhile to reach your 100th year.

THE DESERVING LIST

Make a list of ten reasons you deserve to live at least until the age of 100. Look over your list and see if you believe these reasons really qualify you for longevity.

THE ACTIVITY LIST

Make a list of all the things you would like to do if you suddenly were handed fifty years in addition to what you've always assumed your lifespan to be.

BREATHING STRATEGY

Start paying more attention to your breathing. Visualize every inhalation increasing your energy and aliveness, and every exhalation removing stale air, body poisons, and negative beliefs and emotions. Breathe in an easy, deliberate rhythm. Make a commitment to pay attention to your breathing for at least a two- or three-minute period at least ten times every day. At the end of a week, decide what this has done for you. If it's been worthwhile, continue checking out your breathing on a daily basis. Play with balancing your inhales with your exhales as in Rebirthing. Practice taking in as much air as possible and exhaling more powerfully than usual, so that all the old air gets released from your body.

LAUGHING AND SMILING STRATEGY

Norman Cousins helped cure an incurable, debilitating disease with laughter. Start to look at how much laughter is in your life right now. How many smiles do you get or give in a day? Start this four-week program:

1st Week:
List all the times you've laughed out loud during the week. Also list all the smiles you've received and all the smiles you've given. Keep the tally as accurate as possible, recording it at least once a day.

2nd Week:
Practice laughing out loud when you're alone. You might read some funny stories or watch a funny TV show to stimulate you, but even if it doesn't feel real at first, practice laughing out loud at least 15 minutes each day.

3rd Week:
Start to smile at more people every day. Note their reactions and how all this smiling makes you feel. At the end of this week examine whether you feel younger, older, or the same.

4th Week:
Plan to spend time during the week with as many people as possible with whom you have laughed out loud. Plan some activities that will provide the opportunity for more laughter. Allow yourself to really get into laughing without worrying about whether you will embarrass or shock others.

One of the purposes of this strategy is to let you know what role smiling and laughter play in your life, and whether these are natural ingredients. We know at the very least that laughter releases endorphins in the brain, and it's logical to assume that a life filled with laughter will be enhanced by all sorts of biochemical responses. In Tibet, monks often practice something called a laughing meditation in which they just start laughing out loud. The laugh starts out as a false gesture, and then becomes real as they get their bodies and minds into it.

AFFIRMATIONS

As has been mentioned numerous times in this book, the best way to remove negative material from our consciousness is to replace it with positive material. Affirmations are simply positive messages we feed into our subconscious minds. Here are some specific Psychological Immortality affirmations to repeat to yourself.

EVERY HOUR OF EVERY DAY I AM GROWING YOUNGER AND MORE EXCITED WITH LIFE.

MY BODY, MIND, AND CREATIVE ENERGY ARE AMAZINGLY YOUTHFUL ALL THE TIME.

I DESERVE TO LIVE UNTIL AT LEAST 150.

MY LIFESPAN IS INDEFINITE, MY POSSIBILITIES ARE UNLIMITED.

A LOT OF ENERGY IS FLOWING FROM ME AND THROUGH ME, ACTIVATING MY BODY AND MIND, EXTENDING MY LIFE.

I WILL BE A WONDERFUL AND YOUTHFUL OLDER PERSON.

ALL THE PARTS OF MY BODY ARE COOPERATING IN KEEPING ME YOUNG.

THE MORE I LIVE, THE BETTER I GET AT IT AND THE BETTER I FEEL.

If you are approaching the age when one or both of your parents died (psychologically a very vulnerable time in your life), tell yourself the following:

I HAVE NO NEED TO REPEAT MY PARENTS' PATTERNS.

I AM LIVING FAR LONGER THAN EITHER OF MY PARENTS.

I DETERMINE MY OWN LIFESPAN.

In order to give these affirmations added impact on your life, write them down twenty times and say them out loud twenty times. Choose one at a time to do each day. After you go through these affirmations, think up some more. Write down your own affirmations, making sure they contain specific desires you might have for health and long life. Another highly effective way to use these positive messages to yourself is to deliver them in person as you face a mirror. The more sincerity and enthusiasm you can evoke while saying them, the more deeply they will affect you.

In looking at those people who successfully live their lives and have all the love and health and prosperity they want, one finds they are already giving themselves positive messages of support and reinforcement all the time. Self-delivered sentences such as: "You're looking good." "That's a terrific job you just did." "He's going to love this new idea of mine!" "This is going to be a great day for me!" At one level this may seem to be letting go of reality, being positive on a superficial level, but people who practice self-affirmation seem to know at an intuitive level of awareness what some psychologists are just finding out: We can bypass conscious reality and send positive messages to our subconscious minds which will have as great or greater impact on us than any reality. While the conscious mind can and does distinguish between what is real and what is pretend, the subconscious mind cannot do so.

The underlying foundation of this book and any other book or course or therapy aimed at changing attitudes is the knowledge that the subconscious mind cannot distinguish between fact and imagined fact. Just as we pretend all those negative messages through the years are valid, we can also pretend the positive ones are. They will have the same biochemical significance as reality, and in fact do become reality.

PRAISE FROM OTHERS

In addition to giving ourselves life-affirming messages, we can more effectively use the positive messages we get from others. Most of us have received praise from other people at one time or another throughout our lives, but we rarely make full use of this powerful resource. Sometimes we discount this praise, and feeling embarrassed or undeserving we try to diminish whatever is being praised: "Me—looking good? I wish it were true!" "This old dress? I've had it for years." "It wasn't anything—don't make such a big deal about it!" All of these are ways of avoiding the emotional nourishment that can accompany praise, nourishment which we now know affects actual changes in our body chemistry. Here are two simple strategies designed to help in the receiving of praise and in the perpetuation of the good feelings it can produce.

PRAISE PERCEPTION PAUSE

Every time someone praises you for anything at all, take at least one full minute before making any response. This will avert the meaningless automatic response, the denying response, or the insulting tactic of immediately praising the other person, which needlessly dilutes the original praise. The pause allows you to absorb whatever impact the praise has and to develop a more sincere and authentic response.

THE PRAISE POSTER

Get a large sheet of posterboard. Whenever anyone praises you in some way that feels especially good, ask that person to write down his or her comment and sign it. Paste the comment up on your Praise Poster. This will enable you to revive the good feelings whenever you read the comment, and give you a source of affirming messages whenever you choose to look at your poster.

VISUALIZATION

Another way to affirm life for ourselves is to visualize affirming situations. We think in pictures, not words, and therefore pictures have greater potential for affecting our life consciousness. The following visualization strategies are similar in some ways to the pretending exercises, except that our task is different. Instead of learning how to turn them off and on, these will be more relaxed fantasy experiences, designed to evoke feelings and new perceptions of our psychological and biological opportunities.

During some of these visualization exercises you may notice some changes in your body, perhaps some tingling. This is nothing to worry about, as any experience which is both relaxing and mind-expanding tends to have a releasing effect on the body, letting some repressed energy flow through various parts of the body.

You might want to try the Primary Relaxation Experience described earlier in this section as a prelude to any of these visualizations. Lie down, relax, and close your eyes.

VISUALIZATION #1:
THIS EXERCISE IS FOCUSED ON REMOVING SOME OF THE OBSTACLES TO A LONG AND HAPPY LIFE.
TAKE A FEW DEEP BREATHS AND LET THE AIR OUT SLOWLY,

SAYING TO YOURSELF, "I AM RELAXED." IMAGINE THAT YOU ARE NOW AS RELAXED AS YOU HAVE EVER BEEN IN YOUR LIFE. YOUR CREATIVE IMAGINATION IS NOW READY TO BE ACTIVATED.

IMAGINE THAT YOU ARE ABSOLUTELY FREE TO LIVE YOUR LIFE IN ANY WAY YOU CHOOSE. YOU HAVE NO FINANCIAL WORRIES, NO OBLIGATIONS, NO RESTRICTIONS, NO NEGATIVE BELIEFS, ARE IN GOOD HEALTH. FEEL YOURSELF FLOATING FREE, ABLE TO GO IN ANY DIRECTION, ABLE TO CHOOSE ANY PATH THAT INTERESTS, EXCITES, OR ENRICHES YOU. ABLE TO STAY AS YOUNG AS YOU WANT AND LIVE AS LONG AS YOU WANT. LET YOURSELF PICTURE CLEARLY WHAT YOU WOULD DO WITH THIS FREEDOM. (CONTINUE IMAGINING THIS FOR ABOUT 1 MINUTE.)

BE AWARE OF HOW THIS FREEDOM MAKES YOU FEEL. BE AWARE NOW OF WHAT YOU HAD TO LET GO OF IN ORDER TO OBTAIN THIS FREEDOM. IMAGINE A LARGE HOLE, AND IN THIS HOLE ARE ALL THE OLD BELIEFS THAT HAVE BEEN HOLDING YOU BACK, ALL THE PRECONCEIVED NOTIONS, ALL THE DEATH CONSCIOUSNESS, ALL THE NEGATIVE MESSAGES, ALL THE RESTRICTIONS AND LIMITATIONS YOU AND OTHERS HAVE SET UP FOR YOU. NOW PICTURE YOURSELF COVERING THEM ALL UP WITH DIRT, BURYING THEM IN THIS LARGE HOLE. (PAUSE 20 SECONDS.) BE AWARE OF HOW BURYING ALL THIS OLD STUFF MAKES YOU FEEL.

NOW VISUALIZE YOURSELF DIGGING UP ALL THIS STUFF IN THE HOLE. SORTING THROUGH IT. LOOK AT ALL THESE THINGS THAT HAVE BEEN HOLDING YOU BACK. SEE IF YOU CAN BEGIN TO UNDERSTAND WHY YOU HAVEN'T GOTTEN FURTHFR OR ACCOM-PLISHED MORE IN LIFE. IDENTIFY THE STRONGEST OF THESE PRECONCEIVED NOTIONS, THESE NEGATIVE BELIEFS, THE ONE YOU GIVE THE MOST POWER TO. IMAGINE YOURSELF TALKING TO THIS ONE DESTRUCTIVE PRETEND, TELLING IT WHATEVER YOU WOULD WANT TO SAY TO SOMETHING THAT HAS BEEN HOLDING YOU BACK ALL THESE YEARS. (CONTINUE IMAGINING THIS FOR 1 MINUTE.)

COME BACK TO AN AWARENESS OF YOUR OWN CURRENT REALITY. BE AWARE OF YOUR BREATHING AND YOUR BODY'S POSITION RIGHT NOW. BE AWARE OF HOW YOU FEEL. AND BE AWARE THAT YOU HAVE THE POWER TO COME BACK AND REEXAMINE ANY OF THIS

FANTASY EXPERIENCE AT ANY TIME, TO LEARN FROM IT WHATEVER
YOU CAN.

The purpose of this exercise was to experiment with letting go of
old negative conditioning. You might want to vary the visualization by destroying the old stuff in some other way than burying it,
perhaps bombing it, or scattering it at sea, etc. Though reading
over the exercises once or twice will give you the basic idea, here
too you might want to record the instructions or have someone
read them aloud to you. This can be a powerful series of events to
share with someone else, taking turns leading each other through
the fantasies. Do not rush from one to another. If you do choose to
work with more than one visualization in any given time period,
take a long break in between so as to digest the mental/emotional
material evoked.

VISUALIZATION #2:

IMAGINE YOURSELF TEN YEARS FROM NOW, BUT LOOKING,
FEELING, AND ACTING TEN YEARS YOUNGER THAN YOU DO TODAY.
IMAGINE HOW YOUR LIFE WILL BE WITH THIS RENEWED ENERGY,
AND HOW PEOPLE WILL REACT TO YOU. PICTURE YOURSELF TELLING
PEOPLE YOUR REAL AGE, AND THEIR AMAZEMENT SINCE YOU LOOK
TWENTY YEARS YOUNGER. PICTURE WHAT IT WOULD BE LIKE TO
LIVE LIFE AS THIS APPARENTLY YOUNGER PERSON, THOROUGHLY
EXCITED BY LIFE, TOTALLY ABSORBED IN WORK AND IN A LIFESTYLE
THAT IS SATISFYING AND WORTHWHILE.

Beware here of something called a double pretend. This would
happen if you found you could imagine yourself ten years from
now, but *not* looking years younger because your rational/logical
mind tells you that is unrealistic. Of course, it isn't unrealistic at
all, and the idea of visualizing it is to build up the desire that will
help you make it happen. Also, the part about looking younger is
no less or more real than the mere picturing of the future. Again,
this is the restrictive, nonrisking part of your nature trying to
control your imagination. It may take some practice, but even-

tually you'll be able to visualize anything you choose. And a very simple rule of life is: If you can't see it, you can't have it.

VISUALIZATION #3:

GET INTO AS RELAXED A POSITION AS POSSIBLE. TAKE SOME DEEP BREATHS. IMAGINE BREATHING IN NEW LIFE-ENERGY AND BREATHING OUT ALL THE LOVE YOU WANT TO SHARE WITH THE WORLD. SEE A VERY SMALL VERSION OF YOURSELF STANDING IN FRONT OF YOUR BODY. PICTURE THIS SMALL YOU ENTERING YOUR BODY AND EXAMINING IT. SEE YOURSELF LOOKING INSIDE AT ALL THE INTRICATE MECHANISMS WHICH MAKE YOUR BODY WORK. THE HEART, LUNGS, BRAIN, LIVER, BLOOD, CELLS, NERVES, MUSCLES. (CONTINUE THIS FANTASY FOR 2 MINUTES.)

IMAGINE THAT THIS SMALL VERSION OF YOU HAS THE POWER AND THE KNOWLEDGE TO FIX WHATEVER MIGHT NOT BE WORKING AT PEAK PERFORMANCE INSIDE YOUR BODY. VISUALIZE THIS EXPERT GOING AROUND INSIDE YOUR BODY AND ADJUSTING HERE, TESTING THERE, REPAIRING EVERYWHERE. VISUALIZE YOUR BODY REACTING TO THIS OVERHAUL. (CONTINUE THIS PART OF THE FANTASY FOR 2 MINUTES.)

IMAGINE THAT NOW THAT YOUR BODY IS OPERATING AT PEAK EFFICIENCY IT WILL BE ABLE TO COUNTERACT ANY NEGATIVE FACTORS THREATENING YOUR HEALTH AND VITALITY. PICTURE A VAST ARMY OF HORMONES, ENZYMES, BRAIN SECRETIONS, AND HEALTHY CELLS MOBILIZING INSIDE YOUR BODY TO TAKE CARE OF YOU WHENEVER YOU ASK THEM TO. TRY A PRACTICE DRILL TO MAKE CERTAIN THEY ALL KNOW HOW TO DO THEIR JOB. VISUALIZE THIS LIFE-ENHANCING ARMY GOING THROUGH ITS PACES. (TAKE 2 MINUTES FOR THIS.)

TAKE A FEW DEEP BREATHS AND VISUALIZE THE AUTOMATIC FUNCTION OF YOUR OWN LIFE-ENERGY, AND THAT YOU DON'T HAVE TO TAKE DIRECT COMMAND OF ALL THE OPERATIONS BUT CAN DELEGATE THAT RESPONSIBILITY TO THE PARTS OF YOUR BODY THAT CAN DO THE JOB BEST. SEE ALL THESE PARTS WORKING IN UNISON TOWARD ONE MAJOR GOAL: KEEPING YOU HAPPY AND ALIVE. VISUALIZE THIS HAPPENING IN ANY WAY THAT FEELS RIGHT FOR YOU. (TAKE 1 MINUTE FOR THIS.)

VISUALIZATION #4:

THIS EXERCISE, SPECIFICALLY DESIGNED TO FOCUS YOUR ATTENTION ON INTERNAL ENERGY, IS A RELAXATION AND ENERGY INDUCTION. LIE ON YOUR BACK IN A COMFORTABLE POSITION. ALLOW YOUR LEGS TO SPREAD OUT TO WHERE THEY FEEL MOST RELAXED. ALLOW YOUR HANDS TO REST COMFORTABLY AT YOUR SIDES.

NOW THAT YOUR BODY IS COMFORTABLE, CHECK IT OUT FOR ANY LINGERING TENSION. IF THERE IS ANY, TELL THAT PART TO RELAX. IF YOU NEED TO MOVE OR STRETCH ANY PART OF YOUR BODY TO MAKE IT MORE COMFORTABLE, DO SO.

CONCENTRATE ON YOUR BREATHING. DON'T CHANGE IT, JUST FOCUS YOUR ATTENTION ON IT. VISUALIZE EACH BREATH AS IT GOES IN AND OUT. IMAGINE YOU CAN ACTUALLY SEE THE AIR GOING IN AND COMING OUT. EXPERIENCE AND APPRECIATE THE MOVEMENT OF THE VARIOUS MUSCLES INVOLVED IN YOUR BREATHING PROCESS. CONTINUE TO BREATHE IN AND OUT AS YOU NORMALLY WOULD. (PAUSE 30 SECONDS.)

WHEN YOU BREATHE IN, YOUR BODY IS TAKING IN ALL THE LIFE-ENERGY IT REQUIRES FROM THE UNIVERSE. WHEN YOU BREATHE OUT, YOU ARE GIVING BACK TO THE UNIVERSE WHATEVER YOU DON'T NEED. YOU ARE BREATHING FROM A POSITION OF STRENGTH AND ABUNDANCE. ALWAYS AWARE THAT THERE IS ALWAYS MORE AIR TO ALLOW IN, ALWAYS WILLING TO SHARE YOUR LIFE-ENERGY BY EXHALING FULLY AND DEEPLY. FEEL THIS PROCESS HAPPENING TO YOU. BREATHING IN AND TAKING FROM THE UNIVERSE ITS LIFE-GIVING OXYGEN, ONLY TAKING WHAT YOU CAN EFFICIENTLY UTILIZE TO SUSTAIN YOUR BODY AND MIND, SENDING BACK WHAT YOU DON'T NEED BY EXHALING, SO THAT IT MAY NOURISH PLANTS AND BE REPROCESSED BY NATURE. PICTURE YOUR ENTIRE BREATHING SYSTEM WORKING TO FILL YOUR BODY WITH OXYGEN, BUT OPERATING SO BEAUTIFULLY, SO EFFICIENTLY, THAT YOU REQUIRE LESS OXYGEN THAN YOU THOUGHT. SEE THIS OXYGEN DELIVERING ENERGY THROUGH YOUR LUNGS, INTO YOUR HEART, INTO YOUR ENTIRE BLOODSTREAM AND CARDIOVASCULAR SYSTEM, BRINGING NOURISHMENT AND ENERGY DOWN INTO YOUR ARMS AND HANDS AND FINGERS, INTO YOUR STOMACH AND GENITALS AND LEGS AND

FEET, UP INTO YOUR SHOULDERS AND NECK AND FACE AND HEAD AND HAIR AND BRAIN. FEEL YOURSELF AS AN IMPORTANT AND VITAL PART OF THE UNIVERSE, AND THIS BREATHING, ENERGIZING PROCESS AS AN IMPORTANT PART OF YOU. BECOME AWARE OF YOUR ROLE IN THE UNIVERSE, OF THE NECESSITY OF YOUR EXISTENCE IN THE TOTAL SCHEME OF THINGS, AS YOU BREATHE IN AND OUT, FEELING GOOD ABOUT SHARING WITH THE UNIVERSE ALL THAT YOU ARE, ALL THAT YOU HAVE. (PAUSE 30 SECONDS.)

BE AWARE THAT YOU ARE IN CHARGE OF YOUR OWN LIFE-ENERGY, IN CHARGE OF ITS ENDURANCE AND INTENSITY. IMAGINE, RIGHT NEXT TO YOUR BODY, A SHINY BALL IN A CLEAR GLASS TUBE. AS YOU BREATHE IN, IMAGINE THE BALL RISING TO THE TOP OF THE GLASS TUBE. AS YOU BREATHE OUT, IMAGINE THE BALL MOVING BACK DOWN THE TUBE. WATCH THE BALL AS IT GOES UP AND DOWN, KEEPING TIME WITH YOUR BREATHING, MOVING UP AS YOU BREATHE IN, MOVING DOWN AS YOU BREATHE OUT. (CONTINUE VISUALIZING THIS FOR 20 SECONDS.)

AS YOUR BREATH KEEPS TIME WITH THE RISE AND FALL OF THE BALL IN THE TUBE, MOVE THE BALL AND TUBE INSIDE YOUR BODY. SEE THE BALL AND TUBE INSIDE OF YOU, STILL CONTINUING THE SAME MOVEMENT, WITH THE BALL RISING AS YOU BREATHE IN, AND FALLING AS YOU BREATHE OUT. AS YOU BREATHE IN, THE BALL MOVES TO THE TOP OF THE TUBE; AS YOU BREATHE OUT, IT MOVES DOWN. WITH EACH BREATH, YOU RELAX A BIT MORE. AND AS YOU RELAX, EACH TIME YOU BREATHE IN, THE BALL RISES LESS THAN THE PREVIOUS TIME. EACH TIME YOU INHALE, IT RISES TO A LOWER SPOT IN THE TUBE. AND EACH TIME YOU BREATHE OUT, THE BALL SINKS A BIT FARTHER THAN IT DID BEFORE. EACH TIME YOU EXHALE, IT FALLS TO A LOWER SPOT IN THE TUBE. THE BALL SLOWLY SINKS LOWER AND LOWER, AND EVENTUALLY COMES TO REST IN THE PIT OF YOUR STOMACH, JUST BELOW YOUR NAVEL. IMAGINE THAT THIS SPOT JUST BELOW YOUR NAVEL IS THE CENTER OF YOUR LIFE-ENERGY, THE SOURCE OF YOUR STRENGTH AND LOVE AND CREATIVITY. TAKE ALL THE TIME YOU NEED UNTIL THE SHINY BALL SETTLES IN THE CENTER OF YOUR LIFE-ENERGY. LET YOUR BREATHING RELAX YOU. WATCH THE BALL RISING LESS EACH TIME, AND SINKING SLOWLY TOWARD THE CENTER, COMING TO REST

THERE, JUST BELOW YOUR NAVEL, AND THUS LETTING YOU KNOW THAT YOU ARE COMPLETELY RELAXED AND THAT ALL THE ENERGY YOU POSSESS IS FOCUSED AT YOUR CENTER, WHERE THE BALL HAS COME TO REST. ALLOW THE BALL TO COME TO REST THERE. IF IT IS THERE ALREADY, JUST ENJOY WHATEVER YOU ARE FEELING. (PAUSE 20 SECONDS.)

AS THE BALL RESTS AT THE CENTER, FEEL ALL YOUR ENERGY BEING FOCUSED THERE. YOU CAN TEST WHETHER THIS IS TRUE FOR YOU. FROM THIS CENTER, YOU CAN SEND ENERGY TO ANY PART OF YOUR BODY, ANYWHERE YOU'D LIKE IT TO BE, ANY PLACE THAT NEEDS ATTENTION. TO START THIS PROCESS, SEND SOME ENERGY OUT TO YOUR FINGERTIPS. VERY SLOWLY, SEND THE ENERGY OUT FROM THE CENTER AND UP TOWARD YOUR SHOULDER. FEEL IT AS IT MOVES THROUGH YOUR STOMACH AND CHEST. LET YOURSELF BE AWARE OF THE ENERGY AS IT MOVES ACROSS YOUR SHOULDER AND BEGINS TO FLOW DOWN ALONG YOUR ARM AND INTO ONE OF YOUR HANDS. WATCH THE ENERGY MOVE DOWN INTO THE FINGERS. IT WILL FOCUS ON ONE FINGER TO START WITH, AND MAKE THAT FINGER TINGLE. JUST SO THAT YOU CAN BECOME AWARE OF THE POWER OF YOUR LIFE ENERGY IT WILL BEGIN TO MAKE THAT ONE FINGER ON THAT ONE HAND TINGLE. ALLOW YOURSELF TO FEEL THE TINGLING START. THE TINGLING THEN WILL SPREAD TO THE NEXT FINGER, AND TO THE NEXT, UNTIL ALL YOUR FINGERS ARE TINGLING. GRADUALLY THIS TINGLING, THIS MANIFESTATION OF YOUR LIFE ENERGY, WILL PERMEATE YOUR WHOLE HAND, UNTIL YOUR WHOLE HAND BEGINS TO TINGLE. FEEL THE PRESENCE OF YOUR ENERGY. AND REALIZE THAT THIS IS ONLY A FRACTION OF THE ENERGY YOU POSSESS, THE ENERGY AVAILABLE TO YOU. REALIZE THAT THIS ENERGY HAS THE POWER TO EXTEND YOUR YOUTH AND YOUR LIFE INDEFINITELY. VISUALIZE IT DOING JUST THAT, SO THAT YOUR WHOLE BODY TINGLES WITH ENTHUSIASM, GOOD HEALTH, AND HAPPY ENERGY. (PAUSE 20 SECONDS.)

BREATHE IN AND OUT AND STOP FOCUSING ON YOUR BREATHING. RELAX AND REST FOR A FEW MOMENTS. ALLOW YOUR BODY TO TELL YOU WHAT IT IS FEELING RIGHT NOW.

MUSIC AS A TOOL

As you become practiced at visualizing, you'll want to create your own fantasies. One way to enhance some of these experiences is by playing soothing music softly, as a background to the instructions. Music can also be a powerful tool in and of itself in easing tension and mobilizing the mind and body. In workshops, I often use rousing musical selections to stimulate energy and enthusiasm and to change consciousness. Walt Disney's "Zip-A-Dee-Doo-Dah" (from the film *Song of the South*) is an excellent example of this type of music, as is "Open a New Window" from the Broadway musical *Mame*. Music allows us to synchronize our breathing patterns, and its vibrations can stimulate our own inner energy vibrations.

THE LIFE RITUAL STRATEGY

We all have some rituals in our lives—weddings, funerals, graduations, and of course the even more mundane daily rituals surrounding our morning and bedtime routines. Those people who seem to live extraordinarily long lives have a very strong sense of ritual, often involving family and friends. In the Caucasus, for instance, ritual activities center around the dinner table. No sad stories are to be told, and there is a lot of camaraderie and good feeling. This strategy is perhaps the most pleasurable and may just be the most potent tool of all for a youthful and enduring life. At least once a week, invite a group of the liveliest people you know to a celebration of life and love and friendship. It can be a potluck dinner, and you may choose to have it in different homes each week. At the dinner table, the only talk allowed should be the sharing of your dreams, accomplishments, and pleasures of the week before. Your aim should be to praise and celebrate each other—no gossip, no talk of work other than in pleasurable ways, and no negative messages of any kind. Try to come up with a new toast each week, evoking the spirit of the Hebrew *L'Chaim!* ("To Life!"). Perhaps something like: "To a long and youthful life for each and every one of us!" Or: "May we laugh and love for at least another 100 years!"

THE BEST STRATEGY OF ALL

The best strategy of all, the very best plan of action for achieving Psychological Immortality is to just live. The more joyful our lives are, the more filled with possibilities, the more likelihood of those lives continuing indefinitely. The important thing is to use every tool at your disposal to reinforce the idea of your own possibilities. Lying in bed isn't the best strategy for taking advantage of your built-in longevity potential.

THE CHILD WITHIN

One powerful way to affirm life is to enjoy the child within you. One woman of 90, who looked 20 years younger, told me that her friends and family were aghast when, as a young woman in her 20s and 30s, she skipped down the sidewalk as a child would. She swears this childlike approach to life kept her young. One of the strong factors in feeling one's age is cultural. We do adopt certain behavior at certain ages because it's "the thing to do." Circumventing the process is an effective life-extending strategy: playing with life, not taking it so seriously. As children, most of us were free of the fear of death and aging. The more of that childlike emotional freedom we can reestablish, the more of a dent we can make in the aging process.

THE PLEASURE FACTOR

Children are very pleasure-oriented. This, too, seems to be a vital factor in achieving longevity and maintaining youthful vigor. This book intentionally avoids the subjects of dieting and exercise. First of all, there are many books on these specific subjects. But even more important is the fact that there is often a lot of tension and displeasure connected with these activities. It *is* true that laboratory rats have lived longer on a lower-than-normal caloric intake diet, and that many people living to 100 or more cite moderation in diet as a key factor in their longevity. Moderation, however, does not need to involve self-denial. In fact, the more enjoyment one gets from food, the more intensely its sensory and sensual pleasures are experienced, the less food is actually needed to produce satisfaction. One woman in her late 80s told me that the best part of growing older was that she could eat anything she wanted without being admonished by her parents, her doctor, or her late husband. Many Americans have a "hate affair" with food, stuffing huge amounts down their throats without even tasting it, and then feeling guilty and plunging into desperate programs of diet and exercise. This is the antithesis of the kind of moderate behavior that can keep us youthful. The more of a love affair we have with food—savoring each bite, taking the time to enjoy each meal thoroughly—the more easily we will develop a very natural moderate eating pattern that proceeds from pleasurable self-regulation.

The same is true of exercise. Vigorous activity undertaken as a chore or duty or because of guilt or self-loathing has more negative than positive impact on our bodies. It is true that physical activity has healthy internal effects, but these are negated by the unhealthy attitudes held by many people who exercise as a way of punishing themselves. The most effective and healthy way to include exercise as a integral part of our everyday lives and of our personal longevity programs is to find some physical activity which gives us personal pleasure, something that isn't done just because it is "good for us." My favorite exercise is walking on the beach. I don't have to force myself to do it, and I look forward with euphoric anticipation to each beach-walking experience. Exercise advocates are doing people a great disservice when they ignore the pleasure factor in their proselytizing efforts.

A sure formula for longevity would be to work only at those things which provide pleasure and satisfaction. To thoroughly enjoy the work one does, to take zestful pleasure in one's relationships, one's meals, one's recreational activities, one's relaxing moments. Perhaps each of us should examine our lives and label the negative, self-denying aspects with the warning: NOT ENJOYING YOURSELF MAY BE HAZARDOUS TO YOUR HEALTH!

In using the preceding strategies, check out whether they feel right for you. The ones that make you want to get up and shout, "I'm living an exciting, fulfilling life that will go on as long as I want it to!" are those you'll want to focus your energy on. Check out all your activities on this basis: Are they life-affirming or not? For surely you are now aware that you deserve to live younger and longer and happier. You know your body has all the mechanisms it needs to sustain and rejuvenate itself, and that your mind can become an obedient servant of your wishes and desires. The rest involves what you are going to do about it. Doing is living. To continue doing is to continue living. It *is* as simple as that!

EPILOGUE: GOD IS NOT AN INDIAN GIVER

The promised land contains life, not death. Man's connection with a Supreme Being has been distorted and diminished by a great deal of mythology. One of the many specious arguments against life-extension is that it is not "God's will." Nothing is so pagan as the idea that God's purpose is to cut someone down after he or she has managed to survive the perils of life for a number of years. As Leonard Orr puts it:

> *If you believe that God is out with his divine meataxe, hunting for you, then you have to learn to protect yourself from God. It's amazing that a person can be a priest or a minister and spend his whole life teaching that stuff, and never realize that there's anything inconsistent about God loving you and murdering you.*

If there is no biological need for death, there certainly is no spiritual one. Immortality, *physical immortality*, is, in fact, the ultimate spiritual destination.

In addition to heading up the Committee for an Extended Lifespan, A. Stuart Otto is also a minister. He says:

> *To me, God is life. This idea of dying to go and be with God is just ridiculous.*

241

Otto also subscribes to the concept of "immortality here and now" rather than what he calls "pie in the sky by and by," and says he feels it's serving God to remain here on earth rather than to end up plunking a harp in heaven.

The belief that God grants us the gift of life only to snatch it away once we finally begin to figure it out, once we really become attached to it, is a specious and superstitious one indeed.

God's Plan

Some people, whose religious beliefs more closely resemble ancient idol worship rather than any enlightened spiritual awareness, suggest that if physical immortality or any substantial increase in life-extension were part of what God intended for his creations then people wouldn't have been dying throughout history. I mentioned earlier the fallacy of enumeration, citing the examples that no one thought black swans were possible because none had ever been sighted until they were discovered in Australia, that no one was thought capable of running the four-minute mile, and that most people believed manned space flight was an impossibility until it was actually accomplished. If nothing else, it is arrogant for any of us to presume we know how it's all supposed to turn out. All we do have to go on are the results. We know that the human mind and body are the most marvelously engineered devices ever conceived. We know that built into the organism is the capacity to prolong life and fight aging and disease. If the creation of human life was intentional, then all parts of it were intentional, including the parts that are clearly designed to move toward greater and greater longevity. If human existence is part of God's plan, then so are the thousands of scientists whose skills and curiosity and persistence are moving us closer and closer to immortality.

I talked to a respected Christian theologian who requested anonymity. He said that a proper spiritual perspective has to include the story of Adam and Eve and the Garden of Eden. Whether metaphoric or actual, this tale laid the groundwork for many of our attitudes about death. The eating of the fruit of the Tree of Knowledge provided Adam with the awareness that there was more to life than he had so far experienced, and that death was part of the entire package. This theologian said that the description of Adam and Eve's loss of innocence has nothing to do with loss of virtue, but rather means that they were no longer shut off from the knowledge of the dangers, desires, and benefits of life outside the Garden. In this view of the story, the opposite of innocence becomes awareness rather than guilt. Unfortunately, most people have viewed Adam's eating of the apple as an act of disobedience so abominable that millions of humans have had to die to try and make up for it. It's the further opinion of this theologian that Jesus Christ was sent by God to clear up this misapprehension concerning Adam and Eve, but hardly anyone got the message! Not only did Jesus talk about love instead of guilt and about rewards instead of punishment, but he actually demonstrated that death was surmountable.

In Part Two, we talked about the psychological cycle that leads from sensory stimulus to energy to desire to movement and then to a sense of completion and openness. Adam's sudden acquisition of knowledge could be called the sensory stimulus. The awareness of life and death creates the desire for everlasting life. For thousands of years man has been frustrated in that desire. Whatever the action taken—whether personal sacrifice, placating pagan gods, being a "good" person, no matter what—everybody has still died. And this desire has therefore become submerged and denied. A sort of "sour grapes" attitude has prevailed, an attitude of "Well, who wants to live forever anyway?" and the creation of all sorts of excuses as to why immortality is unpleasant, undesirable, socially catastrophic, morally wrong.

Not every culture had this attitude. In her book, *The Coming of Age,* Simone de Beauvoir says:

> *In Chinese Neo-Taoism man's supreme aim is the quest for the "long life." All the fathers of Taoism speak of this. It amounted to something like a national discipline. Asceticism and ecstasy could lead to a holiness that would protect the*

adept from death itself. Holiness was the art of not dying, the absolute possession of life. Old age was therefore life in its very highest form. It was supposed that if life lasted long enough it would culminate in apotheosis. Chuang Tzu calls ancient beliefs to mind when he says that "tired of the world after a thousand years of life, the superior men raise themselves to the rank of spirits."

The difference between this Eastern view, whereby living long could lead to divinity, is in sharp contrast to our Western view, epitomized in a recent TV movie in which actor Jack Albertson, playing someone who has just lost the woman he loved, looks up at the sky and says, "You're a sniper, sneaking up behind people!"

The age-old desire for divinity and attraction to the mythology of immortal gods has always been a manifestation of man's basic frustration over this basic issue: that life is granted and then suddenly removed, either without warning or after much suffering and pain. Now science promises to remove that basic frustration. Psychological Immortality, if nothing else, is designed to remove those very deep-rooted doubts and fears.

Karma, Reincarnation, and Other Temporary Solutions

The concepts of karma, reincarnation, and various forms of afterlife are merely temporary solutions, substitutes for true physical immortality. Some of these concepts may indeed be valid, but this doesn't really matter. What does matter is that we humans do not have to settle for less than physical immortality *in this lifetime* as our ultimate aspiration! Without awareness, what does it matter how many lifetimes we have? If we had one hundred past lives or incarnations, and couldn't have access to our memories and knowledge from those lifetimes, of what use are they? And a dedication to any of these ideas of immortality without awareness gets in the way of developing a belief system that will lead to here-and-now life-extension. Every moment someone spends worrying about or dreaming about or investigating a presumed past life is a moment spent not enjoying life as a current event. Past lives may exist, we just don't know, but if they do, they are still merely a way station on the path to immortality. And we each will eventually have to make the decision as to whether we are here to stay in this life, or just "passing through."

The Imaginary Problems

Another way people have of avoiding the issue of physical immortality and life-extension is to invent all sorts of formidable problems that will confront us if we dare to extend life or eliminate disease. "How would we feed everyone?" "Where would we put them all?" "We'd run out of everything!" go the arguments. There is some consistency here, because the same people who rigidly hold onto a belief in the inevitability of death and aging view just as rigidly the results of their not being so inevitable. They have a narrow view of the myriad solutions to the problems that would arise from life-extension.

Death to Combat Overpopulation

Perhaps the most ridiculous argument of all is that death is a natural deterrent to overpopulation. Some years ago, when there were about half the number of people on the planet as there are now, a *Ripley's Believe It or Not* cartoon illustrated the true spaciousness of our planet by showing that if the world were reduced to the size of the Grand Canyon, all the people in it could fit into a single matchbox. Today, it would take two matchboxes! One current estimate is that Texas alone could accommodate the entire current world population without overcrowding. And visionary R. Buckminster Fuller says the planet could handle one or two trillion people!

As to the statement that we couldn't feed the population that would increase due to life-extension because of severe existing food shortages, Ray Bradbury told me:

It's just not true! We have enough food right now, California feeds most of America, America is sending food to ninety countries. Any time we want to plant more of California, we can feed the entire United States completely just from this one state. Then if America ups its production, which it can do, it can feed the rest of the world. But if you say that, then you're saying that the rest of the world won't have brains enough to feed themselves. What we have to do is induce others to be imaginative and willful. There's no use thinking that you want extra food if you don't have the guts to go out and plant and harvest it.

We could actually have a planet with twenty or thirty billion people on it and not even notice they were there. In the U.S. right now, most of our population is crammed into cities along the coastal areas and a few interior towns. Most of America's wilderness still hasn't been touched.

We're beginning to reclaim the rivers and the lakes. I'm working with the Cousteau people myself on several projects. I'm also working with the Disney people to build model towns as examples for the small towns of America, so that between now and the end of the century we can revitalize not only our lakes and rivers but the environment of our towns.

As might be expected, Ray Bradbury's view of the way things will be is more optimistic than most views, and he is putting his optimism into action by contributing energy and ideas to a new vision of the world.

A Technological Revolution

Life-extension doesn't mean just living longer. It also means that the finest minds will have the potential to keep producing for a longer period of time. Imagine if Einstein had had another twenty or thirty years of creative and productive life? F. M. Esfandiary puts it this way:

People think along a single track. They allow for the fact that we will live longer and longer but take insufficient account of the fact that all along with this revolution in life expectancy, there is a similar revolution going on in very nearly every area. Breakthroughs are occurring in every area. In the year 2000, individuals will be living well over a hundred years. We will also have moved to an age of abundance. We will have developed solar energy, hydrogen fuel, and a lot of other sources of limitless nonpolluting energy which in turn will provide limitless food and limitless raw materials.

When people raise these objections, they are often in the context of the realities of the world today, not the world of 1985 or 1990 or 2000.

And so it becomes clear how silly it is to believe that it's somehow better for humankind that we all be cut down in the prime of life, rather than be granted additional time to take our accomplishments and ideas several steps further. A world in which rigid death programming has been removed would be one in which the finest minds would be able to move onto the next level in the evolution of human intelligence, solving many of the problems now besetting the planet and easily capable of dealing with new ones.

The Age of Immortality

Comedian George Burns says, "I don't believe in dying. It's been done."

There already seems to be a collective unconscious awareness that physical immortality is closer. This may be responsible for the new concern with nutrition and holistic medicine and physical fitness. A body that will last longer has to be taken care of, and of course taking care of it will help it last longer. There's also an emerging sense of responsibility for the condition of this planet, a growing maturity in the ways we relate to the environment, with less of an inclination to let future generations clean up after us. This concern may not be just an altruistic one, but may contain an awareness that we may now be on earth long enough to bear the burdens of our own carelessness.

In the Age of Immortality, war may be unthinkable. If we could live indefinitely, who would be willing to die at 18 or 20? In such a time, we'd have to let go of old fears, and in the process we may have to confront new ones. In August of 1979, Hurricane David threatened to devastate Miami Beach in Florida. It was headed directly for the resort city and plans were made to evacuate thousands of residents from South Beach, most of them in their 70s and 80s. A major obstacle developed when many of these people panicked at the sight of the buses preparing to take them to safety. For these residents, mostly Jewish, the scene was too reminiscent of World War II, when many of them were carted off in similar fashion to concentration camps. A number of these frightened old people simply refused to leave Miami Beach. A major catastrophe was averted only because the hurricane changed course at the last moment. These people were afraid of Hurricane David, but even more they were afraid of old phantoms. Each of us carries around such phantoms. The fear of death is one of these, and for some it is an old friend not easily discarded. Even should death be totally eliminated, some people will cling to their old fears. But eliminating these fears is an important part of the life-extension effort.

Life need not be a terminal disease. The purpose of life must be to live. To live fully, and with the commitment that only comes with the awareness that life is a permanent entity, not merely a temporary status. A part of this process is to bring the most pleasure possible to our lives. Otherwise, what would be the sense of extending them? A sense that this is something worth embracing, worth holding onto is essential. It is time to get away from the view of this life as a nice place to visit—but we wouldn't want to live there. Just as we move into a house with the feeling that this is our permanent home, even if we might someday move again, it's time to settle into life and get unpacked!

ADDITIONAL RESOURCES

For information on workshops, cassette tapes, books, and other materials offered by some of the people whose ideas are discussed in this book, or to comment on those ideas, readers may write to the following:

Jerry Gillies
22541-A Pacific Coast Highway
Suite 16
Malibu, California 90265

Reverend Terry Cole-Whittaker
836 Prospect Street
La Jolla, California 92037

Dr. Sonya Herman
Healing Breath Centers
5444 Beaumont Avenue
La Jolla, California 92037

Dr. William McGrane
McGrane Self-Esteem Institute
590 Formica Building
Cincinnati, Ohio 45202

Dr. Claude Nolte
419 Vista Flora
Newport Beach, California 92660
(Power of Pretend)

Leonard Orr
Inspiration University
Box 234
Sierraville, California 96126

A. Stuart Otto
Chairman, Committee
    for an Extended Lifespan
P.O. Box 696
San Marcos, California 92069
(Ask for a sample copy
    of the *Life Lines* newsletter)

The SAGE Project
491 65th Street
Oakland, California 94609

BIBLIOGRAPHICAL NOTES

Though most of the material contained in *Psychological Immortality* came through personal interviews with the people quoted on these pages, the author found the following books particularly useful while researching this subject.

Anatomy of an Illness as Perceived by the Patient by Norman Cousins. New York: W. W. Norton & Company, 1979.

Pro-Longevity by Albert Rosenfeld. New York: Alfred A. Knopf, 1976.

How to Stop Killing Yourself by Peter J. Steincrohn, M.D. New York: Wilfred Funk, Inc., 1950.

The Immortalist by Alan Harrington. Millbrae, California: Celestial Arts, 1977.

The Complete Book of Longevity by Rita Aero. New York: A Perigee Book, G. P. Putnam's Sons, 1980.

The Life-Extension Revolution by Saul Kent. New York: William Morrow and Co., Inc., 1980.

Physical Immortality: The Science of Everlasting Life by Leonard Orr. Sierraville, California: Inspiration University, 1980.

Rebirthing in the New Age by Leonard Orr and Sondra Ray. Millbrae, California: Celestial Arts, 1977.